an Archaeology of the early anglo~saxon kingdoms

C.J. ARNOLD

ROUTLEDGE
London and New York

First published in 1988 by
Routledge
11 New Fetter Lane, London EC4P 4EE
29 West 35th Street, New York NY 10001

Reprinted 1988 in paperback

Photoset by Mayhew Typesetting, Bristol, England
Printed in Great Britain by Billing & Sons Limited,

British Library Cataloguing in Publication Data

Arnold, C.J.
    An archaeology of the early Anglo-Saxon kingdoms.
    1. Anglo Saxons   2. Excavations (Archaeology)
    — England   3. England — Antiquities
    I. Title
    942.01   DA152.2

    ISBN 0–415–00349–0
    ISBN 0–415–03248–2 (Pbk)

Library of Congress Cataloging-in-Publication Data
available

AN ARCHAEOLOGY OF THE
EARLY ANGLO-SAXON KINGDOMS

Contents

Tables

Figures

Preface

It has taken a long time for the contents of this book to be translated from diagrams on a blackboard, which gave students considerable amusement, into words. It has been encouraged by the nervous laughter of my seniors, hindered by the lack of dialogue between them. I hope those that gave me the confidence to write this book will not now regret having done so, and wish that those that follow gain as much pleasure and excitement in unlocking the many doors which have remained barred for too long.

A number of colleagues, family and friends have always been willing to discuss the problems posed by early Anglo-Saxon archaeology, and to share their ideas, especially Richard Morris, Paul Reilly, Janet Arnold (*née* Bell), Jeremy Huggett, Julian Richards and the ducks, to whom I am most grateful.

For M. and D.

Introduction

By AD 700 there were seven principal English kingdoms: the West Saxons, the South Saxons, Kent, the East Saxons, East Anglia, Mercia and Northumbria. Although their precise boundaries are unclear the respective areas of their kingdoms correspond roughly with: central southern England, Sussex, Kent, Essex, Norfolk and Suffolk, the Midlands and the area to the north of the River Humber. They had been created from a larger number of smaller and less well documented groups by a process of amalgamation during the preceding two centuries after the migrations of Germanic people to England in the fifth century. Northumbria, for instance, was an amalgamation of two earlier kingdoms, Bernicia, which was roughly equivalent to modern Northumberland, and Deira, modern Yorkshire. At one time during this formative period there were at least ten separate royal families ruling simultaneously in England. The success of individual kingdoms was largely dependent on their success in the political and economic arena. It was the more successful of the kingdoms which were most frequently attacked and which were annexed into larger configurations by the more obscure kingdoms. This process of peaceful and aggressive fusion was to continue in succeeding centuries down to the present day.

Our knowledge of the political structure of England at the end of the seventh century is greatly enhanced by the existence of written records. Little of the written tradition that survives was written down before the second half of the seventh century. Its reliability is determined by the limit of living memory and the vagaries of oral tradition. Many of the written sources stem from the conversion of the English to Christianity during the seventh century, the successful conclusion of missionary efforts from Rome in AD 597 and Iona in AD 635.

The greatest scholar of the period, Bede (c. AD 672–735), was born in Northumbria and trained at the abbeys of Wearmouth and Jarrow. Amongst his influential writings is the famous book completed in 731, the *Ecclesiastical History of the English People*. It was primarily intended as a contribution to Christian teaching, but arising from the main theme, which was the conversion of the English, there is considerable information about the development of the kingdoms. The value of Bede's *Ecclesiastical History* is affected by his own knowledge and the sources available to him. Many details are provided about Northumbria and Kent, but for other areas he was dependent on informers, where they existed, and the sparse earlier records. He was writing about the time before his life and says less about his own time. Nevertheless, we are provided with details of kings' lives, royal courts, statesmanship, the names of people and places and their conversion to Christianity.

The political history of early England can also be traced through the annual entries of the *Anglo-Saxon Chronicle*. As the *Chronicle*, in its various versions, was compiled in Wessex, it is particularly informative about the development of that kingdom, but less so about others. Here also the earlier entries down to the middle of the sixth century are often confused and unreliable, and the inconsistencies between the various sources must urge caution in our dependence on the information provided.

A symbol of the extent of kingship during the seventh century is the various law-codes issued as a means of regulating society, but which indirectly throw light on contemporary attitudes towards justice and perceptions of the structure of society. The first vernacular laws were issued by King Aethelberht of Kent at the beginning of the seventh century, whereas the earliest West Saxon laws were produced by Ine between AD 688 and 694.

To a large extent the writings of modern historians and archaeologists have been influenced by the content of all of the available written sources and restrained by their apparent bias and inaccuracy. The archaeologists' data are prone to similar problems of distortion. Some of the early kingdoms, for instance, remain very obscure, but despite the relative silence of the written records about them, the archaeological data may demonstrate that similar developments were taking place there as in the well-documented examples. But one can never be sure that an adequate cross-section of archaeological data in any one area has been recovered and it is the archaeologist that decides what emphasis should be placed on a particular piece of evidence. The problems of interpreting archaeological data are only exacerbated by the inevitable desire to dove-tail the two forms of evidence together. If such problems can be overcome it should be possible to push back the knowledge of the development of the kingdoms beyond the date at which the written sources are considered reliable, and amplify our understanding of the structure and content of these societies throughout the period.

The early Anglo-Saxon cemeteries provide just such a challenge to interpretation and yet must contain the greatest potential resource for an understanding of the evolving social structure. The numerous excavated cemeteries where the burial rites of inhumation and cremation, often accompanied by grave-goods, were variously practised may have encoded within them much of contemporary attitudes to life, death, status and social identity; it is the archaeologists' difficult task to extract that information.

The conversion of the English to Christianity, through which we learn so much about the kingdoms, is well documented by some of the written sources. The change in religion may account for some of the changes in the archaeological record, but our knowledge of beliefs and the extent and nature of religious practices, both before and after the conversion, is limited. The nature and precise function of the earliest churches are obscure, and we are hardly equipped to extrapolate the beliefs of individuals from their graves. If problems of interpretation exist regarding any aspect of early Anglo-Saxon archaeology, it is only bold experimentation and optimism that will produce the tools required to overcome those problems.

The development of the Anglo-Saxon kingdoms may be appraised on the basis of their permanency and their success in the military, economic and political arenas. Glimpses of the struggles for power and supremacy that were taking place can be gained in the written sources, but a detailed appreciation of the nature of the societies which permitted such developments to occur can only be obtained from the archaeological evidence. The basis for the continued growth of the kingdoms was the subsistence farmers whose settlements and cemeteries, daily and less regular activities, make up the bulk of the archaeological record. The collections of timber buildings on their farms may be difficult to understand and the details of agriculture, animal husbandry, the extent of surplus and storage facilities, fields, the density of settlement and even the nature of the landscape in which such activities took place, may be poorly understood. But it is only by attacking that data from as many angles as possible that any worthwhile information will come out of it, and thus we can prepare ourselves to ask the right questions when the opportunity arises to excavate further examples. The few artefacts recovered from such settlements and the larger quantities deposited as grave-goods in the nearby cemeteries, amply demonstrate the richness of technology and

design during the period. They also form the basis of our knowledge of economic life, from such humble an aspect as the source
of clay used to make pottery to the origins of gold to adorn
extravagant pieces of metalwork. It is such small pieces of information that combine to help us understand the dynamics of the
whole society.

The cemeteries present us with two principal burial rites,
inhumation and cremation. Most of the graves are difficult to date
adequately but in their variations of burial rite, grave structure,
container or grave-goods, they hold conscious and unconscious
reflections of the societies responsible for them. They contain
varying quantities of dress items, containers and weapons some of
which are occasionally lavishly decorated, but there are many
perplexing problems. It is difficult, for instance, to determine
whether the deposition of so many possessions and the raw
materials required to make them should be viewed as a reflection
of a successful society that could afford such extravagances, or one
that was being strangled by, or forced to change because of, its
own beliefs. There is no doubt that it is difficult to put some of the
burial practices into perspective; what are we to make of a society
which at times in its development was prepared to consign large
quantities of precious metal to the ground but rarely buried everyday tools?

An appreciation of the sources and use of raw materials allows
us to examine the movement of internally produced goods and of
those from overseas. From this we may begin to reconstruct the
natures of the economies of the kingdoms whose increasing
complexity is emphasised by the production of first gold and then
silver coinage before AD 700. That growing complexity is also
reflected in the evolving social structure visible in the cemeteries
and by the development of a greater variety of settlement types.
The largely undifferentiated farms in the earlier part of the period
later take their place in the landscape alongside ports, royal
centres and religious institutions. Again, the frequent isolation of
the archaeological and written evidence comes sharply into focus.
Royal settlements are mentioned by Bede, *Gefrin* identified with
Yeavering in Northumberland and Rendlesham in Suffolk. Yet
there are other settlements identified as 'palaces' by archaeologists
which are not named and the written sources are almost silent
about the earliest ports.

These structures and institutions are an indication of the growing power and complexity of the early Anglo-Saxon kingdoms.

Developing as they did after the collapse of Roman Britain and the Germanic migrations of the fifth century, they are a reflection of man's ability to recover from such turbulence and for a new order to be established. It forms an exciting period of rapid change terminating with a period of relative stability in the evolution of the kingdoms and the establishment of towns. The picture we have of these 200 years it still blurred but it is by assessing the state of knowledge at regular intervals that provides the foundations for future scholars to build on and bring that image gradually into focus.

In the text that follows references are only given to cemeteries and settlements that have been published in more recent years. For older excavations the sources may be found in Meaney (1964) and Rahtz (1976, Appendix A). To avoid confusion the pre-reorganisation (1974) county names have been used when appropriate.

1

A History of
Early Anglo-Saxon Archaeology

'Wrapped round with darkness'
Judith translated by R. Hamer

The purpose of this book is to explore the development of English society during the two hundred years AD 500-700 following the migrations of Germanic settlers to the British Isles. The aim is to bridge the gap between the work of specialists whose significance to a general understanding may seem obscure, and generalised accounts which may seem remote from the data. To achieve this we shall be drawing upon the products of archaeologists' research mostly carried out during the present century. The desire to understand the development of early Anglo-Saxon society as a specific contribution to the more general study of past human behaviour has only emerged in recent years.

Each chapter examines a particular aspect of early Anglo-Saxon society. Such a division is purely a literary convenience and each of the topics must be seen as intertwined and forming a complex whole. The ideal framework for the study of early Anglo-Saxon society is provided by the kingdoms which were developing during the period under consideration. Within that evolving framework there is both complexity and variety, for change involves both redundancy as well as novelty, and each region was subject to different pressures stemming from its past and its neighbours.

The archaeological evidence comes from two main contexts, settlements and cemeteries, although most archaeological investigation has been concentrated on the latter, and especially the artefacts derived from them. The emphasis here is not on a description of the evidence but on its interpretation. To achieve

1

this the data requires varying degrees of manipulation if we are to understand the society whose everyday activities constitute the origins of the archaeological record. We will see how the development of Anglo-Saxon archaeology, in which the number of practitioners has always been relatively small, has engendered a conservative approach to the period which was not suited to answering the fundamental questions relating to human social evolution. In more recent years there have been signs of a change in emphasis. This is reflected in those chapters of this book which deal with the agriculture of the farms and the homes in which our subjects lived, trade in commodities and finished products, the craft skills in use and the religious beliefs of the population which were persuasively altered by Christian missionaries.

All such social activities combined to determine the form in which early Anglo-Saxon society developed and a major consideration has to be the definition of all the levels of social organisation in as far as that is yet possible. Naturally the inherent constraints of the archaeological evidence, our caution about the relationship between the archaeological record and the activities that formed it, and the limited research which has been carried out determine the cohesion and balance of a work of this type. However, a definition of the current state of understanding and uncertainty should also serve as a diagnosis to guide future research.

The early Anglo-Saxon period is unspectacular and, except for the rare and fabulous discoveries such as the ship burial at Sutton Hoo (Suffolk) has not been brought to popular attention. Indeed, there are many people for whom the knowledge that the earliest Anglo-Saxons came immediately after the Romans and before the Vikings would be a revelation. The period is also something of a 'Cinderella' within teaching and research in British universities, there being only six specialists teaching undergraduates.

Post-Roman archaeology is one of the younger branches of British archaeology; older established areas of study, such as prehistory, have inevitably tended to form the vanguard of archaeological research and are more firmly printed on the popular imagination. This may, in part, explain why current approaches seem so distant from those applied to other periods of the past. Much research into early Anglo-Saxon England is accompanied by a high degree of innocence, with time-honoured methods being applied despite their failure to deepen understanding of man's past; techniques applied to other periods tend to be excluded as though they are not relevant to an historic period.

While there are signs that the situation is changing, the reasons for the subject being pervaded by such conservatism and isolationism lie in the history of its development. Its comparative youthfulness and exclusiveness cannot be the sole explanations. A great deal of research in the field during the twentieth century has been carried out by scholars trained, in the first instance, as historians, with an equally significant contribution by a number of eminent scholars working in museums; these latter tended to introduce a strong art-historical bias. These may be the principal factors which have tended to control and limit the nature and scope of research.

In 1786, when the true age of man was only just beginning to be appreciated, Anglo-Saxon remains were first identified as such. Possibly the earliest mention of what are probably Anglo-Saxon graves is that by the thirteenth-century chronicler Roger of Wendover in his *Flores Historiarum* where he describes the excavation by monks of St Albans in 1178 of ten human skeletons at Redbourne, Hertfordshire, believing some of them to be the bones of St Amphibalus (Hewlett 1886, 115). Early Anglo-Saxon objects were first illustrated by Sir Thomas Browne in *Hydriotaphia, or Urne buriall* (1658), where he described the 'Sad sepulchral pitchers. . .fetched from the passed world'. To Browne, the cemetery at Walsingham, Norfolk, was a reminder of the power and culture of Rome. One of the 40 or 50 burial urns survived in the 'closet of rarities' at Lambeth known as Tradescant's Ark, which in 1682 formed the basis of Elias Ashmole's bequest to the University of Oxford (Daniel 1981, p. 42). The urns were reported to contain burnt bones, decorated combs

'handsomely wrought like the necks of Bridges of Musical Instruments, long brass plates overwrought like the handles of neat implements; brazen nippers to pull away hair . . . and one kind of *Opale*, yet maintaining a blewish colour'.

It was not until the second half of the eighteenth century that any systematic excavation of an early Anglo-Saxon site, a cemetery, took place. The Rev Bryan Faussett carried out a considerable number of excavations in east Kent between the years 1757 and 1777, amassing a total of over 700 graves. It was he who managed the hurried disinterrment of 28 graves in one day, and nine barrows before breakfast to avoid the disturbance of spectators. Such haste inevitably resulted in cursory recording being a characteristic of research at this time, which is particularly regrettable in Faussett's case because of the scale of his activities in Kent. But Faussett failed to appreciate the true significance of his discoveries; in his journal, kept for the years 1757 to 1773 and later published as *Inventorium Sepulchrale* under the editorship of Charles Roach Smith in 1856, the remains were attributed to the period of Roman occupation, while Smith preferred a purely British origin.

The credit for recognising from their contents that the 'small barrows' were not Roman or Danish, but burial places of the Saxon period, belongs to the Rev James Douglas who also excavated in Kent, from 1779 to 1793. The results were published in his *Nenia Britannica* (1793). Douglas's work marks a turning point in early Anglo-Saxon archaeology; in the words of Horsfield in his *History, Antiquities and Topography of Sussex* (1835, p. 11): (1835, p. 11).

> Up to this time no genuine attempt had been made to acquire knowledge of our early inhabitants, no extensive plan for a generalisation of known excavations.

Douglas made notable advances in archaeological method fully appreciating the value of dating by association within and between grave groups. As his biographer has pointed out it was to be a long time 'before he had an equal in the study of archaeology on a scientific basis or as an illustrator of archaeological relics' (Jessup 1975, p. 109).

In the second half of the nineteenth century progress was made in three ways. Firstly by the publication of the results of the excavation of individual cemeteries, for instance Wylie's *Fairford Graves* (1852). Secondly by their incorporation into the early regional studies such as George Hillier's *The History and Antiquities of the Isle of Wight* in 1856 (Arnold 1978; Hockey 1977), or in more general works such as C. Roach Smith's *Collectanea Antiqua* (1848–80). Thirdly by attempts to survey the material as a whole, for instance Akerman's *Remains of Pagan Saxondum* (1855). The first attempt to study the subject on a broader basis and in a more systematic fashion was by Kemble in his *Horae Ferales* (1863). The material from a number of north-west European countries was arranged by types for comparison from which conclusions about the connectedness of artefact types were drawn. Although he excavated extensively in Germany Kemble's greatest contribution in England was as an historian of the period (1863; 1876). The dominance of the study of cemeteries up until the end of the nineteenth century was unavoidable, but this source of distortion on our understanding of the period has remained almost to the present day.

The early twentieth century was very much a period of collecting together the data and presenting it *en masse*, seen at its best in G. Baldwin Brown's exceptional study of the material of Anglo-Saxon archaeology as a whole *The Arts in Early England* (1903–1937). Apart from the accumulation of material in this manner the study of early Anglo-Saxon archaeology progressed little. It was not until the effects of R.A. Smith's surveys of the evidence county by county, which appeared in the *Victoria County History* during the years 1900–26, had been fully felt that there was any appreciable advance. Such surveys formed the basis for research for many years and still remain the principal source for some categories of data. The format, however, was not conducive to typological study which was beginning to have an impact on archaeology in Britain. In *Origin of the English Nation* (1907), H.M. Chadwick was the first to attempt a general work on the origins of the Anglo-Saxons combining historical and archaeological evidence, a theme which has tended to dominate the subject to the present day.

The beginnings of a mature Anglo-Saxon archaeology was founded on the work of the nineteenth-century archaelologists, Akerman, Roach Smith, Kemble and Wylie. It was the new technique of analysis, typology, which caused the greatest shift of emphasis, in the early years of the twentieth century. Following the publications in England of Oscar Montelius and R.A. Smith (1908;1905), E.T. Leeds (Assistant-Keeper at the Ashmolean Museum, Oxford from 1908) produced the first typology of a form of Early Anglo-Saxon metalwork, a brooch type (1912). Both he, and R.A. Smith in his *British Museum guide to Anglo-Saxon Antiquities* (1923), accepted the important work of the scholar Bernhard Salin, *Die altgermanische Thierornamentik* (1904), whose analysis of the animal motifs used in migration period art provided a chronology to which the English material could be related. Using Smith's county surveys Leeds was able to extract various classes of object and formulate typologies and chronologies by comparison with the dated developments in continental art-styles.

E.T. Leeds was also responsible for the first major excavation of a settlement at Sutton Courtenay, Berkshire (Leeds 1923;

1927; 1947) as well as reporting on a number of cemeteries (1916; 1924; and Harden 1936; and Riley 1942; and Shortt 1953). The style and reporting of such excavations changed little, with a plan accompanied by descriptions and drawings of cremation urns at a small scale, but with no details of the 'grave' or the disposition of the contents. Inhumations were treated in a similar fashion, with some details of the grave, but only late in his career did Leeds provide plans of individual inhumations. Generally, photographs of the grave-goods were published with line-drawings confined to more ornate pieces.

Leeds is best known as a pioneer in the typological study of artefacts, producing detailed analyses of various brooch types (1912; 1949; 1971 posthumously with M. Pocock). He also grasped the opportunity to synthesise and in 1913 published *The Archaeology of the Anglo-Saxon Settlements*. This was the first, and remains the only, attempt to summarise all of the known archaeology of the period in England and is of interest in that it describes the aims and methods of Anglo-Saxon archaeology as Leeds perceived them; it was reprinted in 1970. The distribution of types of artefact dated by the typological method were compared with historical information, particularly recorded battles between the Anglo-Saxons and the native population, which he saw as marking the stages by which the migrants conquered the country. It should be noted that Leeds was making the, arguably false, distinction between the two races on the basis of the artefacts. An individual using and being buried with an artefact of, ultimately, Continental type was a person of Germanic origin.

This misconception has led many researchers in more recent years to discuss the apparent absence of evidence for members of the native population. Leeds, the culture historian, is seen at his peak in his *Early Anglo-Saxon Art and Archaeology* (1936) and his paper entitled 'The distribution of the Angles and Saxons archaeologically considered' (1945). He believed that if the distribution of an artefact type could be attributed to a particular race it could indicate the course of the invasion and settlement of England and the origins of the settlers on the Continent. This type of preoccupation has also been prevalent until recent years. Other valuable studies concentrating on art-styles and artefact types were produced during this period by Åberg (1926) and Kenderick (1938).

The method of study developed by Leeds can be traced back as early as 1912 in his career; however the formulation of the theoretical framework was achieved by the prehistorian Gordon Childe who stated that prehistoric archaeology should be 'devoted to isolating such cultural groups of peoples, tracing the differentiations, wanderings and interactions' (1933 p. 417). That Leeds was working within the constraints of this theory as early as 1912 is often overlooked. He was undoubtedly encouraged to adopt this approach by the historical information provided about the distribution of the various races in England by the *Anglo-Saxon Chronicle* and Bede's *Ecclesiastical History of the English People*.

A similar approach was taken by Fox in his *The Archaeology of the Cambridge Region* (1923). In this detailed regional study Fox was concerned with the Anglo-Saxon invasion and settlement and also attempted to reconcile distribution maps of artefact types with supposed ethnic groups to the extent of discussing political boundaries. The work of Leeds on Anglo-Saxon metalwork did not encourage other scholars to follow him immediately, perhaps as a result of the more spectacular possibilities opened by the birth of prehistoric studies at Edinburgh and Cambridge in the late 1920s and 1930s. It was not until the 1950s that new interest was awakened, particularly with the work of J.N.L. Myres on pottery and of D.B. Harden on glass (1956b). This division of labour by artefact type epitomises attitudes towards archaeology generally at that time, and such divisions have to a large extent persisted to this day, emphasising how artefact-based early Anglo-Saxon studies have remained.

An important assessment of the state of the subject is provided by the Leeds *Festschrift* (Harden 1956a) which can be seen to develop many of the traditional themes; the study of the Jutes of Kent, by C.F.C. Hawkes, stimulated by the latest typologies and chronologies of grave-goods on the Continent (Werner 1935; Kuhn 1940) was one of the last studies employing the traditional methodology, although its influence can still be found in more recent work (Hawkes and Pollard 1981).

Despite the increase in the number of scholars studying the period, the same preoccupation with art-history and the origins of peoples persisted and continued to do so through the 1960s in studies of pottery (Myres 1969; 1970) and metalwork (Hawkes 1961; Hawkes and Dunning 1961). Myres believed that 'it should be possible to extract. . .some valuable information on the origin and distribution of the settlers, their relationship to the pre-existing population, their social and economic development, and their notions of religion and of decorative art' (1969, p. 11), although only the first and last of these aims were satisfied to any degree via the pottery. Published works of the 1950s, 1960s and 1970s all tended to follow this approach, and while there were occasional signs of shifts in direction, these were mere rustlings in the undergrowth compared with the revolution taking place elsewhere in British archaeology. The study of social and economic aspects of early Anglo-Saxon society are still viewed as spin-offs from art-historical and technological study rather than topics worthy of treatment in their own right; when thematic studies have been produced in recent years the themes have tended to remain based on site-types or artefacts rather than themes which may be more directly relevant to past human behaviour (Wilson 1976a).

The numerous studies of artefact types that have been produced are important as they form the basis for the chronology of the period, but beyond that their relevance to the study of man has not been demonstrated (Evison 1955; 1958; 1963; 1967; 1968; Swanton 1974; Avent 1975; Avent and Evison 1982; Hills 1981a). Redefinitions of chronology are claimed to be part of the process of improvement of understanding, but may as easily be viewed as an infinite series of alternatives none of which are demonstrably correct unless they are somehow related to the reality of the society in question.

The Archaeology of Anglo-Saxon England (Wilson 1976a) was the first major attempt at synthesis since Leeds in 1913, but its range was limited ignoring most of the early evidence, and there was very little discussion of method. Traditional topics were omitted, supplanted by studies of the form and pattern of settlement, made possible by the great increase in their rate of discovery and excavation during the 1970s. The traditional dependence on a literal version of written sources is absent, although elsewhere such a dependence can still be found, particularly in discussion of the origin of the Anglo-Saxon kingdoms (Biddle 1976; Hope-Taylor 1977, 276–324).

In the 1950s and early 1960s the, then, Ministry of Public Buildings and Works (now English Heritage) sponsored the rescue excavation of a considerable number of cemeteries, but the enthusiasm of that support has not been matched by the rate of publication, to the extent that it is very difficult to comment on excavation methods during that period. More recent years have seen the continuation of such rescue work with a much better publication standard, and there have been two major projects at Mucking, Essex and Spong Hill, Norfolk. Published reports reveal the greater desire for detail and the development of new techniques to cope with the particular problems of early Anglo-Saxon cemeteries. A major improvement in recent years has been the inclusion in such reports of analysis and interpretation of the data (see, for instance, Cook and Dacre 1985). Earlier reports tended to be content with inventories of graves and their contents (for instance, Green and Rogerson 1978).

The more recent years of early Anglo-Saxon studies have been surveyed by Dickinson (1983) and Hills (1979), who both rightly emphasise the shift away from cemetery excavation to the examination of settlements. But both overlook the important point that while there is an apparent shift away from the limiting aim of integrating the archaeological and historical data, this has not been accompanied by any reassessment of the appropriate aims and methods of studying the archaeology. Dickinson's view that early Anglo-Saxon archaeology lacks a good theoretical framework is an extraordinarily isolationist one, when archaeology has been undergoing a revolution in thinking since the beginning of the 1960s and which has been dominated by theoretical considerations appropriate to all archaeological periods, including the post-Roman periods. A scan of the literature concerned with early Anglo-Saxon archaeology over the last 25 years has hardly reflected this change until very recently when there have been definite signs that dissatisfaction is leading to experimentation; otherwise the Sutton Hoo harp has been played while the archaeological world burned.

The principal reasons for this state of affairs lie in the explanations given at the beginning of this chapter; scholars with museum backgrounds laid the foundations for an artefact-based subject in the first half of the twentieth century and introduced the strong historical background to such studies. To many scholars of the early Anglo-Saxon period the study of artefacts with a view to placing them into dated sequences *is* archaeology and is accompanied by little or no questioning of the basis of the method. There have been few serious attempts to break away from this restrictive framework; it is the absence of the application of any theoretical framework that has made such work so sterile, and it is doubtful whether evidence will be found for the social and economic developments during the period by studying art-styles, date and distribution alone, unless specific questions are formulated first. In 1913 Leeds appreciated that because of the confused distribution of the Germanic tribes in Europe before their settlement in England, the picture would be even more confused. Attempts to reconcile archaeology with history during the period have always presented problems, and will undoubtedly continue to do so. What is easily overlooked is that all such work is based on a series of unstated assumptions whose validity has never been examined.

There are growing signs of a desire to abandon the descriptive approach to this material and to examine unknown fields rather than continuing to prove by alternative means what is already known. Moreover, frameworks are being sought which may open new doors. The major changes in other branches of archaeology, particularly prehistory, which resulted from the development of independent dating techniques, has stimulated a move away from the mere grouping of artefacts to represent 'cultures' using typologies, in part, to provide the time scale, with varying degrees of success. Anglo-Saxon archaeology hasn't come to a crisis point as did prehistoric studies in the early 1960s; rather it is gradually slipping into new directions with the establishment of a generation of archaeologists more aware that alternative approaches exist to be tried and which have been available for 20 years.

The last ten years have seen the beginnings of a trend away from the study of objects for their own sake, stimulated partly by the discovery and excavation of settlement sites which have encouraged the formulation of a new range of questions; the nature of and change in human societies have replaced the barren side of the artefacts. Similarly, there is a stronger awareness that graves are not merely places where artefacts can be obtained for study but are reservoirs of data reflecting numerous activities of a past society in addition to mortuary rituals. An accurate and meaningful account of a human society should be more than a generalised narrative of the changes in composition of the archaeological record through time. Concern has for too long been with problems of stylistic chronological placement and historical continuity between and among archaeologically defined units. The methodological tools developed for the investigation of such problems are inappropriate for supplying information relevant to broadening research interests in the process of cultural evolution.

The method of studying early Anglo-Saxon archaeology by equating process with typologies, and the demonstration of clustering along the dimensions of time and space, only inform us that some systematic process was at work. The validity of the method for Anglo-Saxon archaeology has never been questioned. It was normally assumed that the quantity of differences as measured by some typological evaluation among assemblages (usually subjective intuition) is a measure of ethnic affinity between the groups responsible for the archaeological remains. Attempts to understand the processes which caused the differences and similarities are rare. Our ability to measure qualitatively these differences and similarities between assemblages and to synthesise the results into such taxonomic units as phases or traditions is in no way a test of the validity of the proposition that measured differences are indicative of degrees of ethnic affinity. Faced with an apparent nonconformity the explanation has generally been in terms of cultural replacement rather than change. The processes usually called upon to explain the distribution of art-styles have been, for the 'conforming type' (those that have a long observable development) diffusion, and for intrusive new types, migration and invasion. The resistance on the part of some Anglo-Saxon archaeologists to formulating hypotheses and to examine methods currently in use is reflected in Wilson's suggestion that 'the tendency on the part of some American archaeologists to force it [archaeology] within certain philosophic boxes . . . quite at odds with the loose methods of induction often needed to deal with the archaeological material must be ignored' (1976a, p. 2). This plea for methodological anarchy seems rather at odds with current competition between generalising approaches and those that assert the unique cultural specificity of cultural practices. The latter currently figure larger in early Anglo-Saxon studies although, ironically, this is probably the result of the traditional isolation of the subject from other branches of archaeology. Irrespective of this, theories and assumptions must be stated and analysis be rigorous if progress is to be made.

The preoccupation with the study of artefacts in isolation has a number of causes: the need to provide a chronology; the absence of frameworks of thought by which grave-goods might be considered in the first instance as part of a mortuary ritual; and, particularly from the nineteenth century, obsession with artefacts. Prehistoric studies experienced a shift of emphasis in the 1960s as a result of scientific methods of dating being introduced into archaeology. This encouraged a move away from the study of artefacts and 'cultures' based on them which had developed in the absence of such dating methods, to a more all-embracing study of past human societies. Unfortunately the degrees of confidence that can be applied to such scientific dates are inadequate for a period which can be viewed in terms of generations (Campbell, Baxter and Alcock 1979). As a radio-carbon date is usually accompanied by a high standard deviation greater than ±60 years its value in early Anglo-Saxon archaeology is limited. Often, timbers dated by radio-carbon are carbonised oak and a date obtained relates to the age of the rings of the surviving tree and not the felling date. Dendrochronological research for the first millennium AD is still under development with a number of floating chronologies in existence; but the general rarity of timbers suitable for such work from the types of site belonging to this period also limits the value of the method at present. Thus, scientific methods of dating are probably less accurate than the traditional methods based on the study of artefacts, although their accuracy is very difficult to establish. It is important to stress, therefore, that there is no absolute, only a relative, chronology for the period.

The unreliability of the written sources and the more obvious difficulty of actually relating the majority of historical events to archaeological data, make their use for dating early Anglo-Saxon archaeology very limited. E.T. Leeds worked hard to use the sources to provide a chronology of the development of brooch types (1933) and the extremely dubious assumptions he made have coloured a great deal of thinking to this day. Even if they are accurate, the historical data are principally concerned with conscious expressions of political life, while archaeology is concerned with a mixture of conscious and unconscious action and processes. The little history of the period that has survived is an invaluable asset, but there are great dangers in using archaeological data to elucidate chronologically-based historical problems when the span of as little as a generation is so crucial.

One of the earliest detailed discussions of how the artefacts of the period might be dated was provided by Åberg (1926, pp. 149–58), although typically there is no consideration of what such chronology could be used for beyond using it to relate the archaeological data to an historical narrative:

> . . . the chronological position of the Anglo-Saxon anti-
> quities has been estimated partly from the typological
> characteristics of the material and from the occurrence of the
> various objects in closed finds in association with other
> objects, partly from datable coins. (149)

From these, similar artefacts could be dated by comparison; by this method it is rarely clear whether the date applies to the manufacture or deposition of the artefact. Some of the earliest material (i.e. object-types which are found both on the Continent and in England) was dated by reference to the historical sources: 'the oldest brooches belong to the time of the invasion' (156). Artefacts found on both sides of the North Sea provide an important reference point, although it would be easy to question the basis of the chronology of such objects in Scandinavia and North Germany. The use of English material to support Continental chronologies creates additional problems.

Åberg (1926) discussed the value to chronology of the Crondall (Hampshire) coin hoard (Sutherland 1948) and graves at Sarre (Kent) and Compton Vernay (Warwickshire) which contained coins (Rigold 1975, pp. 71–2; Avent 1975, p. 47). A number of other graves containing coins have been added to the list since Åberg was writing in 1926 (Rigold 1975, pp. 69–70; Avent 1975, p. 6; Rigold and Metcalf 1977) as well as the one case of coins from a single building at Mucking (Rigold 1977). The *termini post quos* of these finds could be tabulated with the diagnostic contents of each context, but the value of such an exercise must be tempered by the fundamental problem of the chronological association of the coins and the other artefacts and their respective use-life.

A great stride forward was made after 1931 by J.N.L. Myres who began the systematic investigation of early Anglo-Saxon pottery (Myres 1969, pp. 1–5), yet there was no clear statement concerning the methods used to establish the chronology of the vessels under review, despite quite specific dates being ascribed. The material was fitted in a general manner, to a five-phase evolution of Anglo-Saxon society to which dates were ascribed, but the basis for it was not discussed. The supposedly most securely dated vessels are those which can be related to Continental chronologies; vessels which occur on the Continent but not in England date to before the migration, those on both sides of the North Sea to the migration period itself, and those which are only found in England must have developed after the migration period. The method involves making important assumptions about the nature of the migrations and the rate of change in the style of the English pottery if potentially 'early' vessels are not to be confused with those of the following centuries. By this method very few vessels had date ranges ascribed to them (Arnold 1981). The flexibility employed in making comparisons with Continental pottery has also been questioned; for instance, the problem posed when the shape of two vessels is similar but whose decoration is totally different. The artefacts found within cremation vessels were generally ignored and appear at times to conflict with the dates ascribed (Morris 1974; Kidd 1976; Dickinson 1978; Richards 1987).

Most discussions of the chronology of specific artefacts, or artefact-types, of the period are couched in predictably vague terms. This is in a sense unavoidable, but inevitably the flexibility that must be allowed can lead to varying opinions. Fundamental to all such discussions are assumptions about the rate of evolution of decorative styles and the definition of the circumstances in which such evolution took place. It could be argued that until those important issues have been resolved the role of subjective opinion in dating many artefacts is unavoidable.

When dates for particular artefact-types are given it is rarely made clear whether that date is one of manufacture of the artefacts, its period of use or the context in which it was found. The dating of an artefact to the span of a single generation would be to a degree of accuracy which would provide a powerful tool for the study of Anglo-Saxon society. Because the length of the period is so short and can be measured in generations, consider-able caution has been shown in the accuracy of dates given by some writers (Avent 1975, p. 56). Some writers quote dates to an accuracy of 25 years, others 30 years, but rarely is it made clear why, or how such dates are obtained. There is unlikely to be any advance in the accuracy of dating of early Anglo-Saxon arch-aeology in the near future whereas the assumptions upon which such dates are allowed are very likely to come under close scrutiny. Most writers have a framework for the development of the society in question to which their chronology is related, whether stated or not. It may, therefore, be more productive to work within the limitations imposed by the data than to continue to explore art-styles as a root to chronological precision when this does not seem possible because of the unknown number of unknown variables. What is most apparent is that when chron-ologies are put forward the resulting data either cannot be, or is not used to study early Anglo-Saxon society in any more detail, and even when a pattern appears it is noted as an aside to the central issue.

There is still a great deal to be learnt about early Anglo-Saxon society, both as a result of new excavations, the publication of older ones and research carried out on the wealth of material already published or in museums. There have been many advances over the last 20 years, particularly in the subjects of settlement, technology and social and economic organisation. Yet there is a long way to go, particularly in breaking down some of the fixed images of early Anglo-Saxon society. Despite being faced with a complex and rapidly evolving society, the prejudice that is apparent on the pages of textbooks threatens to stultify research. We read that the meaning of the embellishment on metalwork 'cannot be recaptured from the archaeological material' and it cannot be interpreted from the 'surviving literature, which was written down long after the inception of the style' (Wilson 1976a, p. 3). Yet, for information about religion, political structure, boundaries, marital practices, the rights of the individual and social structure 'the historical sources are more useful'; the 'archaeology has more value for certain tangible material' (ibid.). Notwithstanding this statement the pagan Anglo-Saxon cemeteries are claimed to inform about 'wealth and . . . social condition' (ibid., p. 6). The historical sources tend to be accepted unless there is evidence to the contrary, by which process much of what can be read about Anglo-Saxon England is based on uncorroborated historical evidence written down hundreds of years after the events they describe. Despite the difficulties of relating it to the archaeology, Bede's statement about the origins of the Germanic settlers in England is generally accepted. Much else of what Bede claims is rejected.

Alongside such apparent contradictions the very condition of society is claimed to leave much to be desired as life was full of danger and trouble (Page 1970): 'life was cheap and illness, plague and famine were never far from the surface' (Wilson 1976a, p. 13); weapons in graves point to the 'ever-present threat of death by violence' (ibid., p. 20). However, these are impressions which would be difficult to demonstrate from the archaeological evidence. Most surveys of the period present a flat, superficial descriptive account of the origins of the migrants, the historical sources, village, cemeteries, art-styles, Christianity, and lack any depth of understanding about the society involved. Explanation flows not from analysis of archaeological data but by reasoning on the basis of what seems most likely given the manner in which the data has been presented.

The rapid, undisturbed development of early Anglo-Saxon society provides an ideal area for the study of the processes of social and economic development. But because 'philosophic boxes' (Wilson 1976a, p. 2) have not been created or examined in relation to this period, the subject has yet hardly developed beyond the accumulation and description of data. A period which is initiated by the collapse of a major civilisation, had an historically documented migration and which in many respects provides a 'clean slate' has an irresistible attraction. It allows the study of a rapid societal development limited in time and space within very narrow boundaries.

The aim here is to demonstrate how recent excavation and research have markedly changed the face of early Anglo-Saxon archaeology during the period AD 500–700. This is a time period which witnessed rapid change in all spheres of life; following the migrations (Arnold 1984a) rural communities were expanding their social and political networks to form the Anglo-Saxon kingdoms. These changes are paralleled by a growing economic complexity. Christianity became a powerful religious force towards the end of the period. Archaeology is the principal source of data for informing us about the manner in which these changes took place, and how man adapted to the revolutionary changes occurring in society. What follows is inevitably a personal interpretation produced in the face of numerous difficulties, not the least being the breaking away from traditional methodologies and doctrines. A total synthesis is not possible given the rate at which new data and techniques are being produced; the principal difficulty remains the quantity of material that was excavated in the last century under conditions which do not assist in answering the questions now being asked and which now lie, unpublished and unstudied in museum collections throughout England. Despite the rapid increase in the number of large-scale excavations of settlements, only three have been published (Bell 1977; Millett 1983; West 1985); a similar problem pertains with the number of cemeteries examined since the Second World War and which remain unpublished, denying a generation of researchers the data from modern excavations. Rightly, few of the hypotheses examined in this book will stand the test of time but it will have achieved its aim if it provides a foothold for fellow students who also appreciate the need to abandon what may glibly be characterised as the 'Beowulf and brooches' approach. It is hoped that it will provide a flexible structure which can be refined and developed and which may help to break down the monolithic structure and mystical nature of the subject.

2

The Land's Wealth

The basis of the early Anglo-Saxon economy was the land. The production of food and clothing in an essentially self-sufficient life-style guaranteed survival. Essentials that were not available locally and the growing desire for non-essentials must have been satisfied by surplus produce. There is nothing to suggest that the rural economy was anything but generalised, with evidence for specialisation appearing late in the period. A thorough understanding of the landscape and the economic structure of society lies in the future, but the need to understand the context and role of the numerous artefacts that have been excavated, particularly in cemeteries, makes this a crucially important area of research.

Farm and Field

An Anglo-Saxon settlement could draw on a variety of environments to maintain the supply of essential resources. The evidence recovered by excavation emphasises that the landscape was being fully utilised by the inhabitants of farms dispersed across the landscape. This depth of utilisation is exemplified by the settlement and cemetery excavated on a hilltop overlooking the English Channel at Bishopstone, Sussex (Bell 1977). In the fifth century rectangular and sunken buildings were erected over an earlier farm and its fields. In the pastures stood sheep, cattle and a few horses and around the farm buildings were geese, fowl and cats. Growing in the arable fields during the summer months would have been a crop of barley amongst which various weeds were growing, including fat-hen, common orache and black bindweed. The food produced in this way on the farm was supplemented by

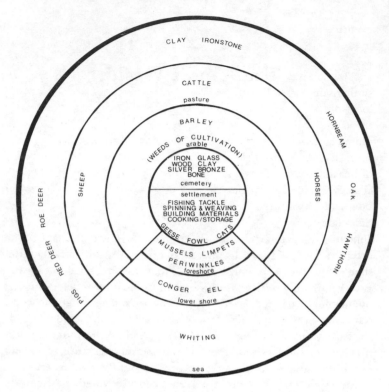

Figure 2.1: Diagram illustrating the resources exploited by the early Anglo-Saxon settlement at Bishopstone, Sussex. The evidence from the buildings and the cemetery are shown in the centre, surrounded by the resources derived from the sea-shore, arable fields, pasture and the Weald. (Data: Bell 1977.)

marine resources, mussels, limpets and periwinkles gathered on the foreshore, conger eel from the lower shore and whiting taken from the sea; nets were made on the farm using bone netting needles. In nearby woodland pigs were reared, and red and roe deer were hunted. The woodland also provided oak, hawthorn and hornbeam for building, fuel and the wooden implements found in the adjacent cemetery. Clay and ironstone were brought from the Weald to manufacture pottery, spindle whorls, loom-weights and a variety of iron implements including nails, knives, spears and shield bosses. The animals not only provided dairy products, meat, leather and wool for clothing; bone was used to make such things as combs, weaving tools and netting needles. Bronze and silver items were manufactured or acquired and eventually buried, along with considerable quantities of other material, as grave-goods in the community's cemetery (Figure 2.1).

This picture of subsistence agriculture varies little between settlements and any minor variations are the result of regional and local differences in the environment. On some farms, especially those without direct access to the seashore, a wider range of wild animals and birds were taken, although they are always in a minority. At Walton (Buckinghamshire), for example, the bones of beaver, crane, plover and redwing were identified (Table 2.1) (Farley 1976). The principal hunting weapon may have been the bow and arrow; arrows, as with all tools, are rare in early Anglo-Saxon cemeteries; they are often viewed as weapons of warfare but constitute the most obvious hunting weapon amongst the range of artefacts and their rarity in cemeteries may only be a reflection of their importance to the community. Wooden bows are rarely preserved, although one was described by the excavator as a 'bow, about five feet in length, which could be distinctly traced by the dark line of decomposed wood' (Hillier 1856, p. 30). In a Warwickshire cemetery, at Bidford-on-Avon, were 'Several arrowheads of different patterns with closed sockets' (Humphreys *et al.* 1923, pp. 96–7).

Whatever contribution hunting made to the diet, the domestic animals and crops in the fields must have provided the majority of the food eaten. Sheep are normally the most common animals represented although occasionally cattle predominate over sheep. But whatever the particular proportions cattle were generally good-sized, perhaps the result of the provision of reasonable grazing and implying successful husbandry. There is generally no particular emphasis in the killing ages of sheep as both young and old are found, although at West Stow (Suffolk) the evidence was indicative of sheep being used mainly for a combination of meat production and dairying with a small amount of wool being produced for domestic purposes (West 1985, p. 93). Pigs are particularly rare at a few settlements. The figures from West Stow (Table 2.1) emphasise the degree of continuity involved during the period.

Barley was not always the only cereal grown, but it is generally the most common. The potential ingredients of the diet are clearer than our understanding of it. The study of past dental health can provide only general indications about the food eaten. During the early Anglo-Saxon period a diet having a 'coarse physical

Table 2.1: Assessment of quantities of animal bones from early Anglo-Saxon settlements by per cent of fragments

	cattle	sheep/ goat	pig	horse	deer	bird	other
Walton, Buckinghamshire	38	31.8	21	3	0.7	4.2	0.9
Bishopstone, Sussex	25	39.5	17.2	2.2	1.4	7.8	2.1
Cowdery's Down, Hampshire	71.3	4.3	3				21.3
Old Down Farm, Hampshire	37.5	42	7.5	2.4		4.2	6.3
West Stow, Suffolk. Phase 1	34.27	44.04	21.69				
Phase 2	36.30	49.98	13.71				
Phase 3	34.66	45.69	19.65				

consistency' resulted in a lower incidence of dental caries compared with modern populations. The use of naturally occurring sugars in milk, honey and fruit resulted in cavities occurring at different positions to those in modern teeth (Moore and Corbett 1971).

The range of tools found on these farms is often limited and unrepresentative of the range of activities we know took place. They are found in deeper deposits of buildings sunk below ground level; tools associated with weaving are most commonly recognised. In addition there are rotary querns for milling flour on site, stone rubbers connected with leatherworking and hones for sharpening edge-tools and weapons. The rarity of tools is particularly emphasised by the numbers of woodworking tools found in both settlements and cemeteries; whilst carpentry was a skill demonstrated in the construction of houses and fine items like cups of stave construction, woodworking tools are extremely rare. The cemeteries of Horton Kirby and Lyminge, Kent produced axe-hammers and a T-shaped axe, a plane and wedges. A boring-bit and saw have been identified at cemeteries in East Anglia (Wilson 1968; Dunning 1959). It is not clear why there should be such a high proportion of woodworking tools from Kent, especially the cemetery at Sarre beside the Wantsum Channel, but it may reflect ship-building and repairing as much as more general carpentry. It seems probable that all tools were handed on from one generation to the next; their frequency in Kent may reflect a greater overall wealth and the ability to dispose of such items as grave-goods. The only exception to this pattern is the iron knife, an everyday tool which is frequently found in graves, and which may have been more personalised than the more specialised tools and therefore buried with the owner.

Agriculture in the early Anglo-Saxon period appears to have been designed to satisfy immediate, local needs, but evidence that the situation was changing towards the end of the period can be found by comparing the food resources with those of the earliest post-Roman urban and commercial centres in England; *Hamwic*, the middle Saxon port of Southampton, and Ipswich have both received large-scale excavation. Middle-Saxon rural settlements, like those earlier, were supplied with a relative abundance of wild animals, whereas they are rare at *Hamwic* (Bourdillon 1979). Although they were eventually eaten, the *Hamwic* sheep were not reared primarily for eating, and there are lower quantities of fowl and poultry than at early- and middle-Saxon farms. Cattle on both rural and urban middle-Saxon settlements are of the same approximate state but larger than their earlier counterparts. The conclusion would seem to be that the early Anglo-Saxon countryside was not run as efficiently as in the following centuries. In the eighth and ninth centuries the killing age of domestic animals was earlier in rural contexts, whereas at *Hamwic* the bones do not reveal such early mortality, implying that the town, divorced from the wild, was not affected by the immediate hazards of the land. Thus the early killing age at Walton need not be a reflection of success in animal husbandry. Of the crops found in the urban environment after AD 700, *Triticum aestivum*, the naked bread or club wheat, is the most common, whereas the hulled wheat, *Triticum cf. spelta*, occurred rarely, possibly merely as a contaminant to the crop. Naked wheats are free-threshing and, unlike the hulled varieties preferred earlier, grow best on heavy soils. Systematic sampling for plant remains at the early Anglo-Saxon settlement at Cowdery's Down, Hampshire, produced six-row barley (*Hordeum vulgare*), bread wheat (*Triticum spelta*) and barley (*Hordeum sp.*) (Millett 1983, p. 259).

Despite the extensive sampling during the excavation of the sixth and seventh century settlement at Cowdery's Down the results prompted the excavator to offer a warning about interpreting the results; it was concluded that 'it is impossible to make any assertions about the economy or waste disposal systems associated with the site' (Green 1983, p. 261). The rarity of evidence for domestic and agricultural activities provoked a number of suggestions. It may simply be the result of little domestic refuse being left around the farm; cereals may not have been processed there, or, if they were, not in a place likely to have resulted in their being burnt and therefore preserved. There is little likelihood that cereals played a minor role in the economy. Such domestic refuse may have been spread on the fields and the removal of floors by later agriculture may have robbed the archaeologist of vital information. This may only be a curiosity of Cowdery's Down, for, on other contemporary settlements, pits and other deep features contained numerous seeds and animal bones.

The survival of such evidence may be due to a wide range of factors which need have little to do with contemporary activities; at the time of occupation the possible use of raised floors may affect survival. Nevertheless it may be observed that in the earliest phases of the life of the Cowdery's Down settlement when all the buildings were closely associated with fenced enclosures the majority of bone and cereal recovered came from buildings straddling the fence. In the third and final phase the majority of cereal and animal bone came from the buildings in the compound, especially from smaller buildings. This change may reflect the growth in size of the settlement and the greater separation of domestic and farming activities.

Very little is known about the layout of fields or of the ploughs that may have been employed on them. It has been suggested that a totally new system of open fields for arable agriculture was laid out in at least one area of England in the seventh century (Hall 1979; 1981). The absence of evidence of a distinctive layout of fields before that time has led to the suggestion that Romano-British fields continued to be used in the Saxon period and that open fields may have been something that developed gradually through the Anglo-Saxon period as a whole (Taylor and Fowler 1978). None of the parts of ploughs from the period have survived except for the soil stain from a wooden object in a recently excavated, and unusual, grave at Sutton Hoo which has been interpreted as representing a complete ard-type plough. Although horses were kept it is not at all clear whether they, as opposed to cattle, were used for traction. It seems most likely that horses were used as a means of transport. The rarity of their bones is matched by the rarity of pieces of horse-gear from settlements and cemeteries. The central link of a three-link horse-bit was excavated at Walton; if actually Anglo-Saxon it is a very rare example (Farley 1976, p. 198); late prehistoric terrets have been found in Anglo-Saxon cemeteries on the Isle of Wight and in Kent (Arnold 1982a, p. 68). Snaffle-bits of two linked iron bars with a small ring at each end are known from a scatter of cemeteries across the country from Lincolnshire to Kent (Welch 1983, p. 112).

The farms themselves may be categorised into three broad types on the basis of their layout: one or a few buildings seemingly in isolation or associated with earlier structures, for instance late prehistoric enclosures or, as at Lower Warbank (Kent), a single sunken building adjacent to a Roman villa (Philp 1973, pp. 156–63), which may only be part of larger settlements; individual farmsteads, a group of buildings associated with a fenced enclosure or paddock, such as Cowdery's Down (Millett 1983); thirdly, larger settlements with either multiples of the previous category or a farmstead apparently with a larger number of ancillary buildings, such as Chalton, Hampshire and West Stow, Suffolk (West 1985). The size of such settlements can easily be overestimated as the number of buildings must be viewed as a factor of the length of time the site was occupied and the frequency with which buildings were replaced. Both are difficult to calculate. The rarity of artefacts found during excavations of such farms not only affects the archaeologist's ability to date the buildings, but also makes it extremely difficult to understand the details of the activities carried out on the farm.

Two main types of building are encountered on such farms; sunken buildings and those built at ground-level, often called 'halls' in a rather indiscriminate manner. 'Sunken featured building' is a cumbersome and inelegant term adopted for relatively small structures erected over a sub-rectangular pit dug in the ground, ranging in size from 3 × 2 m up to the largest so far excavated at Upton (Northamptonshire) which measured 9.1 × 5.5 m (Jackson *et al.* 1969). The superstructure was supported by 1 or 3 posts at each end, represented by postholes on either the upper or lower edges of the pit. A gable roof is implied by such an arrangement and the number of posts may relate to the presence or absence of vertical side-walls as much as to the size and weight of the roof (Figure 2.2). At West Stow, the six-post array could be claimed to be the earlier form. A few representatives have central posts, and stakeholes around the edge of the hollow to support a revetment.

A variety of activities took place in the buildings. For instance, of the 68 such buildings at West Stow, six had been used for weaving, some producing up to 100 loomweights used to tension the warp-threads of an upright loom (Figure 2.3). Once these structures went out of use they became ready depositories for rubbish

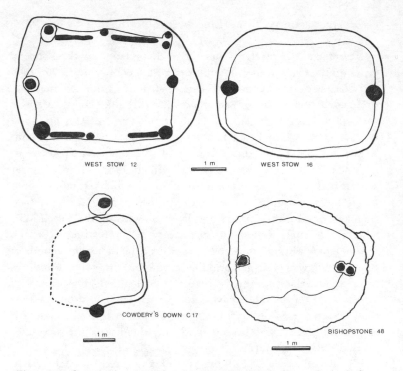

Figure 2.2: Comparative plans of sunken featured buildings from early Anglo-Saxon settlements, showing the variety in the methods of construction

(Jones 1979b), which can be difficult to distinguish from material reflecting the use of the building. The presence of hearths and the absence of material trampled into the floors in a number of examples may support the view that many were used as dwellings. Alternatively the cleanliness of the pit base has been viewed as an indication that the pit had plank floors at ground level. The evidence actually tends to be ambiguous (West 1969; Jones 1979b) as indications of timberwork at the lip of the pit may be connected with the superstructure and planking in the base may have fallen from the walls or roof lining. Some certainly did have plank floors in the pit base. The purpose of the pit would appear to be to provide the maximum headroom using the minimum raw materials in the superstructure; this would make a ground level plank floor something of a nonsense, an opinion shared by Welch (1985, p. 23, n.1).

The term 'hall' includes all the rectangular timber buildings

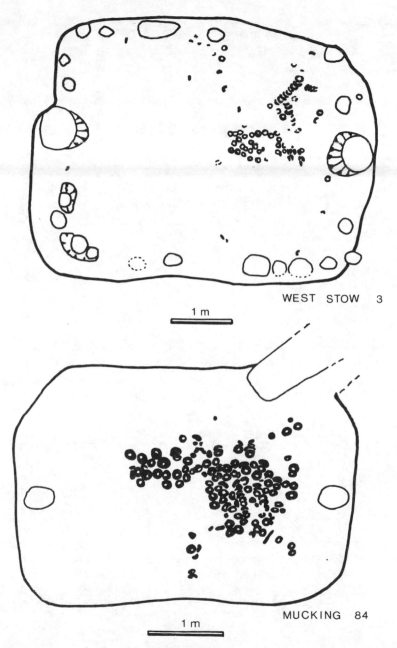

WEST STOW 3

1 m

MUCKING 84

1 m

Figure 2.3: Plans of sunken featured buildings containing textile manufacturing equipment. Clay loomweights are frequently found lying in the bottom of the pit in rows and irregular heaps

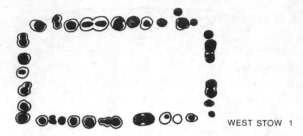

WEST STOW 1

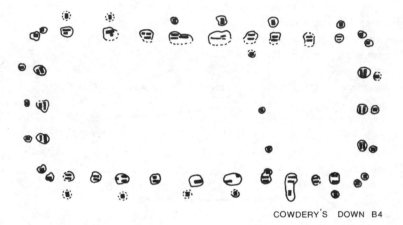

COWDERY'S DOWN B4

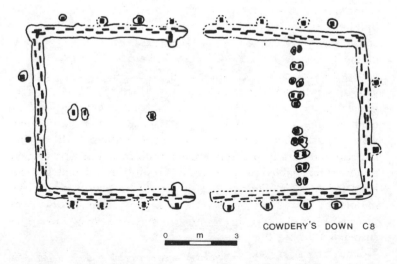

COWDERY'S DOWN C8

0   m   3

Figure 2.4: Comparative plans of halls from early Anglo-Saxon settlements showing the variety of methods used to construct the foundations

whose only remains are the postholes and beam-slots dug into the subsoil. Traces of the form of the timber which they contained are rare. There is considerable variation in size, method of construction and design. Some of the smallest have been found at West Stow, perhaps because of the weakness of the sandy subsoil on which it was built (Figure 2.4). At Chalton, the largest structures measured 9 m or more in length, and are characterised by opposed doorways in the centre of the long sides, flanked by pairs of postholes (Addyman, Leigh and Hughes 1972). Internal divisions were positioned at the eastern ends sub-dividing 1/3 or 1/5 of the area. The provision of separate rooms was not visible at Bishopstone and only present in one building at West Stow. The second group of rectangular buildings, also with opposed doorways, but no internal partitions, vary more in size, clustering at 8.5 × 5.3 m and 6.5 × 3.5 m. At the smaller end of the scale are buildings having single doorways in the middle of one side. At Chalton the doors were hung inside the building closing against the back of the door frame. Such doors could have been secured by the use of a drawbar; keys for the operation of such devices are known from some better provided for women's graves. Where buildings overlap it can be shown that post-built structures preceded those constructed using continuous trenches.

Some of the best preserved buildings have been excavated at Cowdery's Down and can be arranged sequentially into a minimum of three phases (Millett 1983). The majority of the buildings were of post-hole or trench construction and display considerable variation in size and design (Figure 2.5). The walls of the buildings most commonly consisted of a single row of vertical timber planks or baulks with wattle panels inserted into grooves down their edges. Alternatively, pairs of vertical timbers in holes in the ground clasped horizontal members with wattle and daub infilling, or the uprights were staggered with panels of interwoven wattles between them. The interpretation of the superstructures naturally presents greater problems, but it is argued that most had gabled roofs with rafters resting on wall plates below head height. The floor would be clear with crucks across the middle of most of the buildings supporting purlins and a ridgepiece. Some of the more complex structures may have had suspended timber floors.

The internal arrangements and uses of these buildings are poorly understood. It is not, for instance, possible to say to what extent the differences in construction relate to their function.

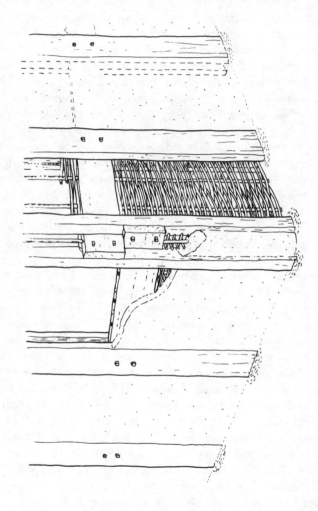

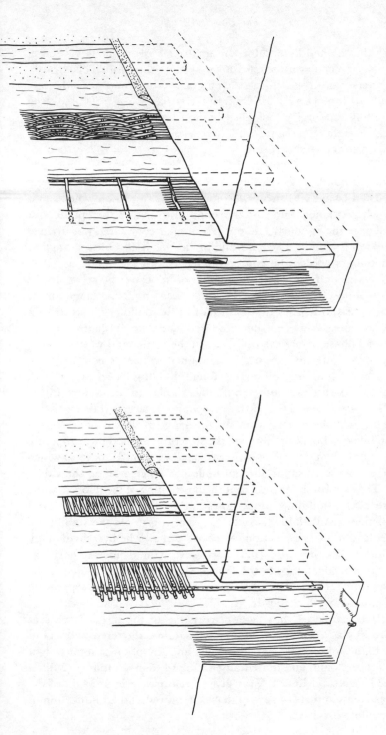

Figure 2.5: Constructional details of buildings from the early Anglo-Saxon settlement at Cowdery's Down (Hampshire) (after Millett 1983) showing the various methods used to build the walls

Within one hall at Chalton an area of less-worn chalk subsoil at the eastern end near the partition may mark the position of a hearth. Scatters of iron slag in the vicinity of two buildings at Catholme, Staffordshire (Losco-Bradley 1977) strongly suggests that iron smelting and forging took place in these buildings. Two rectangular buildings there had a pit sunk in one corner which might be taken as a distinguishing feature.

The layout of the farm at Cowdery's Down changed gradually with the number of buildings increasing in each phase, there being 3, 6 and 10 in each, always accompanied by two fenced compounds which contained some of the buildings. In the first phase, for instance, the regularly laid out rectangular compound was divided through the middle with a building in each half. One rectangular building straddled the compound fence with an annexe attached on the inside from which there did not appear to be access to the compound. The annexe need not have been roofed, although there was access to it from the main part of the building. This in turn had doors midway in its long sides, outside the compound. In the second phase one of the buildings in the compound was replaced, while the other two may have remained in use. A new structure was built straddling the external and dividing fences, again with its doors outside. Another building, similar to the annexe in the first phase was erected in the compound adjacent to its end wall. In the final phase there was a major change in alignment and structural type of building. Some of the structures around the compound were rebuilt and the enclosure extended westwards, beyond which were a series of six additional buildings erected along the ridge.

The excavator suggests that the positioning of the doors and the size of the buildings 'does not seem to indicate an agricultural function' (Millett 1983, p. 247), preferring to see the stability of the layout as a reflection of social units, whether divided by 'kinship, sex or status' (ibid.). However, the deliberate positioning of the doors outside the fences which they straddled could be seen from an agriculturalist's point of view, to assist the separation of animals from domestic areas.

It is estimated that to construct one of the larger houses at Cowdrey's Down, C12, would have required the removal of about 81 tonnes of topsoil, clay and chalk and the use of a total weight of timber, daub and thatch amounting to some 70 tonnes (Millett 1983, M5/02, M5/03). This gives a reasonable impression of the massive quantities of raw materials required and an indication of the effort involved.

There were very few artefacts recovered from the settlement, even in areas protected from later ploughing; they included shears, nails, a variety of fragmentary fittings and pottery made up of nine fabric groups. It is thought that this represents a very real social phenomenon, either because of the nature of the settlement or because it was a general policy to dispose of rubbish away from the settlements, perhaps as manure in the fields, and is clearly not the product of poor preservation as has tended to be assumed (Astill and Lobb 1982, p. 140).

On chalk subsoils sunken buildings and artefacts are relatively rare, but rubbish pits are more common than elsewhere. Where sunken buildings occur many artefacts are found as a result of their being used as rubbish pits after abandonment. The most extensive array of rubbish pits has been recorded at Abbots Worthy, Hampshire where there were twelve pits which appeared to have specific functions. They comprised oval pits associated with shallow circular ones; rectangular, vertical sided ones and three very large circular ones measuring 2.7 m diameter × 1.5 m deep. Most produced only animal bone, whereas the five sunken buildings contained bone, pottery and other small artefacts.

The type of farm layout represented at Cowdery's Down is fairly common (Figure 2.6). It accounted for more than half the structures at Chalton but at Bishopstone, where the extent of erosion was even greater and the excavation not total, there is less evidence of such planning although traces of fence lines attached to buildings were located. At West Stow, where sunken buildings outnumber the 'halls', the former clearly cluster around the halls in distinct groups. Catholme, Staffordshire reveals a similar pattern of enclosed units with a large central building surrounded by lesser structures, some interpreted as granaries. One unit was composed of many more buildings than the others and it is suggested that it represents a social difference with specialist activities taking place there.

The common attributes of the building tradition of early Anglo-Saxon England have been summarised as:

> . . . rectangular, precisely laid-out and constructed in substantial earth-fast foundations. Their plans frequently employ simple geometric forms or length-width ratios; the square is very common and often occurs in pairs. Most buildings have a door exactly in the centre of each long wall, and some have an annexe at one or both ends. Most of the

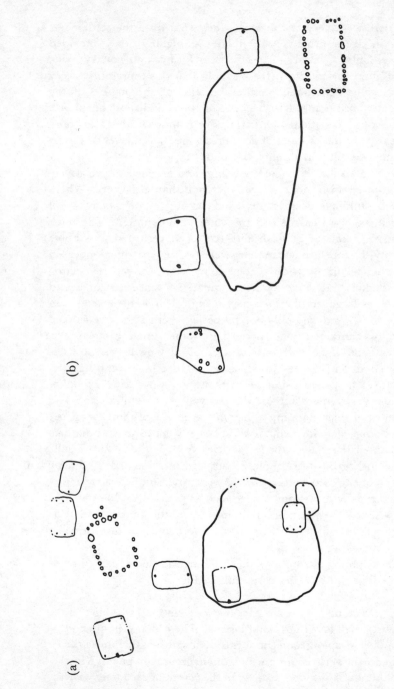

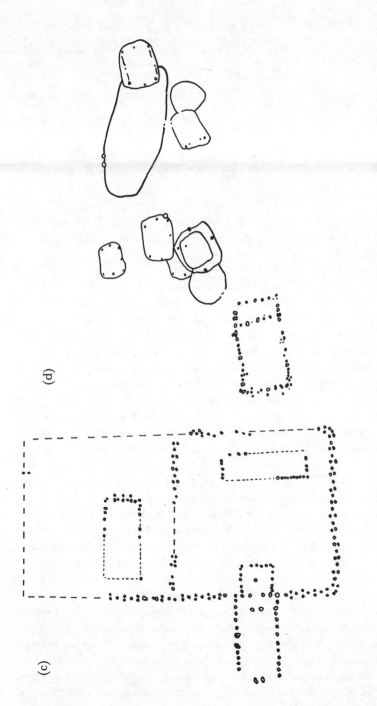

(d)

(c)

Figure 2.6: Comparative plans of farm modules from early Anglo-Saxon settlements. The buildings are typically associated with fenced areas

Table 2.2: Ratios of building types in early Anglo-Saxon settlements

Site	'Halls'		Sunken buildings		Ratio	Sub-soil
	no.	%	no.	%		
Mucking, Essex	*c.* 50	19.0	213	80.9	1:4	gravel
West Stow, Suffolk	6	7.8	70	92.1	1:12	sand
Eynsham, Oxfordshire	4	16.6	20	83.3	1:5	gravel
Bishopstone, Sussex	17	85.0	3	15.0	6:1	chalk
Cowdery's Down, Hampshire	16	88.8	2	11.1	8:1	chalk
Chalton, Hampshire	57	93.4	4	6.5	14:1	chalk

structures stand within, or abutt palisaded enclosures, and *Grubenhäuser* are present. (James, Marshall and Millett 1984, p. 184)

The writers view the evidence in terms of an early medieval building tradition which has not been apparent until recently because of the variable quality of the surviving evidence. They view this building tradition as a merger of traits with Romano-British and Germanic origins, although Dixon (1982) has placed greater emphasis on the former. He emphasises how the uniformity of this architecture contrasts with the marked regionalisation seen in artefacts and views this as evidence for the native origin of the tradition. There are some regional differences which can be discerned in settlement structure, although these need not have an ethnic or social basis. The chalk downland sites of Chalton, Bishopstone and Cowdery's Down are marked by the rarity, but not absence, of sunken buildings (Table 2.2). The reason for the high number of sunken buildings in some areas may be the greater drainage potential of gravel and sand than chalk. This may also account for the small size of halls at West Stow, the uncompacted sand subsoil being incapable of taking the strain of a large building with earth-fast timbers. On chalk subsoil an accumulation of water in holes and pits may have been a severe problem making timber 'halls' the more popular structure. If such were the case the difference between east and south is related to geology and not to any differences in the societies or their subsistence. The ratio between house types on gravel sites in central England, such as Eynsham in the upper Thames valley, supports such a view. It is possible that these differences reflect the availability of suitable timber, but it is difficult at present to determine the extent of woodland at a sufficient level of detail.

Jones has suggested that the sunken buildings found on early Anglo-Saxon settlements were dwelling houses, especially in eastern English settlements such as the large Thameside settlement of Mucking, and West Stow. This would imply that in central southern England buildings were put to different uses and that there was a radical difference in the economy and social structure. It is unfortunate that the activities which took place in the buildings can rarely be determined. On the farms where 'halls' predominate they tend to be of three sizes, large, medium and small. At West Stow the one large hall is the exception to a rule of small size and uniformity. At Catholme the dimensions of the buildings were in proportions of 2:1, 3:1, 3:2 and 5:2 and at Chalton the most common proportion was 2:1. While at one level a functional difference was probably intended, the relationship between groups of buildings at certain sites strongly suggests that there is a social distinction cutting across the functional dimension. The variation in size and construction technique in the sunken buildings is much greater, with no clear clustering when a large sample is analysed (Jones 1979b). On occasions their function is much clearer than with the larger rectangular structures; for instance, at West Stow 9 per cent of the sunken buildings contained weaving and textile-related equipment. The *majority* of the 'halls' can be divided into two on the basis of their floor area, one group of settlements having mostly large buildings, the other smaller, which may reflect the status of the settlements (Figure 2.7) (James, Marshall and Millett 1984).

The study of the buildings found on the farms tells us little at present that is definite about the rural economy. An additional approach to the question is the analysis of the settlement pattern, the search for underlying regularities in the choice of location of the farms. Regional differences may be informative, and the manner in which the patterns may change through time. The available archaeological data are the excavated settlements and the more numerous cemeteries. A full appreciation of the cemeteries, in this context, demands an understanding of the relationship between the settlements and cemeteries during the period. In the absence of information about land tenure, which archaeology is poorly equipped to examine, the location and interrelationship of the farms can be assessed in terms of soil, geology, height, aspect and proximity to water. The relationship of settlements to cemeteries can be considered using the results of

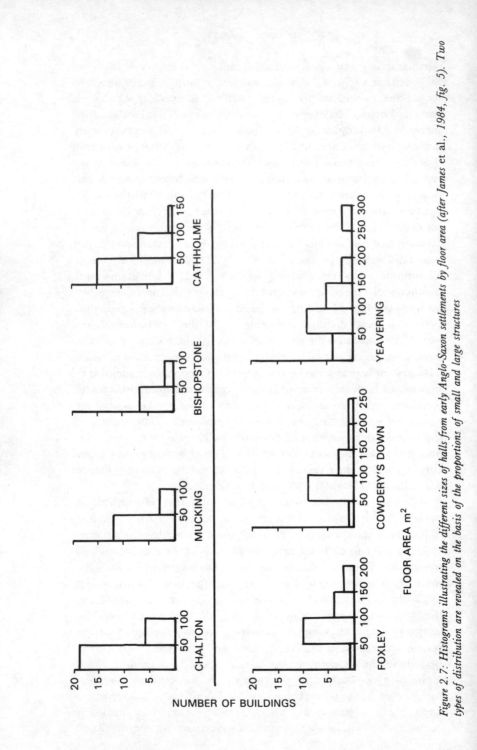

Figure 2.7: Histograms illustrating the different sizes of halls from early Anglo-Saxon settlements by floor area (after James et al., 1984, fig. 5). Two types of distribution are revealed on the basis of the proportions of small and large structures

large-scale excavations as a control, and the actual distances between such features may act as a guide even when a relationship cannot be directly inferred. An understanding of why settlements are deserted and have presumably been relocated can be revealed from an examination of the chronology of the settlements and by comparison with the locational qualities of later sites. Additional information regarding the settlements of the period might be gleaned from the study of place-names. The chronology of the various early medieval elements has been broadly established, but we remain ignorant of the actual names given to the settlements of the period. It is actually questionable whether the locational analysis of Old English place-name elements has any validity for early Anglo-Saxon settlement patterns. The number of unknown factors is so great and the processes by which place-names have survived so irregular and difficult to assess, that their use here is of limited value (Gelling 1978; Arnold and Wardle 1981; Taylor 1983; Welch 1985, pp. 17–18; Copley 1986).

In a number of areas of England it has been observed that early Anglo-Saxon cemeteries are frequently close to parish boundaries, particularly in Wiltshire. This has given rise to speculation about the origins of such territorial units and the rationale behind the siting of cemeteries. This relationship, whose validity ultimately depends on statistical arguments may be one of the greatest red herrings of the subject. In Wiltshire 29 per cent of the sample lay on parish boundaries and 14 per cent within 500 feet (Bonney 1972; 1976). In Lindsey (Eagles 1979, pp. 177–8) it has been shown that 11 per cent are on such boundaries and 18 per cent within 500 feet. Whether these figures are statistically significant is doubtful. A randomly generated pattern in Wiltshire produced figures of 7 per cent on boundaries and 16 per cent within 500 feet. The pattern may suggest that cemeteries and boundaries may coincide in up to 30 per cent of cases, but the 70 per cent away from them is perhaps the more relevant figure; in reality, pagan Anglo-Saxon cemeteries are not significantly biased towards the boundaries and their location there may be the result of chance. Goodier (1984) has applied a statistical approach to this question and concluded that 'the Anglo-Saxons buried a significant proportion of their dead on the boundaries of their land units' (ibid., 14). However, the statistical methods applied to the concept of a bounded area of land are dubious unless the shape of that area is taken into consideration and only those cemeteries within 100 m of parish boundaries were considered (Reilly and Zambardino

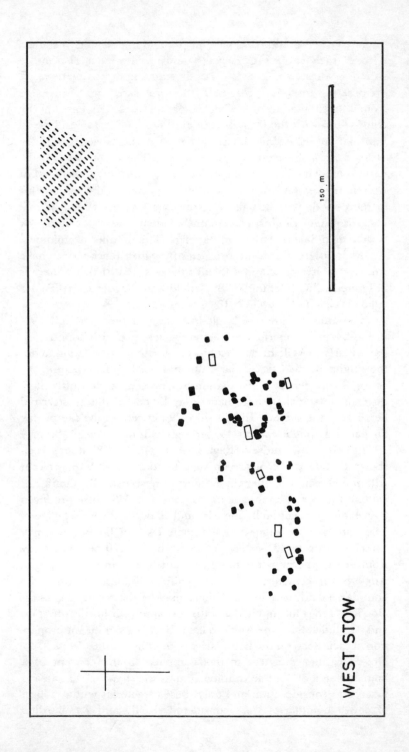

WEST STOW

150 m

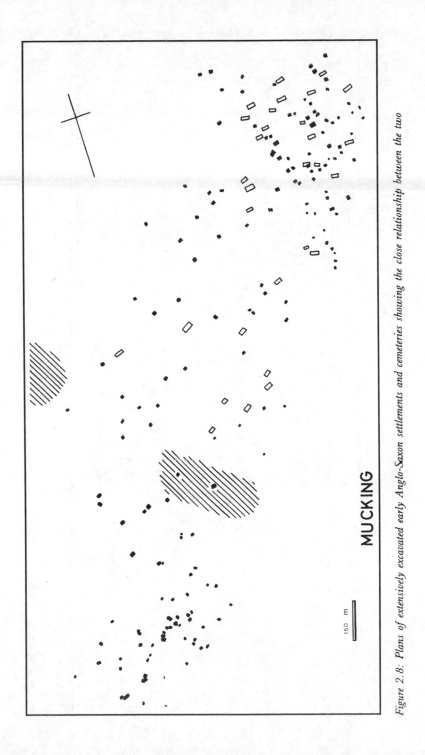

MUCKING

150 m

Figure 2.8: Plans of extensively excavated early Anglo-Saxon settlements and cemeteries showing the close relationship between the two

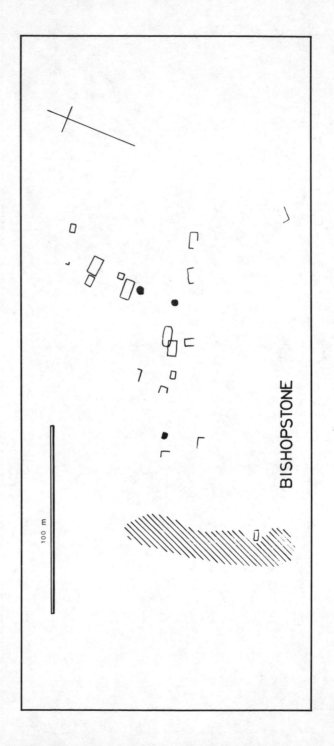

100 m

BISHOPSTONE

Figure 2.8: *Continued*

1986). The location of cemeteries alone near the boundaries might be easily explained, but the accumulating evidence from excavated settlements strongly suggests that many had an adjacent cemetery (Figure 2.8) and the excavation of a number of cemeteries in recent years has indicated the presence of a nearby settlement up to 0.5 km away. This may have come about as a result of a phase of shifting settlement gradually giving way to greater stability, so that when land boundaries (some of which may have also become parish boundaries) were formed the earlier settlements may, purely by chance, occur at a distance to later ones and are therefore more likely to lie near boundaries (see also, Welch 1985, pp. 18–21).

The close relationship between settlement and cemetery may not have existed throughout the country. Cemeteries in eastern England tend to be very large, infrequent and dispersed, whereas those in the south are smaller and more common (Figure 2.9). This may indicate that the settlements of eastern England were also large and dispersed. Alternatively, if the size and density of settlements were uniform throughout the country, then in some areas the dead were being carried over considerable distances for burial. It is notable that in eastern England cremation is the preponderant burial rite and if cremation took place near the settlement it would be more practical to take the remains to a distant cemetery. It has been noted that on occasions the cremated bones are found in the urns in a small cluster as if placed there in a small bag.

The location of rural settlements depends on a balance of considerations, ultimately on the nature of the rural economy and the system of land tenure. The patterns could be analysed in terms of a number of factors, such as water, fuel, arable land, pasture, the needs of defence. To this might be added the impact of Roman period agricultural activity on the landscape in the form of fields, hedges and roads. Early Anglo-Saxon settlements are much more common than was once thought (Figure 2.10). Extensive field-walking is beginning to show just how dense their distribution was, although not all of the farms identified need be contemporary. In the Itchen and Avon valleys in Hampshire the farms are apparently regularly spaced along the valley bottoms. Further fieldwalking in Northamptonshire emphasises the widespread distribution of such settlements, some near earlier and later settlements, others having no such connection (Taylor 1983). Within the broad perspective of rural settlement studies it is most

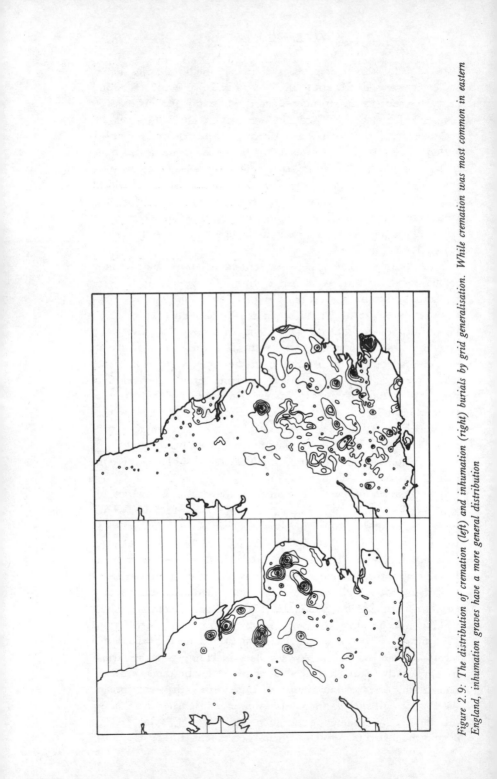

Figure 2.9: The distribution of cremation (left) and inhumation (right) burials by grid generalisation. While cremation was most common in eastern England, inhumation graves have a more general distribution

Figure 2.10: The distribution of known early Anglo-Saxon settlements in England. The greatest number are known from the Midlands and eastern England. The bias in fieldwork producing this pattern is emphasised by comparison with the distribution of graves in Figure 5.3

apparent that they are not static entities and their mobility results in their frequent desertion. In Sussex and Hampshire fieldwork has revealed that no village can claim uninterrupted development from earlier than the middle Saxon period. A similar study of Norfolk parishes admirably demonstrated the manner in which medieval settlements were frequently relocated, although in that case early Anglo-Saxon settlements were conspicuous for their absence (Bell 1978; Cunliffe 1972; Wade-Martins 1980).

Such mobility in the settlements of the period is most graphically demonstrated by the results of the very large-scale excavations at Mucking (Jones 1979a). The first identifiable phase of occupation of the gravel terrace above the River Thames began early in the fifth century and consisted of a dense settlement within which three periods of rebuilding were observed. Then in the late fifth, or early sixth, century the settlement moved northwards; it was smaller, of briefer duration and more dispersed, and the cemetery belonging to it was defined by Romano-British ditches. In the third phase in this shifting pattern, in the later sixth or early seventh century, the settlement moved to the north-east and was relatively dense with some deliberate alignment of buildings. In the final phase, in the seventh century, the settlement moved westwards and consisted of more isolated and separate farmsteads. It is apparent from the data that Mucking was not a village but a series of shifting hamlets, a close community changing to one in which there was far less interaction, which may be intimately connected with changes in the methods of landholding.

It has been observed that in Berkshire, topographical names, particularly those referring to water are the most common Old English names in areas where early Anglo-Saxon settlement has been attested archaeologically. But this is hardly surprising when the most common location for these, and other, settlements is beside a source of water. The great majority are riverbank sites, and there is no clear difference between early and middle Saxon sites in terms of this variable (Figure 2.11). The greatest proportion are sited on good quality soils, stagnogleys and brown earths (Figure 2.12). Stagnogleys are non-calcareous loamy or clayey soils at moderate depths, light to moderately heavy, fertile, moderately well-drained and suitable for cultivation; the category includes soil on river terrace gravels. Brown earths are loamy non-calcareous soils, well-drained, fertile and excellent for farming. Of the remainder, 10 per cent of the sites are located on Rendzinas, shallow calcareous soils over limestone and chalk which are also light and fertile.

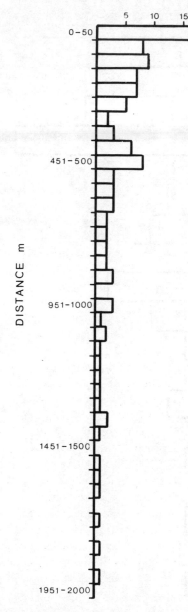

Figure 2.11: Histogram showing the distances between early Anglo-Saxon settlements and the nearest (modern) source of water. Over half of the settlements are within 500 m of a water-source

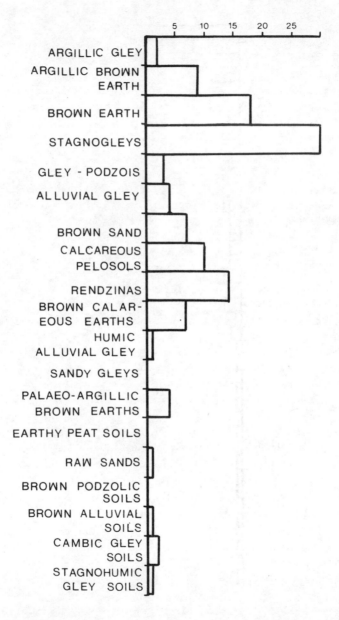

Figure 2.12: Histogram showing the number of early Anglo-Saxon settlements on specified soil-types. The largest number of settlements is found on light soils such as rendzinas and stagnogleys and fewer are located on heavy soil-types

Poor agricultural soils appear to have been avoided, especially those affected by fluctuations in groundwater which would cause waterlogging. In contrast to the proportion of early Anglo-Saxon farms located on Rendzinas, no middle Saxon settlements are known on such soils. This may be the result of siting for ease of farming in the earlier period. Further, it may suggest a drift away from the shallow, light soils favoured in the early period to heavier soils which are more fertile and produce a greater yield per acre. By the late Saxon period, most settlements occur on the heavier soils; indeed by that date settlement is found on a far greater variety of soil types.

The need for wood for fuel, building materials and tools would have required extensive woodland close to the settlement. It is hard, however, to gauge the effect man's demand on the woodland had on the landscape at this time. Considerable clearance would have been necessary to build a single timber 'hall', up to 18 mature oaks being necessary to build a large example at Cowdery's Down. Another major demand on woodland which is rarely discussed is the fuel requirement for cremating bodies, especially in eastern England where many thousands of cremations may be represented at a single cemetery. While this might be thought to have a major impact, the effects would have been lessened if the cremating was carried out at dispersed homes. However, little research has been carried out on the quantities of wood required. An experiment stemming from the excavation of prehistoric cremations in Orkney indicated that one cubic metre of brushwood and peat was required to reduce a 4 stone goat to 0.04 cubic metre of bone and ash in five hours (Hedges 1977, p. 143). From a practical point of view Wells's study of Anglo-Saxon cremation (1960) was concerned only with determining the technique of cremating and the temperatures achieved. He found that there were reasons to believe that bodies were placed supine below the pyre and that the average temperature achieved was about 900° C, but the quantity of fuel required was not determined. There are too many unknown quantities in the complex equation regarding number of bodies, quantity of fuel, rate of woodland regeneration and time, to be able to calculate what impact the presence of a large cremation cemetery would have had on the landscape. There is palaeobotanical evidence for a phase of increased woodland clearance in the sixth and seventh centuries in Britain (Biddick 1984, p. 108 and fig. 1).

The high number of sites very close to water can be equated

with the number of sites at low altitudes, sea-level and up to 15 m above sea level. Most are actually riverbank sites which also correlates with the number of sites on drifts and clays, and the soil types developed on drifts, the stagnogleys. Wells are almost unknown on early Anglo-saxon settlements, emphasising the importance of rivers, but they are more common on urban and rural sites from the eighth century onwards. The numerous wells at the port of *Hamwic*, Saxon Southampton, may have been encouraged by the high density of population, but the wells on farms like Odell, Bedfordshire, may imply an awareness of the risks from polluted water brought about by a growing population, or even the need to extend settlement onto good soils which were not close to water.

The extent to which the landscape was being farmed and the efficiency of agricultural practices may be measured by the frequency with which farms were abandoned for new sites. The growth of population and commensurate expansion of settlement is reflected by the increasingly varied soil environments settled through the Anglo-Saxon period. The analyses support the idea that the relocation of farms occurred quite frequently, with a considerable horizon of shifting settlement taking place in the 100 years around AD 700, for nearly all early Anglo-Saxon settlements appear to have been abandoned during that period. This may be when settlement patterns began to stabilise. The pagan Anglo-Saxon cemeteries are much easier to date because of the larger number of artefacts found in them as grave-goods. They therefore provide the best evidence for shifting settlement. Very few pagan cemeteries were in use throughout the period, and those that were tend to be the large examples in eastern England which may have been centralised depositories, not belonging to individual settlements. However, the foundation of a new settlement/cemetery may be the result of shifting patterns brought about by such things as soil exhaustion and plague, or they may be new settlements caused by a growth of population. Similarly, abandonment can be viewed as a shift or a decline in population. If the pattern of use and disuse of the cemeteries also reflects settlement movement one would be drawn to conclude that either population levels fluctuated frequently and/or that shifting settlement was common.

The stability of the rural economy may, in part be dependent on the effects of climatic change. Bede describes how in the 670s the South Saxons were saved 'from a cruel and horrible extinction' as a result of their conversion to Christianity by Wilfrid:

'. . . for no rain had fallen in the province for three years prior to his arrival, and a terrible famine had ensued which reduced many to an awful death' (HE IV 13). Extreme fluctuations in climate are more likely to have a detectable effect on man's settlement patterns than gradual changes. There is evidence for a minor advance in European glaciers during the period AD 700-900 (Denton and Karlén 1973) and Tooley has demonstrated that there was a period of climatic extremes in addition to a complex marine transgression sequence at this time; sea-levels rose to a maximum of + 1.2 m above sea-level in *c*. AD 150, falling during the following 500 years to a minimum altitude of + 0.4 m above sea-level by *c*. 650 (Tooley 1978, pp. 182–92). Specific examples of the effects of such transgressions have been noted in studies of settlement patterns in coastal and estuarine regions (Hallam 1961; Hawkes 1968; Thompson 1980).

With an assumed growing population in early Anglo-Saxon England there would have been increasing pressure on rural resources, especially by the second half of the seventh century. With the development of urban centres and religious foundations greater demand would have been placed on the hinterland. The predictable result would have been an intensification of agriculture and we may be witnessing this in the drift of settlements ending on more fertile and productive soils and the changes in cereal crops being cultivated. Any agricultural surplus would have been required to support the development of urban centres which in turn encouraged craft specialisation. In this way the move to more fertile soils may have been made to improve productivity per person and increase output for similar or less effort.

Exchange

The exchange of raw materials and finished products in a society is an activity which is inextricably bound up with economic, social and political life. The nature of the movement of goods can only be understood if it is seen in relation to the complex and changing framework of society. The basic model for early Anglo-Saxon England is that small cohesive social units with low population densities merged by peaceful and forceful means into larger political agglomerations. Exchange will have been an important factor in this general process of consolidation. Small isolated communities would have been extremely vulnerable if crops failed and, in such circumstances, alliances with neighbouring groups would have assumed great importance when food was required in emergencies. If allies were able to provide the necessities of life, primitive valuables could have acted as a medium of exchange; primitive valuables may also have been used as a means of contracting alliances as may marriages between members of different political groups. In this way, alliance relations between descent groups would simultaneously have involved political, economic and social affairs and it would be entirely artificial to try and divorce them. This type of organisation may be epitomised by early sixth-century settlements whose cemeteries reveal less social differentiation than later ones. Despite their displaying a generalised and largely self-sufficient subsistence economy, precious metals and other valuable goods are known to have moved between such communities.

The gradual development of cohesive political units with important leaders of lineages will have extended and strengthened this pattern. Such leadership may be typified by superior access to, and use of, ordinary goods and valuables such as food and women through ceremonial forms of exchange. Goods may also be acquired for the benefit of the élite sections of society by barter with neighbouring districts; such goods could then be channelled through the hierarchy thereby reinforcing the position of the élite.

We should therefore seek evidence for long-distance exchange as indications of political alliances and the growth of centralised political organisation. Bede's commentary on aspects of seventh-century English life reflects the nature and extent of the traffic of gifts, particularly between royalty and senior members of the Christian Church; the items and the materials serve to remind us of some of the primitive valuables seen in the pagan graves. The items mentioned by Bede include clothing, gold ornament, a silver mirror, a gold and ivory comb, a horse, regalia, presents as the price of peace and gold and silver vessels (HE II 11, II 12, III 14, III 24, IV 1). The *Anglo-Saxon Chronicle* occasionally mentions the giving of land and gifts in return for peace.

The primitive valuables involved in such exchanges were neither money nor cash, but items that were often spent in political and social spheres of activity to form alliances in peacetime and during war, as well as compensation for death and bridewealth. In this way much of the movement of exotic items which can be traced archaeologically, can be seen as part of a system of ceremonial exchange in the formation of alliances, that is used by the heads of lineages for important political and social transactions.

The seventh century sees the appearance of leadership by birth, perhaps resulting from a series of successful leaders from a single descent group. As such kingdom states were evolving, primitive money appears. It was used for political obligations such as taxes and fines, for reward and increasingly for ordinary market exchange. Significantly, by the end of the period coinage as cash had appeared for commercial transactions. Such coinage was issued by rulers and may be viewed both as a measure of their power and prestige as well as an attempt to extend their influence.

Overseas Exchange

The occupants of the farms of early Anglo-Saxon England lived an essentially self-sufficient existence, and the farms were located to make maximum use of available resources amidst land most suitable for the form of agriculture practised. The majority of items required on an everyday basis such as food, clothing, building materials, fuel and water, were either to be found locally or were produced on the farm. There is no evidence that such goods moved any great distance from their place of manufacture and no reason why this should be necessary. However, some raw materials and goods, whether they fall into a utilitarian or luxury category, were not always available locally and these give us the clearest testimony of the extent of exchange in early Anglo-Saxon society. The actual mechanisms by which such goods were acquired, that is by some form of gift or an exchange involving such things as surplus agricultural produce, rare local resources or finished products, can only be inferred. In addition to identifying the mechanisms for the movement of goods, there are difficulties in establishing the quantities involved, especially when considered in terms of their relative value. In the same way we are not able to talk of the volume of agricultural yields and the excess *per capita* from the farms.

Indisputable evidence for the movement of goods is provided by commodities which came from the Continent, and at times originated from even further afield. Such articles will be discussed on the basis of their distribution patterns as they fall into two distinct groups. Some are densely concentrated in small areas, for instance the volume of amethyst beads, gold coin, garnet, rock crystal spheres and wheel-thrown pottery in Kent, which have Continental or Mediterranean sources. Others have a more widespread distribution in England, for instance amber, crystal beads and ivory rings, and which are generally from north-west Europe. These commodities are arguably the primitive valuables of early Anglo-Saxon society, used to oil the wheels of social and political activities (Huggett 1982 and forthcoming).

Amber, a fossil tree resin, is commonly found in graves particularly in central and eastern England. It is found predominately in female graves, either rough or facetted and polished, pierced and worn as beads. The position of the beads in the grave normally suggests they were worn on a necklace, but a case can be made for some having been worn in the hair. The actual quantities varies between one and twenty but occasional graves have very large numbers; for example grave 71 at the cemetery of Long Wittenham I (Berkshire) contained 280 beads.

The largest quantity in a single cemetery, nearly 1,000 in total, is from Sleaford (Lincolnshire). When viewed in terms of the number of beads *per capita* on a regionalised basis (Arnold 1980), it appears that in southern England, Kent had a monopoly over the movement of beads, but the large quantity in Kent is an isolated peak when compared to the more general distribution with smaller peaks found elsewhere. This suggests different sources or means of acquiring the amber. Throughout the area in which amber beads are found there appear to be single, sometimes adjacent cemeteries with relatively large numbers of beads surrounded by cemeteries with lesser quantities.

The principal source of amber in Europe is the shores of the Baltic Sea, although it is found elsewhere, for instance Rumania and Sicily. Some amber can be found washed up onto the shores of East Anglia, but its role as a source appears to be minimal given its relative rarity in cemeteries near to that coast. The marked differences between the distribution of Anglo-Saxon amber and that of the British earlier Bronze Age implies that neither distributions need be controlled in detail by the location of the source. Unfortunately no characterisation studies of early Anglo-Saxon amber have been made, but the Baltic Sea is believed to be the source (Beck 1970).

Another example of an imported good with a widespread distribution is ivory, which normally occurs as rings. The rings were used in a variety of ways: some were worn on the arm or wrist; others appear to be the frames for the mouths of pouches which are often found to contain small metal items; a third use was as a girdle hanger. The evidence is frequently ambiguous because of the degree of preservation and the inadequacy of early reports. Over 70 examples are known, varying in size from 9 cm to 15 cm diameter, averaging 10 cm.

They are distributed in eastern England, particularly Lincolnshire and Cambridgeshire, and in Wiltshire, with only a few examples in Kent (Figure 2.13). The highest number, eleven, at Illington (Norfolk) is followed by Sleaford and Caistor-by Norwich (Norfolk) with five each. The source of the ivory is difficult to determine, and the question of whether the material derives from elephant or walrus has not been resolved. The interpretation of some examples that have been studied is that they were rings cut from the upper part of an elephant's tusk with the pulp cavity forming the natural ring (Myres and Green 1973, pp. 100–3). However, others appear to be made up in regular jointed sections which do not conform to the natural lines of cleavage. This suggests the use of smaller pieces of ivory, possibly fragments of elephant tusk, or the smaller walrus tusk, or even the tusks of wild boar which are on occasion found pierced and threaded on necklaces. If the source of ivory was elephant (MacGregor 1985), Indian or African, a larger number might be expected in Kent which appears to have had a dominance over many of the goods imported from the Continent and Mediterranean. The easterly distribution, implying importation from Scandinavia, might point towards walrus. Walrus were quite commonly encountered in the Shetland Isles and the Scandinavian coasts until quite recently. It has been suggested that after AD 700 until the eleventh century, 60 per cent of ivory was derived from walrus (Beckwith 1972).

Rock crystal was used for beads and was made into spheres mounted in metal cages, but the distributions are different. The balls only occur in graves singly, normally accompanying female-rich graves, in eight cases associated with silver spoons, which are often perforated, both lying between the knees. The beads, sometimes described as spindle whorls, are pierced, sometimes smoothed and slightly domed, or facetted. They are found in graves concentrated in central and eastern England (Figure 2.14), the largest number being from Sleaford where there are approximately 25 from five graves, although absolute numbers were not reported. The greatest number from a single grave are the twelve from Chatham Lines, Barrow II (Kent). The balls are normally

Figure 2.13: The distribution of ivory rings in early Anglo-Saxon England (after Huggett 1982, fig. 7, with additions). They are found predominantly in the area of England between Dorset and the Wash

spheroid and enclosed in a cage consisting of either a cross-shaped piece of sheet metal, often silver, or two metal bands. These are wrapped around the ball and fastened at the top with a collar through which passed a wire ring for suspension or to pass round the wrist. About 30 examples are known, 75 per cent of them from Kent, especially at Bifrons and Chatham Lines with four each,

Figure 2.14: The distribution of rock crystal beads in early Anglo-Saxon England (after Huggett 1982, fig. 5). They are most common in the area of the country between Dorset and the Wash

and outside Kent at Chessell Down (Isle of Wight) with two.

Sources of adequate rock crystal for the manufacture of beads are widespread in England and Europe, but as the spheres require large crystals it may be possible to narrow down the range of sources. Germany, Switzerland and Scotland may be suggested.

That more than one source for the crystal was involved is suggested by the differing distributions and the manner in which few cemeteries contain both beads and spheres. Only Faversham, Bifrons and Chatham Lines (Kent), and Kempston (Bedfordshire) fall into this category. The beads are more common than the spheres in a ratio of about 3:1.

The crystal beads and spheres are probably the only objects made of one material and which have different distributions. They highlight the division between the localised and widespread types of distribution pattern. In addition to the crystal spheres there is a wide variety of goods which also have a localised distribution, particularly in Kent.

Considerable quantities of gold were utilised in Kent. It is found in the form of coin imported from the Continent and in jewellery. Analysis of both the coin and jewellery shows that the gradual debasement of the coin may be matched by the quality of the gold in the jewellery, pointing to the coin as being the source of the jewellers' raw material (Hawkes, Merrick and Metcalf 1966). Kent was the major producer and consumer of gold jewellery and it is not surprising to find that the greatest number of coins is found there also, often mounted on suspension loops and worn on necklaces.

While the greatest concentration of gold is found in Kent (Figure 2.15) there are localised peaks caused by the Crondall hoard in Hampshire, the contents of the purse from mound 1 at Sutton Hoo in Suffolk and the possible hoard at Kingston-on-Thames (Surrey) (Rigold 1975). Prior to AD 625 the coins are found mainly in Kent and the upper Thames valley; afterwards they are found spread over a wider area as far afield as Ireland, Scotland, Derbyshire and Yorkshire, although they remain concentrated in south-east England. This change in distribution appears to be a reflection of the changes in the mints from which they were drawn. Prior to AD 625 the sources are southerly, Lyon, Provençal, Vienne, Marseilles and Arles, whereas after that date the mints from which the coin was derived are mainly in the Meuse and Moselle regions, such as Limoges and Paris (Rigold 1975). It may be no coincidence that the occasion of this shift in distribution was also the time when the devaluation of the gold had become serious.

The coins are found in graves, hoards, reused in jewellery and as 'casual' finds, the last category being the most numerous. The more obvious uses to which the coin was put, the contexts in which

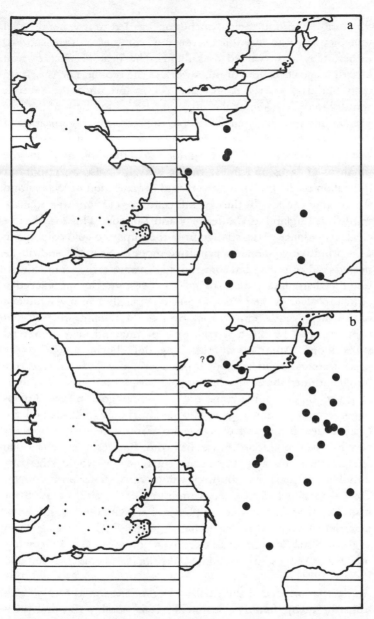

Figure 2.15: The distribution of unmounted gold coin in the British Isles (small dots) and the Continental sources (large dots). a = AD 595–625; b = AD 625–671. In the earlier phase the coin is concentrated in Kent, but later they have a more widespread distribution. The location of the mints moves northwards through time. (Data: Rigold 1975)

they are found and their distribution has led to a general belief that they were not used as currency in commercial transactions; rather, they were valued as bullion. The near absence of true hoards (deposits of coin or metalwork in the ground not associated with burial) in early Anglo-Saxon England until the seventh century may be taken as an important indication both of the role of hoarding in other societies and of the economic organisation of this period. Such gold is an important development in its use as primitive money, the first uniform commodity used in the payment of taxes and fines. In this way it is also an important indication of the growing powers and organisation of leaders and the kingdom states. In the seventh century gold coin was actually minted in England at Canterbury and London. This may be the clearest evidence of the change from the imported gold coin acting as a primitive valuable to primitive money. Near the end of the period gold coin may have been used in commercial transactions, but the dwindling supply of gold in western Europe caused a switch to silver as the principal precious metal. The silver coinage of the late seventh century took over the developing role of gold coin and may be the first true cash in England for commercial transactions. Alternatively this may only be a change in the precious metal brought about by necessity, and silver coinage may have continued the earlier function of the gold coinage, as bullion.

It is difficult to understand the function of gold in early Anglo-Saxon society in much greater detail. Certainly gold, as bullion, is a practical means of storing wealth. From *c.* AD 620 there were rare English imitations of Frankish coin, but despite any possible tendency for this coin to become currency, it would still have found its greatest use for high-value transactions and storage. Once a surplus had been converted to gold it could be used, for instance, to reward, and to supply jewellers with the necessary raw material to produce lavish items of jewellery; it has even been suggested that Scandinavian decorated gold pendants, bracteates, may have been a source of bullion like the later coins (Hawkes and Pollard 1981).

Most knowledge of the earliest Anglo-Saxon gold coins comes from the hoard found at Crondall. It is notably the first post-Roman coin hoard in England and may in itself signify a change in the economy. One coin bears the mint-name DOROVERNIS CIVITAS, Canterbury, and another gives the mint name LONDVINIV around the cross; the obverse shows a priestly head. These 'thirds' of a Merovingian solidus fall within the period *c.* AD 604 to 616 and *c.* AD 675. There are also two series of coins in which a secular character is more explicit, one bearing the name AVDVARLD REGES, and another showing a diademed portrait with 'sceptre' and a reverse with the moneyer's name WITMEN around a cross. Aufvald may be Eadbald, King of Kent 616–40, but whether or not this is the case, the coins point to both a royal and ecclesiastical responsibility for their production.

Gold allowed the easy storage of wealth because of the high ratio of value to bulk, and its being minted by royal and ecclesiastical courts may reflect the need to administer justice, maintain officials and finance commerce, and goes hand-in-hand with the development of written law and taxation; in the oldest Kentish laws, fines were listed in gold 'shillings' and in silver. By the end of the seventh century, possibly *c.* AD 675, a shortage of gold forced a change to silver coins (*sceattas*) and their frequency in Kent points to both Kentish supremacy in exchange and, perhaps, the direction in which commerce was moving when the change was necessary.

Grierson (1961) has suggested that seventh century coins have a social rather than a commercial significance. This may in part be true, but it ignores the mechanisms by which gold was obtained, assessed and utilised. It must be seen against the social background of early Anglo-Saxon society in the seventh century. This was a society with true leaders of kingdom states within which commercial activities were becoming more institutionalised. Society had changed from the earlier structure where primitive valuables were of greater importance.

The clearest testimony to the level of exchange being carried on between England and the Continent, especially in transactions involving gold, is the existence of sets of balances accompanied by weights. Fourteen partial or complete sets are known, especially from graves in Kent, but also from the upper Thames valley where they tend not to be complete. The majority are dated to the seventh century, the exception being that from Shrivenham (Oxfordshire) which dates to the second half of the sixth century or later (pers. comm. C. Scull). These small copper alloy balances had an inverted T-shaped beam supported from its centre by a suspension arm. From the ends of the beam were suspended the pans (Figure 2.16). The weights are custom-made or ground down Roman coins; one or two appear to be actual Byzantine weights, or imitations, indicating the extent of exchange networks in the later sixth and seventh centuries in Europe. Where accurate

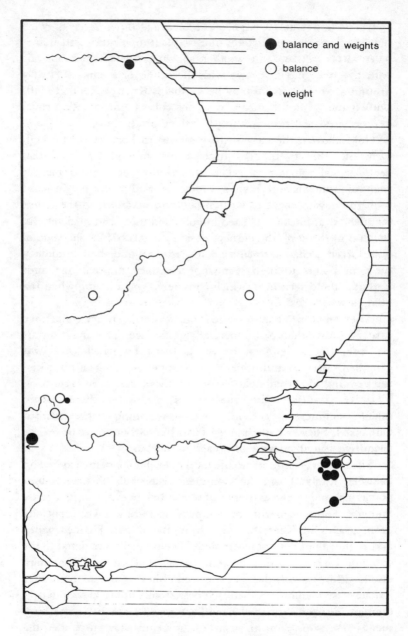

Figure 2.16: The distribution of early Anglo-Saxon balances and weights. The majority of the complete sets are found in Kent, weights being more rare from inland sites

values for the weights are available, or the weights can be reweighed, they suggest that at least one unit was in use, particularly in Kent, based on *c*. 3.11 g. The majority of the balances, buried in Kentish male graves without any particular range of grave-goods, belong to the late sixth and seventh centuries, the earliest being from Shrivenham, dated to the mid- or second half of the sixth century. There are few examples outside Kent and none of those found in the upper Thames valley seem to have been buried as complete sets. Some of the Kentish examples were reported as being found with touchstones, used for assessing the purity of gold (Moore and Oddy 1985). Thus, at times, not only was the quantity assessed using the balances, but the tools were available to measure the quality. This evidence for weighing gold shows how the coin was not being used as currency, and it may also be significant that many of the balances date to the period when the debasement of the gold coin was at its most serious. Given the small size of the balances they must have been used to weigh small quantities of a precious substance, but gold need not be the only material involved. Larger balances, if they existed, have not survived.

The fact that so many of the balances are associated with graves-goods dating from *c*. AD 600 onwards may reflect a growing demand for luxury goods and the scale of such transactions, and also the need to regularise the transactions. The apparent rarity of balances in the sixth century emphasises the change that had taken place, especially in Kent. That a regular unit was in use, which differs from the Continental value, reflects a centralised authority and even, perhaps, that the bearers of the balances were official representatives of the court, which would point to the destiny of the gold; the possibility that the gold coins found in Sutton Hoo mound 1 were a royal weight standard has been suggested (Spratling 1980). The distribution of the balances and gold coin mirrors the areas in which goldworking was most common. The need to regularise transactions in east Kent may also suggest the existence of organised points of entry for traders, but no such settlement of this date has been identified, although there are strong hints that Kent was moving towards that development in the seventh century with commercial centres on the Wantsum Channel and the River Stour (Hodges 1982a).

Another imported luxury item which is also very strongly represented in Kent is amethyst, usually polished pear or droplet shaped beads, pierced down their length. Most have been found in graves especially at Faversham which accounts for about two-thirds of all such beads found in England. Their origin is thought to be the east Mediterranean and if the majority were being imported into Kent very few were allowed to pass further. There are rarely more than two in a grave, the largest number from a single grave being the 17 examples from grave 1 at Breach Down (Kent). They, like most beads, are usually found in female graves, strung with others in a necklace or used as pendants mounted in metal loops. Some may have been worn as earrings.

The vast majority of the pottery used in England for both domestic and funerary purposes was hand-made locally. However, some wheel-thrown pottery was imported from the Continent and is found in contexts dated after AD 625, mostly in Kent (Evison 1979b). They are grouped into five general types: bottles, jugs, biconical and globular bowls and shouldered jars, the total number being about 130; the cemetery of St Peter's, Broadstairs (Kent), produced 26 alone. Most are found as 'accessory' vessels with inhumation graves, often showing signs of extensive use with damage repair. Bottles make up 51 per cent of the total, all but three being from Kent, the important exceptions being from the seventh-century rich graves of Asthall (Oxfordshire) and Sutton Hoo (Suffolk). The high incidence of vessels compared with dishes may, as Evison suggests (ibid.), imply that they arrived as containers of oil or wine; the crude workmanship of some examples may emphasise that the contents were more important than the packaging, even though they may have been viewed as valuable objects in some secondary function.

This pottery is a rare instance of an import that is found more often in male graves (46 per cent) than female (27 per cent); bowls and jugs are more common in female graves. In the light of the division between Kent and the rest of England in terms of some luxury imports, it is interesting that Evison (ibid.) observed that the wheel-thrown vessels found outside Kent, and which are widely scattered, have originated from different and often distinct parts of north-west Europe. This may serve to emphasise that this long-distance trade reflects political alliances and the organisation that lay behind it, as much as geographical location.

A similar pattern is found with imported bronze vessels (Richards 1986). Most of the Coptic vessels found in Kent are types which Werner (1957; 1961) has shown to have been common on the Continent, but outside Kent there are a large number of rarities. Examples of a type belonging to a general class of the later sixth and seventh centuries on the Continent, with drop-handles and tripod rings, are known from the Kentish sites of Coombe, Gilton, Faversham, Sarre and Ash. Three-legged Coptic forms are known only from seventh-century contexts, often rich barrow burials such as Sutton Hoo, Taplow (Berkshire), Asthall and Cuddesdon. Byzantine vessels in contexts dated to the second half of the sixth century are known from the Isle of Wight (Arnold 1982a).

Kent also seems to have been the major importer of garnet, although the actual amount that survives has not been quantified. Large quantities were brought to Kent from the early sixth century onwards, with the jewellery contained in mound 1 at Sutton Hoo creating a notable seventh-century peak. Its distribution again emphasises that the dispersal of some rare imports may have been governed by social or political factors. Used as embellishments to ornate metalwork, the garnet may have originated from any of the main world sources, Egypt, Britain, Turkey, Scandinavia, Ceylon and may parts of Europe. One analysis carried out has pointed to Bohemia as a source in that instance (Roosens *et al.* 1970). The study of the garnets used in the jewellery found at Sutton Hoo has suggested that the source was similar to that which the Frankish world drew on, but was different to that used in Gotland and south Russia. No light was thrown on the mechanism of exchange, except that the assemblages of garnet on a number of the Sutton Hoo jewels were distinct (Bimson, La Neice and Leese 1982).

Alongside these luxuries we may consider a range of other imports to Kent, especially the numerous Frankish imports such as ornaments and weapons which were buried as grave-goods. As a whole they indicate contacts with both the kingdom of Neustria in north-west France and with that of the Austrasian Franks in the Rhineland. The sheer quantity of such imports might preclude tribute being the mechanism of transmission to Kent, but if a material exchange was involved we must look to the area of consumables to fill the other half of the transaction, for durable Kentish items are known, but are rare, on the Continent. In the absence of evidence of valuable raw materials being extracted in England at this time, both explanations remain possible. There are other potential imports which are less apparent; mercury, for instance, was used to gild at least some of the metalwork in England at this time (Oddy 1980). The major sources of mercury in Europe are Italy, Yugoslavia and Spain. Exchange in such a commodity with Spain may explain the amount of Anglo-Saxon metalwork in the Bordeaux region of south-west France (Leeds 1953), as at Herpes-en-Charente, as well as the Frankish interest in the area expressed by the campaigns of Clovis from the late fifth century onwards (James 1977).

A final example of a luxury product with a restricted distribution is glassware. Glass vessels appear in a variety of forms in graves and were classified by Harden (1956b) into eleven types divided into three chronological groups, which have since been extended and reviewed (Harden 1978). These are also concentrated in Kent with 65 per cent of the total (25 per cent at Faversham alone), and there is little change in this pattern through time except that the total quantities fall off during the seventh century. The strong similarities between English glassware and that in Belgium, northern France and the Rhineland, especially the area around Trier where Carolingian glass factories are known, has suggested that the majority of glassware in England was imported. However, some types, the squat jars, bag beakers, pouch bottles and cone beakers (Evison 1972) are rare on the Continent and may well have been made in England; the Faversham area is a strong contender for the centre of this production. The rarity of glass outside Kent may again imply that, when imported, it arrived through Kent, but the occurrence of glass elsewhere in England indicates a complex pattern of dispersal (Figure 2.17).

There remains one import which we may consider which is found concentrated in two distinct regions, and which also has exotic origins. Cowrie shells originating in the Indian Ocean or Middle East, are occasionally found in late sixth or seventh century graves, most frequently in Cambridgeshire and Kent. Often they are accompanied in graves by other 'trinkets', at the foot of the grave in a wooden box, or worn as pendants. Unfortunately there have rarely been precise identifications although two are stated to be of Middle Eastern origin, the *Cypraea Arabica* from Sarre grave 238 and a tiger cowrie from Haslingfield (Cambridgeshire), whose source is the Red Sea. Another example found amongst cremated bone in an urn from the cemetery at Girton (Cambridgeshire) has also been identified as *Cypraea tigris L.* (Arnold and Wilkinson 1984, p. 26).

Some details of the mechanisms of dispersal of such imported goods can be obtained by a more detailed examination of their distributions. The different nature of the materials imported to particular parts of England in the sixth and seventh centuries is

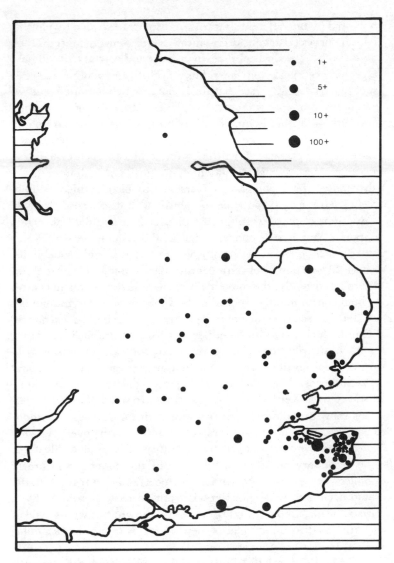

Figure 2.17: The distribution of glass vessels in early Anglo-Saxon England (after Huggett 1982, fig. 3). Glassware has a widespread distribution with a marked concentration in Kent

mirrored by the different patterns of dispersal revealed by plotting fall-off curves (Huggett forthcoming). The Kentish concentration of amethyst, glass, wheel-thrown pottery and crystal balls all have a pronounced peak and sharp fall-off. Until the manner in which such goods are dispersed within regions is better understood we can only assume, at present, that places with very high consumption are also the points of distribution where a paramount controlled such prestige exchange, consuming most locally and allowing the passage of a little to other places. As we shall see, those cemeteries which display high quantities of such imports are also those where potential leaders are to be identified. Within Kent itself it may be possible to identify a shift, or more probably a division, of power through the distribution and date of certain imports. Amethyst is concentrated at Faversham, in west Kent, and dates to the seventh century, whereas crystal and probably the wheel-thrown bottles of sixth century date are found in east Kent. More importantly, the movement of these luxury items to centres of high consumption emphasises the superior access of individuals in stateless societies to valuables through ceremonial exchange, behind which may also lie superior access to ordinary goods.

Such distributions are in marked contrast to those with, arguably, a northern and Baltic Sea origin, especially ivory and crystal beads. The centres of highest consumption are some distance from Kent where the quantities are small. Their distributions show pronounced concentrations with a number of secondary, yet significant clusters of smaller size over a wide geographical range; the greatest quantity of ivory is at Sleaford. The secondary peaks occur throughout the country and are of smaller size, separated by voids, which certainly contrasts with the rapid decline in prestigious goods from an easterly source. Even crystal beads, whose actual source is unknown, but whose type of geographic distribution places them with this group, has a similar fall-off with a peak at Sleaford.

Within the overall distribution of the amber beads there are two concentrations, one at the cemetery of Sleaford which also forms the centre for such items as ivory and crystal beads, and the other in Kent. The distribution of these Scandinavian materials might be equated with south Scandinavian derived metalwork found in Kent (Hawkes and Pollard 1981) and with Norwegian derived metalwork in eastern England (Hines 1984). The implications of a more general dispersal of prestige items, as is generally the case outside Kent, is of a less developed society more dependent on

primitive valuables moving horizontally and cementing relationships between major and minor allies. These societies may have
comprised small political units and low population densities when
compared with the more concentrated areas of consumption
discussed above. This difference may, to some extent, be reflected
in the variation in political development of such kingdoms as Kent
and Mercia (see Chapter 5).

The implications of the very sharp fall-off with increasing
distance from Kent are that such items were controlled at
particular centres which maintained a near monopoly over their
supply. The one exception to the pattern is the cowrie shells which
although they have an eastern origin are not concentrated in Kent,
occurring in similar numbers in the Cambridgeshire-Suffolk
border area and the Yorkshire Wolds. The more northerly
distributed material implies far less restriction than pertained in
Kent. Overall there appears to have been very little exchange
between Kent and other areas of England in the sixth and seventh
centuries, but where there is a potential link it may indicate the
direction of alliances between groups. Gold coin, for instance also
occurs in the upper Thames valley and in Suffolk; crystal balls are
also found in Cambridgeshire-Suffolk and the Isle of Wight;
garnet in Kent and Suffolk.

The distribution of amber beads in southern England has been
considered when weighted in terms of their density per person per
area (Arnold 1980) emphasising that Kent was a major consumer
despite not having the greatest density in raw terms. This type of
analysis can be carried out for the whole country showing that
there are a number of areas which are prominent in the consumption of the imported goods and which may have been developing
centres of political and economic power (Huggett forthcoming).
One of these concentrations is in Kent, divided into two parts in
the eastern and western parts of the county. This concentration
extends across the River Thames to the south part of Essex and
another is centred on the Ipswich area of Suffolk, partly the result
of the rich burial at Sutton Hoo. Elsewhere there are equally
significant concentrations in the Sleaford area of Lincolnshire,
Driffield (North Yorkshire), Surrey, the Linton region in
Cambridgeshire, Sussex and in Berkshire. This map (Figure 2.18)
should be compared with that of the overall distribution of graves
to emphasise how one is not merely a reflection of the other. The
problem is one of relating the spatial pattern with the spatial
process. While they must have been closely linked, it would help

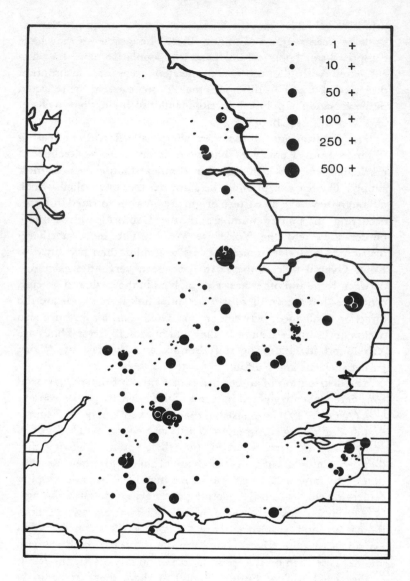

Figure 2.18: The distribution of amber beads in early Anglo-Saxon England (after Huggett 1982, fig. 1). They are found in most areas of England, especially in the area between the Wash and Dorset and in Kent

if we could distinguish between the circulation of such goods and their deposition in graves, for it is the latter which is actually being studied. It remains one of the basic archaeological assumptions, however, that the two are linked.

The unequal distribution of such prestigious goods found in the cemeteries may be seen as a reflection of hierarchies in early Anglo-Saxon England and how the maintenance of such hierarchies was closely bound up with the consumption of such valuables. We may predict that there will be a close correlation between the strongest position in the most developed hierarchies and the best contacts for obtaining exotic goods. Much of the exchange was probably in the form of reciprocity bound up with gift-giving as Grierson implies (1959). One of the implications of the Kentish monopoly of certain materials and sources is that other areas must have been either dependent on the Kentish elite for such goods, or sought their own exotic goods by making contacts with elites elsewhere, that is, entering into an entirely different network. Given the pre-eminence and advanced economic development of Kent, we might conclude that the exchange of prestige items was directed towards the areas with the most marked social differentiation.

Such an advanced social and administrative development is certainly apparent in seventh century Kentish law-codes; but it is odd that these make little provision for economic transactions. This may only reflect the nature and purpose of the law-codes, but it may also point to the undeveloped nature of institutionalised commerce or the manner in which such exchange was connected only with those who issued and administered the law. It is only in the laws of Wihtraed *c.* AD 695 that travellers from afar, or foreigners, are instructed to shout or blow a horn before leaving a road, to avoid being treated as a thief or worse; this says as much about the controls placed on the English population as the desire to protect foreigners. Such travellers may have been missionaries or emissaries, but the term presumably also encompasses those involved in commerce irrespective of whether they originated from across the English Channel. Similarly a late seventh-century law of Wessex provided that the king should receive a large part of the *wergeld* of any stranger 'who came across the frontier'. There is no mention on the regulation of prices or of a method of arbitration in the event of dispute, suggesting that commerce was regulated by custom or the social mores of gift-giving, and had not reached a sufficiently organised scale for legal controls to be necessary; the earliest hint of such controls is to be found in King Ine's laws, in which traders were to make their transactions before witnesses or the king's reeve. These laws were issued *c.* 694. We are witnessing here the variations that existed in early Anglo-Saxon England in social and economic development. The areas which display the greatest success in acquiring valuables are also those that first develop leadership by birth. They are also the first to achieve levels of commercialism higher than those based on ceremonial exchanges as a means of forming social and political alliances; the latter type of system may have remained in use longer in some areas.

Commerce can be seen to be more closely regulated from the late seventh and eighth centuries onwards in the form of manufacturing and trading centres (Hodges 1982a), although these certainly do not necessarily imply free trade; in fact, quite the opposite, for the evidence from Saxon Southampton, *Hamwic*, indicates that the craftsman there were as tied and organised as the rural 'peasantry'. Such trading emporia may have been established purely for the profit of the king and the servicing of his estates. Toll charters were issued for Kentish settlements such as Sarre and Dover in AD 761 and AD 696 X 716 respectively, in keeping with the centralisation of commercial activities demonstrated by the excavations at *Hamwic* and Ipswich. Notably a large number of the earliest silver *sceattas*, the silver coins which replaced the gold issues more common earlier in the seventh century, are concentrated in east Kent around the Wantsum Channel (Rigold and Metcalf 1977). Like the River Solent, the Wantsum enjoyed a double tide and provided a natural, sheltered harbour, although later silting of the Wantsum makes present appearances deceptive. The earliest suggestion of the regulation of commerce applies to Fordwich (Kent) in AD 675; Fordwich is higher up the River Stour and about 5 km from Canterbury which was developing as a royal and ecclesiastical centre from *c.* AD 600 onwards. Each of the major kingdoms appear to have had such trading centres in the eighth century (Hodges 1982a; Biddle 1976), even an inland centre such as Northampton was a royal centre and is also described as a trading centre. The development of such trading centres is only relevant here in as far as they point to the direction in which economy was evolving in the sixth and seventh centuries. The formation of the commercial basis of the kingdoms is not uniform and geography must have played an important part in the speed with which they evolved out of the less commercial exchanges of primitive valuables between earlier corporate descent groups and cohesive political units. The desire of landlocked kingdoms to share in the potential of overseas trade may explain their belligerence towards coastal kingdoms in the seventh century.

It may be possible to link the distribution patterns of imported goods with those trade routes reconstructed on the Continent (Hodges 1982a, p. 29ff.). This may well extend our understanding of alliances on the larger scale (Huggett forthcoming) although we should be wary of assuming that the sources of the material are relevant to the question of alliances with all of England. It seems probable that Kent imported material directly from the Frankish world; Scandinavian imports to Kent may have come directly or were also channelled through Francia. There were probably direct connections between the Continent and other parts of England, reflected, for instance, in the large volume of Scandinavian material in East Anglia. But some of this material may have been dispersed from Kent.

Many writers are unnecessarily pessimistic about the value of archaeology in the understanding of exchange systems in the absence of literary evidence; Wood points out that 'distribution maps rarely make it possible to distinguish between trade, exchange and plunder' (1983, p. 3). But this is an oversimplification of the study of distributions and of the nature of exchange. The literary sources for contact between Francia and surrounding regions do not allow more detailed understanding than archaeological sources. There is little doubt that Francia was powerful, demonstrated by Byzantium believing in, and feeling threatened by, the Merovingian claims to hegemony; Wood argues that the literary references to alliance between English kings and Francia may be viewed as a medium through which many Frankish goods entered England. But if the Franks were the *dominant* partner it is difficult to explain why so much material should have been channelled towards England with little apparently going back in return.

This is actually a problem which faces any interpretation of the movement of goods to England from overseas. It is quite common in primitive exchange systems that the movement of goods can only be seen in one direction. This may in part be explained by one half of the reciprocity taking the form of labour services and trade in consumables; a large proportion of the goods which may be considered of high value by reason of the distance over which the raw materials had been transported, and their resulting rarity, may have been given for services, gifts or payments for work, what may be termed institutional exchange. Similarly, primitive valuables may be paid by weaker groups to create alliances. Alternatively, they may be given as a mark of generosity so as to increase the cohesive forces in society, known as levelling mechanisms. In this way nothing visible in the archaeological record constitutes the other half of the exchange; such consumables as animals and crops fall into the same category. This type of explanation may help us to understand the one-sided nature of exchange relationships with the Continent, noting also that the English probably had no direct access to a valuable and durable raw material without going to the extent of deep mining. There are very few observable exports in both the sixth and seventh centuries and Wood's argument for Frankish hegemony over at least Kent may explain the situation if goods moved in one direction, as one leader enhanced his superiority by making lavish gifts to neighbours. Problems remain, however, because of such evidence as the weights and balances found in Kentish graves. If the conclusions derived from the analysis of the content of Merovingian gold coin and Anglo-Saxon jewellery are correct (Hawkes, Merrick and Metcalf 1966), the jewellers do not appear to have refined the gold. It may, therefore, also be the case that the jewellers were not over concerned with the purity of the gold and that, therefore, the balances, weights and touchstones did not belong to them. We should not however confuse the transaction with the eventual use of the raw material. There can be little doubt that some people in early Anglo-Saxon England were dealing in gold and were concerned about quality and quantity, and it does not matter if the balances were the property of foreign traders because the implication remains that transactions were taking place.

In the search for foreign exports many commentators place a great deal of emphasis on textiles, stimulated by a limited amount of written evidence recording gifts and the exchange of textiles in the eighth century. Certainly textiles were produced on a widespread basis, although it is impossible to measure the scale of manufacture. The only instance in which textiles of known, or suspected, origin have been identified are braids brocaded with gold strips (Crowfoot and Hawkes 1967). They were used as woven decorations to headdresses and the borders of garments found in richer graves in England during the second half of the sixth and early seventh centuries, significantly mainly in Kent. Such textiles as these are found on the Continent between the fifth and the eighth centuries. On a technical basis it is possible to exclude those Continental examples which are not made in the same tradition as the English ones. Some of the Continental examples, for instance the headband from Cologne, St Severinus grave 73, is very similar in design to one from Chessell Down grave 45, and that from Saint-Denis, Paris grave 9 and Planig, Rheinhessen, Germany are similar to some Kentish braids; they are, however, made of silk and no silk has yet been identified in an Anglo-Saxon grave. Silk is categorised as a luxury import into western Europe and, it is assumed, arrived as ready made lengths of braid. The woollen tablet weaves of England, which are relatively crude in the sixth century but which were improving in quality in the seventh, may be an insular product. However, in the absence of detailed comparative work on the Continent it is impossible to be certain, but such textiles are viewed as a Continental fashion entering southern England through Kent. While it is not possible to demonstrate that any of the Continental braids are of Anglo-Saxon, even Kentish, manufacture, the very close similarity between some examples on each side of the Channel makes it possible that they are at least from the same source.

Some of the connections which can be observed through the textiles are reflected by other goods; the braids from Chessell Down have been compared with those from Envermeu and Herpes-en-Charente in France, the latter producing additional Anglo-Saxon objects matched in Kent and the Isle of Wight. We may be seeing a reflection of a more widespread export of consumables. At least this possibility and the sporadic occurrence of English metalwork on the Continent point to the areas to which goods were moving, whatever the basis for the exchange and its volume.

Internal Exchange

The evidence for overseas exchange, particularly in one direction, is the easiest to observe in the archaeological record, although we should not believe that the details are yet fully understood. The identification of regions involved in the overseas trade is important for understanding the potential centres of production of home-produced goods, such as lavishly ornamented metalwork, and for the identification of the emergent political centres. Below the exotic level of manufacture and exchange is the question of the movement of goods of insular origin within the British Isles.

There are a number of classes of object made in England which can be shown to have regional and/or local distributions. But in the absence of direct evidence for the place of manufacture, or at best the source of the raw materials, there has been a degree of reticence about interpreting the distribution of such goods. The majority of the evidence for such a study are the grave-goods found in cemeteries, although the growing number of excavated settlements is slowly extending our knowledge. Nevertheless, we remain largely ignorant about the manufacture of the items from such evidence as the tools that were used and industrial debris.

The written sources are almost silent about the subject of internal trade, just as the details of overseas trade do not match the volume of archaeological evidence. We do learn from them that there was a trade in slaves in early Anglo-Saxon England which also had an international dimension. As a class of people, slaves are mentioned in the laws of Wihtraed, *c.* AD 695, and Bede mentions the intention of a Mercian to sell a Northumbrian slave to a Frisian merchant in London in AD 679. Wilfrid is claimed to have baptised 250 slaves of both sexes at Selsey and there is the celebrated case of 'Angles' from Deira, an area approximating to the historic county of Yorkshire, being sold in the market-place of Rome *c.* AD 700 (HE IV 22; II 1; IV 13). People such as these may have been enslaved as a result of capture in war or through failure to meet legal obligations; the scale of the practice is unclear (Davies 1982, p. 66; Sawyer 1978, p. 173). Presumably slavery is what is meant when the *Anglo-Saxon Chronicle* records the capture of villages and booty as a result of war. This information is important because the extent of slavery in any society is difficult to determine through archaeological evidence (Pelteret 1981). But for a more detailed and broader perspective on internal exchange the archaeological evidence is of paramount importance, even if little research has yet been carried out.

There are various ways in which abstract art-historical analyses can be made more relevant to the study of man and the organisation of exchange. Characterisation studies of clay, glass, metal and stone are beginning to have an impact on the subject by demonstrating the similarity of raw materials in groups of artefacts and, at best, their actual source. Decorated metalwork and pottery can, in addition, be studied by the measurement of elements in designs to determine which objects may have been made at the same source, using the same tools, or even by the same craftsman. In this way the results of characterisation studies can be corroborated by alternative, and independent, measures of similarity.

Technical difficulties have not encouraged the widespread analysis of the composition of metal artefacts. For instance, the analysis of the metal alloys used in a series of silver brooches from Howletts (Kent) and Chessell Down indicate strong similarities in their alloys. But the interpretation is obstructed by the possibility of segregation of the minerals in the artefacts during burial, thus normalising the results. Nevertheless, there would appear to be an optimum recipe, especially in the silver and copper content used to manufacture the brooches found in each cemetery. Without knowing the actual source of the metal it is difficult to proceed further, except by detailed analysis of decoration (Leigh 1980, p. 185ff., Table 9, App. 2).

Analysis of the metal content of Kentish gold bracteates presents similar problems (Hawkes and Pollard 1981). Results are available from an examination of the bracteates themselves and from their suspension loops, thus making comparison possible. Further scope for comparison is provided by groups of bracteates found in the same grave and cemetery, and especially between die-linked specimens. Some of the die-linked examples have similar metal compositions, while others do not, and it was shown that the loop occasionally differs from the bracteate itself. In fact there is a wide variety of permutations represented by the data. This may suggest that the re-working of the bracteates and their loops, both together and separately was common and emphasises that contemporaneity need not be demonstrated by two objects having the same metal composition. Alternatively it may be suggested that the metal alloys from which the bracteates and their loops were made need not always be from the same source.

The ability to re-cycle metals is fortunately not a property which applies to clay and stone, but they have their own limitations. Petrological studies of stone are constrained by the difficulties of distinguishing the actual source of the material from the basic choice of parent material and that which is glacially derived. In the absence of widespread sampling of clays uncertainty will remain as to whether all of the potential sources of a particular clay have been located. The studies that have been undertaken on early Anglo-Saxon pottery emphasise that, unlike the more exotic materials discussed above, it rarely travelled far from a clay source to the point of consumption, regardless of whether it was for funerary or domestic purposes; some classes of funerary pottery may have been transported further.

A study of undecorated domestic pottery from settlement sites in Northamptonshire suggested that there were a limited number of fabric groups, each originating from sources up to 50 miles from the place of discovery (Walker 1978), although a lack of detailed knowledge about the area's Drift geology led the author to have serious doubts about the results. Grain-size and heavy mineral analysis of selected sherds of pottery from stamp-linked groups excavated at the cremation cemetery at Spong Hill in Norfolk indicated that there were a minimum of nine clay sources, possibly relating to the settlements using the cemetery. In one case there was a unique relationship between a fabric and a stamp-linked group (Brisbane 1980).

A long-held belief has been that decorated cremation pottery, at least, was a product of specialist workshops which traded their wares (Myres 1969). Much of the more recent research is beginning to cast doubt on this view and is revealing a more complicated picture.

The greatest scope for study exists with cremation pottery for, being decorated, it presents a greater number of variables for study, thereby reducing the number of possible interpretations of the patterns produced by analysis. A study of cremation urns, grouped on a stylistic basis as being the products of the 'Sancton-Baston' pottery or workshop, incorporating the analysis of fabrics and measurement of all of the stamp impressions, produced a complex pattern (Figure 2.19) (Arnold 1983). Vessels from the cemeteries in north-east England, Baston and Elsham (Lincolnshire), and Sancton (East Yorkshire) were found to have fabrics specific to the respective cemeteries, although they had been decorated using the same set of dies. This would suggest that the dies, rather than the clay or the finished vessels, had been transported up to 160 km. We have already discussed the question of fuel used in cremations which, at least for the larger cremation cemeteries, argues that the cremation itself may be more likely to have occurred at home than at the cemetery. In the Midlands and East Anglia individual examples from cemeteries were also made with a separate clay and also a specific set of dies; one exception was at Newark where two die sets and two clay sources were in use, but these were not mutually exclusive.

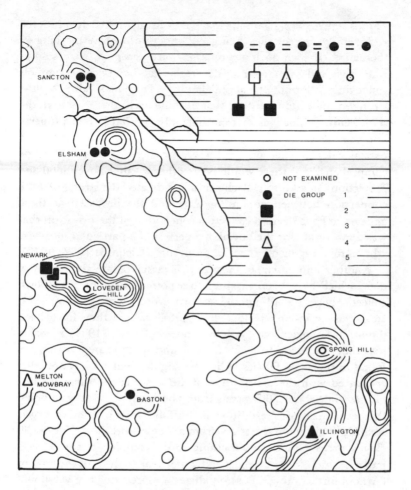

Figure 2.19: The distribution of Sancton-Baston die-groups against a trend surface map of early Anglo-Saxon graves, showing the considerable distances over which the dies were moved. Examples occur in almost every region of eastern England in which graves occur in significant numbers. The sequence of production of the dies suggests that three 'generations' of dies are represented, each generation represented by a few new designs and the abandonment of some of the original ones

Rather than view the Sancton-Baston pottery as the products of individual potters or workshops (Myres 1969; 1977), the fact that five sets of dies were cut to produce a minimum of nine vessels suggests that the decoration of the pottery may have had a totemic significance to individual families. Additions to the range of stamps represent exogamous marriages in successive generations, with family sets of dies being cut in each, with a merging of 'heraldry'. If such an interpretation were accepted, such stamps can be viewed as more than decoration as they become symbols conveying information about family. This may also be the strongest indication we have that in some areas there were, in the sixth century, lineages owning not only, perhaps, real property but also such intangible property as magic crests and names. A person's dependence on his lineage in such a system would be comprehensive as there would be no other means of livelihood and protection. In addition, Richards has indicated the strength of the connection between cremation urns and the deceased as there appears to have been 'a collective conception of the urn form that was appropriate for the burial of a person of a particular age, sex, ethnic, totemic, or other social grouping' (Richards 1982, p. 43).

Another, but much larger, group of vessels of late-sixth-century date, which have been assigned to a potter/workshop are known collectively as the Illington-Lackford group, after the two principal cemeteries in Norfolk and Suffolk where they have been found. Petrological analysis by Andrew Russel (1984) revealed that they are made from 20 fabrics, and undecorated vessels are found in the same fabrics. The petrological analysis has not been compared with the distribution of die-sets, yet the sheer volume of material, about 200 vessels from about twelve sites, one being the settlement of West Stow in Suffolk, might seem to argue strongly that the products are from a single workshop. Yet the 20 clay sources points to something more complex again. It is a pattern which could be clarified by metrical analysis of the stamps (Arnold forthcoming). Possibly this is a more extensive version of the system applicable to the Sancton-Baston pottery, reflecting branches of a much larger family or clan, spread over eastern England. At West Stow itself, the presence of antler stamps and clay dumps indicates that decorated pottery was made there; the same stamps are represented on vessels from there and the cemetery at Illington. The limited number of urns per fabric may reflect, Russell suggest, a number of pottery-making occasions or different potters, perhaps even the maintenance of a clay-pit or different years of pottery-making. There are hints that certain sets of dies were used to decorate pots made from specific fabrics, while some were retained for a later occasion and occur again on another fabric. The Illington-Lackford type of pottery occurs on 4 per cent of cemeteries and 15 per cent of settlements in East Anglia, strongly suggesting that it was being used for domestic, as well as funerary, use, and it is estimated that undecorated pottery made from the same fabrics outnumber the decorated Illington-Lackford pots by 15:1. Two basic fabric types were used, one silty the other sandy; most of the former occur at Illington, whilst others were 'traded' further afield into neighbouring valleys. The change from silty to a sandy fabric may also reflect a change of production centre which may be mirrored in a change in the style of decoration of this pottery group.

The results of the study of early Anglo-Saxon pottery have yet hardly come near the commercially based model envisaged by Myres, with specialists producing for a consumer market; social explanations appear to be more appropriate for similarities between vessels, and their movement. Analysis of ceramic material from a cremation and inhumation cemetery on the Isle of Wight revealed that cremation urns, which may also be early in the cemeteries' histories, were made from local clay sources, whereas more unusual forms of pottery were made from sources foreign to the island and were found as grave-goods with inhumations; they are types most commonly found in Kent. While this may appear to emphasise the role of the exchange of primitive valuables, perhaps ceremonial in nature, there are also links between the island and Kent in a limited amount of metalwork, dress and burial form which have encouraged the connections to be viewed in familial terms. Again, the possibility of commercial exchange disappears (Arnold 1981; 1982a).

It is frustrating that so little pottery from settlements has been examined in this manner, although Brisbane (1981) has proposed a model for various modes of production that may be appropriate for such pottery. Domestic wares were produced on the farm from clays available in the immediate vicinity; funerary wares were manufactured from a variety of local clay sources; and imported wares. Petrological analyses that have been carried out support the model to some extent, especially for the production of domestic pottery; much of it is grass-tempered which Brown (1976) suggests represents an equal mixture of clay and horse manure. When fired the organic elements are burned out leaving a porous fabric. This practice made the clay into a more workable material, improved the firing qualities as well as making economic use of the materials readily available on the farm. Given the ambiguity of the evidence from West Stow as to whether decorated funerary pottery was also used domestically, it should be noted that such grass-tempered vessels have open-mouthed, simple, rounded forms, whereas the 'funerary' wares are larger and have more restricted mouths. The evidence currently suggests that the factors controlling the dispersal of similarly decorated pottery related more to the social system than to purely commercial factors, even if economic considerations controlled the distance travelled to a chosen clay source. Russel (1984) suggests that some sporadic longer distance movements of the Illington-Lackford group of pots is related to exchange between social groups, It has been noted (Arnold, D.E. 1985) that societies living in areas where resources are rare or absent may compensate by the production of pottery for exchange with neighbouring groups better endowed with the necessary resources. The problem here remains one of the identification of the sources of the raw materials used during the period.

Characterisation studies have also been applied to early Anglo-Saxon stone artefacts. These allow an understanding of the range over which materials were gathered for use on the farm, reflecting the extent of human movement and interaction. They also allow us to see whether stone with special properties was transported over greater distances. At the farmstead excavated at Walton (Farley 1976), the occupants had acquired a rotary quern of a stone comparable with greensands in Buckinghamshire and Bedfordshire, probably from the Leighton Buzzard area *c.* 16 km distant. This stone had not, apparently, been transported over a great distance. Another stone tool found on settlements and in cemeteries, the whetstone used for sharpening metal tools and weapons, seems on occasion to have been transported further. A single example excavated on the settlement of Old Down Farm, Hampshire was a glauconitic limestone from Northamptonshire (Davies 1980).

A recent survey of early Anglo-Saxon whetstones showed that a number were made of a sand-silt greywacké which has its source in the north-west Pennines, the Lake District and south-west Scotland. They are assumed to have been quarried there, *in situ*, and not removed from the glacial Drift. Amongst this group are the large decorated examples from Loveden Hill (Lincolnshire) and Sutton Hoo mound 1, considered to be ceremonial in function. The majority of the examples of this stone type have been found in eastern England. In the south a different range of stone sources was used; whetstones of Kentish Ragstone have been found in Suffolk, Oxfordshire and Kent (Evison 1975). An example of Devonian sandstone originating in the Bristol area has been excavated in Berkshire and examples of Metamorphic rock from the Ardennes-Rhineland area, or the Boulonnais in Normandy, are known in Kent and Essex.

The problem, as with the provenancing of clays, is that the whetstones have been accepted as evidence of trade from their quarry site as opposed to random stones selected from glacially deposited material (the Drift). A similar problem exists with the interpretation of Neolithic axes; while there cannot be any doubt that glacial drift has resulted in the deposition of rocks at a considerable distance from the parent rock, it is difficult to determine the actual source of the stone in either period. It is noteworthy that the distribution of the early Anglo-Saxon whetstones of rock from north-west England, although of smaller number, is similar to that of Neolithic Group VI axes from the same area. This is difficult to explain otherwise than as the result of the source being glacial Drift; the same explanation may apply to other whetstones also. The distribution of the whetstones which have the same petrology as the Group VI axes is not merely a reflection of the distribution of cemeteries as the type is absent in southern England. But, just as there is evidence that Group VI axes were being quarried from the parent rock, there is some evidence of contact between south-west Scotland and eastern England at this time, which may explain why at least some of the whetstones have been transported up to 400 km from the parent rock. Settlements in south-west Scotland were reworking Anglo-Saxon bronze scrap and perhaps glass; the fragmentary whetstone with a facing human head from Collin, Dumfrieshire, is stylistically related to the examples from Loveden Hill and Sutton Hoo and may point to the exchange of goods between the areas. The strong British element in some of the metalwork from Sutton Hoo might also be seen in this light. Such evidence must be balanced with the certainty that stone of the appropriate type does occur in the Drift of eastern England (Penny 1974, p. 248) (Figure 2.20).

The same problem exists with touchstones, or more accurately basanite or lydite, which is a flinty jaspar or finely crystalline quartzite, black or dark grey in colour, used to test gold-silver alloys for their gold content. Rubbing the alloy on the stone produces a streak whose colour determines the gold content to an accuracy of one part in one hundred. A study (Moore and Oddy 1985) of examples from seventh century graves in Kent at Kingston and Osengell, both bearing gold streaks on their surfaces, determined their petrology. One was a siltstone whose

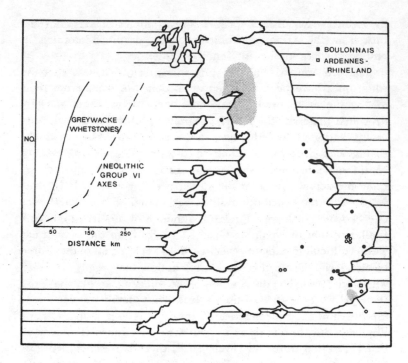

Figure 2.20: The distribution of early Anglo-Saxon whetstones from known sources and fall-off curves for greywacké whetstones and Group VI neolithic axes. Although the quantities are different, the source, fall-off curves and distribution of greywacké whetstones (black dots) and the neolithic axes are very similar, emphasising how the source of stone for the whetstones may have been glacial erratics. Whetstones from sources in Kent and the Continent are concentrated in south-east England. (Data: Evison 1975.)

provenance is given as south-west England, and the other a tuff, of Wales or Cumbria.

Goods that had been imported from the Continent may then have become powerful social tools by their redistribution through the social system, and in this way they form part of the subject of internal exchange.

The study of the distribution of exotic imported goods within England has extended as far as noting that there are two basic patterns to their distribution, apparently depending on their sources, and that particular areas or individual cemeteries have disproportionately high quantities of some of these goods. The fall-off curves away from such centres of consumption imply that the redistribution of such goods was controlled, but there has been little research carried out to determine the patterns of dispersal in any more detail. The amber bead is an example of such an imported commodity which is found in very large quantities at some cemeteries often with relatively low proportions amongst surrounding communities. It would be useful to know whether there are any similarities in the graves with and without amber in each type of cemetery as it may help us to understand whether such goods are being handed down through society and something of the controls on access to them.

Examples of such cemeteries are the large and amber-rich Sleaford and the small neighbouring example of Ruskington (Lincolnshire) and in the Thames valley, the Berkshire sites of Long Wittenham I and Wallingford. As is so often the case with archaeological data, the smaller cemeteries present such a small sample as to make detailed conclusions of dubious value, and their small size may be misleading as more graves may await discovery. At Sleaford a higher proportion of graves with amber beads contained small-long brooches and pendants than those without, the latter being more strongly characterised by the presence of cruciform brooches. The graves lacking amber beads also had smaller numbers of disc brooches, earrings, bracelets and bags, implying that the differential access to amber also extended to other objects. At Ruskington the inadequacies of the data make it difficult to draw firm conclusions, although there appears to be a smaller proportion of graves with amber than at Sleaford. At Long Wittenham I the presence of amber beads makes little difference to the nature of the brooches accompanying the graves, but those graves with such beads had significantly higher quantities of rings, coins, pins and toilet implements. There are hints of a similar pattern at Wallingford where graves with amber beads were also more likely to have brooches.

The most common items found in early Anglo-Saxon graves are those made of metal, especially iron, copper-alloy, silver and gold. The volume of the evidence is, unfortunately, not matched by our understanding of the organisation of production and dispersal. The smith obviously needed fuel and metal to carry out his work but we do not know the extent to which the smith was dependent on local resources as opposed to trade, nor the size and structure of the industry. It is possible to characterise metals, be they copper-alloy, iron, lead, silver or gold, but the interpretation of the results presents many problems. It is also very difficult to use the particular form of the artefact, or the style of decoration, when present, to determine the mechanisms involved in their production and dispersal; the factors determining similarity between artefacts beyond learned tradition and functionality are barely understood. 'Style-zones' may be identified, but the roles played by the craftsman and the consumer (if such a model is correct) in the generation of such patterns is unclear.

The sources of metal used are very difficult to determine. We do not know whether the metals were mined and smelted by the smith, or purchased from miners. The supply of metal may not have been a problem if supplies of scrap were plentiful and if there was a continuous re-cycling of the raw materials. But how would this affect the smith's relationship with the supplier, who may have been the customer?

The smith may be elusive in the archaeological record but there are a few references to such craftsmen in the early law-codes, which in itself may emphasise their standing in society. In Aethelberht's laws, the king's smith was protected by a special *wergeld*, called a *leodgeld*, amounting to 100 Kentish 'shillings', which would be paid for causing the smith's death (Loyn 1962, p. 103). In King Ine's laws the smith was rated as the equal of the reeve and a child's nurse, who, being servants, could be taken with a *gesithcund* man if he moved to a different area (ibid. p. 104).

The earliest record of iron extraction is found in a charter of AD 689 in which the monks of Canterbury were granted the right to mine ore at Lympne (O'Niell 1967, p. 189). Silver must have come from silver-bearing lead and copper ores but there is no evidence of mining lead itself until the late Saxon period. Importation seems the most likely answer for many of these metals, but the existence of scrap in the forms of late Roman silver coinage, plate and, increasingly, Germanic silver may easily have satisfied the demand.

Metal analyses of silver alloy brooches reported by Leigh (1980, p. 185ff.) suggest that the silver was moderately pure and was alloyed with a copper-based alloy, possibly of Roman origin. Pairs of brooches often have similar values of silver, but some reveal significant differences in copper values indicating they were not made from the same batch of metal. Less work has been carried out on copper, but the little that has (e.g. Manser 1977, pp. 22–3) indicates a very wide range of composition, matched by the range found in Roman copper alloys which may suggest extensive use of scrap such as that found in bags accompanying skeletons (Myres 1978). Analysis of Merovingian gold coin and early Anglo-Saxon gold artefacts has made it clear that they have a similar composition, the latter accurately following the debasement of the coinage (Hawkes, Merrick and Metcalf 1966).

Few craft activities of the early Anglo-Saxon period have left any archaeological traces except in their finished products, and metalworking is notable for its near absence. Only the settlement at Mucking has produced evidence, part of a two-piece mould for casting a great square-headed brooch (Jones 1980). This is despite there being thousands of pieces of metalwork which have been cast in moulds. Metalworking is indicated by crucibles found at Walton, Sarre, Portchester, (Hampshire) and Sutton Courtenay but these do not significantly improve our understanding of the organisation of such industry. It is possible that the very rarity of this type of evidence is an important clue. Indirect evidence for the methods of manufacture might be drawn from two failed castings from the upper Thames valley (Dickinson 1982, n. 4), a pendant from Woodeaton (Oxfordshire) (Vierck 1967, pp. 111–13) and a saucer brooch, now lost, from Cassington (Oxfordshire) (Arthur and Jope 1963, p. 3).

Graves with metalworking tools are similarly rare in England, while on the Continent (Wilson 1979b) they are more frequently found. A die for impressing sheet metal with Style II ornament was found at Barton-on-Humber (Lincolnshire) with a set of weights and a balance (Capelle and Vierck 1971) and other dies are known from Salmonby (Lincolnshire), two from Suffolk and there is an example from Salisbury (Wiltshire) (ibid.), all of seventh-century date. A jeweller's hammer was found at Soham (Cambridgeshire). The sum total of data connected with metalworking is hardly a representative guide to such industry or exchange.

The absence of information concerning metalworking may reflect uncentralised production, which may be expected when settlement was dispersed. In which case we may predict that this craft activity was on a small scale producing no concentrated evidence. Itinerant craftsmen have been argued for on the basis of the use of bronze models for the production of two-piece clay moulds (Werner 1970; Capelle and Vierck 1971) and Hines views travelling craftsmen as the most suitable explanation for the dispersal of ornamental metalwork (Hines 1984). With such equipment, jewellers would be able to replicate a series of similar designs from a single model. In contrast, however, is the evidence for a large and centralised metalworking industry at Helgö in Sweden (Holmqvist 1961; 1964; 1970; 1972; 1975). There is yet no evidence of permanent production centres in early Anglo-Saxon England, and resort must be made to the objects themselves to determine the structure of the industry. The absence of tools, particularly from graves, may actually point more to the decisions which lie behind the choice of grave-goods to be interred with the dead; tools have a very high use-value and may not therefore have been disposed of in this manner.

In regions where there is a very distinctive form of metalwork, an extreme example being the disc brooches of Kent, the distribution might be suitable for analysis as the problems concerning the measurement of similarity are less important. However the very fact that the extent of replication is greater with certain classes of metalwork in one region than those of another may be the result of differences in the organisation of their manufacture, even if the actual system is unknown. The manufacture of disc brooches was a complex procedure requiring the procurement of a wide variety of raw materials and processing before the brooch could be made. Few of these brooches are found outside Kent, in keeping with the observed pattern of distribution of imported luxury goods; where they do occur in other regions they frequently accompany other items which may be labelled 'Kentish'. Within Kent the largest number of examples have been found at Faversham, with the second and third largest peaks in the Wantsum Channel and River Stour area, and the coastal region of east Kent around Dover.

This distribution pattern may be compared with a similar brooch type found commonly in the upper Thames valley, the cast saucer brooch. Dickinson has examined the possibility of determining whether similar brooches have been produced using the same procedure or equipment on the basis of measurement (1982). The research was geared particularly towards determining how matching pairs of brooches were produced. There were indications that the method of manufacture changed during the sixth century, perhaps from itinerant craftsmen to workshops, implying a degree of centralisation. A recent study of square-headed brooches came to a similar conclusion (Hines 1984, p. 180); they could be divided into three phases on the basis of their distribution: general, localised and, finally, more numerous and widespread. Such a change may also have social implications, the rise of individuals having the wherewithal to employ a craftsman, who then benefitted from the arrangement personally and who could distribute the products to the surrounding region. Certainly there is a change from a limited range of simple motifs in ornament to a 'varied production of complex and compound motifs' (Dickinson 1982, p. 36). Both the Kentish case and the example of the disc brooch serve to emphasise that earlier sixth century distributions are localised and may, from a social standpoint, be confined to lineages or clans. But gradually the pattern changes until we see the growth of commercialism by which time the symbols in ornament had less meaning as such social networks were supplanted by more cohesive political groups; production could at that time be taken over by entrepreneurs who continued the evolution of regional designs but who were distributing the goods in an entirely different manner. It is not necessary, however, to see this change as predominantly the result of changes in the organisation of their manufacture. It may merely indicate that during the early phase of production there were social reasons for indicating one particular identity amongst many, whereas later on such small-scale variation in *social* identity had been replaced by larger political institutions which were not indicated in the same manner. Thus the jeweller was free to use more efficient methods, replicating designs with a freer hand in ornament variation.

The majority of attempts to gain greater insight into the organisation of the manufacture of ornamental metalwork and the meaning of the decoration have been based on the decoration itself. A study of a small series of sixth-century, square-headed, brooches showed how the various brooches could be placed into a sequence because of the interchange of parts of the decoration on them. Hence it could be shown that the connection between the brooches was more than one of a vague 'stylistic type' as has tended to be the case in most studies in the past. How or why the interchange of decorative elements was carried out is more difficult to understand; the moulds for casting the brooches may have been made with models constituting separate elements of the decoration of the brooches, or entirely remodelled each time a brooch was made, with variations. Irrespective of the actual method of replication, the series is found spread across southern England from the Isle of Wight to Suffolk, indicating the extent of social interconnectedness whether at the level of the manufacturer, the 'purchaser' or the wearer; people travelled considerable distances during the period (Arnold 1980; Hines 1984).

All studies of the relationships between pieces of ornamental metalwork serve to emphasise the extent of the movement of people and, therefore, of contact. Hines has extended understanding of such relationships in a thorough review of the square-headed brooches in England. While the research was designed to answer questions of origin of type and chronology, the resulting groupings are based on similarity of design elements. A variety of patterns are apparent in these groupings ranging from small groups like Group VI concentrated in the valley of the Warwickshire Avon, and Group XV in Cambridgeshire-Suffolk and the Midlands, to larger groups which reveal connections between distinct areas, for instance Group I in Kent, Sussex, Surrey and the upper Thames valley, and further north Group XVI in East Anglia, Leicestershire and Nottinghamshire. Hines divides the brooches into three overlapping chronological phases which reflect a development in the manufacture and use of the brooches. The first phase is marked by about nine brooches which are 'distinctly individualist' and dated *c*. 500–520. Larger groups of brooches characterise the second, overlapping, phase *c*. 510-550, which can be viewed as attempts 'to reproduce the same recognisable prototype', thereby playing down the change that actually occurs. In the final phase, *c*. 530-70, the largest number of brooches are found in a smaller number of groups, marked by 'mass produced' reproductions of a single type. Geographically the first phase of brooches tend not to cluster in any particular region and are found dispersed over much of England. In the second phase they tend to be more regional, although they are still dispersed over considerable distances, up to 200 km apart. In the third and final phase the area of dispersal is larger and the distribution more dense.

Similar patterns are discernible with other brooch types, although there has been less detailed research. Types of florid cruciform brooch in the Midlands and East Anglia, for instance types c, d and g surveyed by Leeds and Pocock (1971), have distinctly regional distributions similar to the phase 2 of Hines. Certain types of cast and applied saucer brooches reveal similar distribution patterns.

Some of the most detailed studies have been carried out by Leigh (1980) on sixth-century square-headed brooches from Kent. The work was geared towards trying to isolate the products of specific workshops or craftsmen. This was achieved by examining brooches which are pairs, those not paired but which are very similar and those which are of a different design but which share the same characteristics. By this means it was possible to isolate the features which give the groups cohesion. One group, represented by nearly 30 brooches, mostly from Kent, was characterised by the care and precision of the design and laying out, the notched ridge making up the designs, the well-made and neat niello bands and garnet inlaid cells, and the carefully carved animal and geometric ornament, with sharp tops to the ridges. Some minor differences, for instance the angles at which tools had been applied to surfaces, might indicate the hands of separate craftsmen (ibid., p. 75).

Leigh concluded that the brooches he considered were the products of a single workshop although there may, yet, be other reasons for the degrees of similarity he observed; it is these which are actually being assessed, not whether or not they originated from one workshop. The principal conclusion of the study was that all three of the series of square-headed brooches which were isolated (two of silver and one of copper alloy), the majority of keystone garnet inlaid disc brooches, of silver, and at least some of the garnet inlaid buckle plates, some of silver and some of copper alloy, are the products of a single workshop. The work of individual people can be detected on certain examples. It should be noted that this grouping of sixth-century metalwork includes nearly all of the known examples, and only raises again the question of how similar items have to be for us to be able to distinguish the skills of one workshop as opposed to the learned traditions of a single society. However, as the conclusions are based on the minutiae of craftsmanship it seems likely that Leigh has come closest to identifying the work of individuals.

The identification of apparent patterning amongst types and sub-groups of ornamental metalwork can easily induce a false sense of satisfaction. It is a far cry from actually understanding the patterns, and at present we can only really present possibilities. When such replication and variation is found we may rightly ask, what were the factors controlling the results? Are such brooches the product of itinerant craftsmen who produced objects to order? Was the smith free to produce his own designs? Does the variation have a function similar to the interpretation placed upon the cremation pottery, that it represents the wearer's social group? Is the movement of such metalwork carried out by the manufacturer at all, as opposed to the purchaser or wearer, for instance as gifts or the movement of people in marriage? It is noticeable that the dies for decorating the surface of pottery are as rare as the tools for producing ornamental metalwork. It may be of use to compare the regional groupings of brooch types with those areas which are revealed as high consumers of imported luxury goods; whilst such a correlation tells us nothing about the mode of production of the brooches, it does provide some articulation to the distribution maps. These types of problem extend even to the more commonplace types of metalwork in which the lack of replication might lead to the suggestion that everyday items were produced locally as required; but were such technical skills possessed by someone on every farm or hamlet, at only a few locations, or was the craftsman a mobile specialist?

The vast majority of ornamental metalwork has only been studied from a typological standpoint on the basis of form and decoration. This allows estimation of chronology and the identification of regional types, but it says little about the organisation of manufacture and dispersal. The absence of exact replication with most brooch types strongly suggests that each, or each pair or trio, was manufactured as required, thereby introducing a high degree of innovation. But we are no nearer understanding what or who determined the form of decoration. The distribution of stylistic types may reflect either the beneficence of wealthy individuals, the region of activity of a craftsman, or the distribution of social groups (or other exchange networks), who wore such items as an indicator of their identity. By this means the combination of elements would reflect one's social background. If such a model is correct, we may speculate that the movement of such female associated items may have been enchanced if the giving of women in marriage was at all common. Women may have been seen as valuables by which means weaker groups would try to marry their girls 'upwards' in the creation of alliances, resulting in the occasional movement of ornamental metalwork some distance from the regions where they are most commonly found, the core area of a social grouping.

Another means by which light may be shed on the problems concerning the modes of production and dispersal of metalwork would be to consider very distinctive examples. Their very individuality might imply the hand of a single craftsman. When so much decorated metalwork is associated with women it would be helpful to examine types connected with men, for instance weaponry, to redress the imbalance. However the very nature of weaponry does not lend itself so readily to such analysis. A limited number of swords are very individualistic, but shield bosses conform to a relatively limited range of designs which appear to change slowly through time. Spearheads were made in a wide range of identifiable forms emphasising that each iron object was a unique forging. A classification of spearhead types has been made (Swanton 1974) which shows how they have broad geographical distributions.

It is easy to see why it is the more unusual types of artefact that are used for this type of research. For instance, there is a group of bronze-bound wooden vessels whose binding hoops were decorated with a distinctive *repoussé* ornament and which are found distributed over central southern England (Arnold 1982a; Davies 1984). Similarly, there are pieces of metalwork decorated with enamel which are found in the Lark valley in Cambridgeshire (Brown 1981a; Scull 1985).

The time and expense involved in manufacturing some of the more individualistic pieces of metalwork may ultimately reflect the greater social standing of their users, and this must be appreciated when considering the controls over their distribution pattern. Such metalwork may be the more prestigious items, not the more common varieties, resulting in a marked bias in our view of the economics of both metalworking and the period as a whole. Indirectly this problem reveals something of the organisation of craft activities in early Anglo-Saxon England, but we must be wary of categorising the period on the basis of the more influential members' activities alone.

The close association between exotic metalwork and élite members of society is particularly apparent in the seventh century where the development of a distinctive style of animal art, Style II, is documented. The most ornate and rich pieces are strongly associated with otherwise rich burials in Kent and Sutton Hoo, Cuddesdon, Broomfield (Essex) and Taplow. Speake has commented that: 'Patronage to support and pay a goldsmith or craftsman who utilised such expensive materials as gold, silver and garnet, could only be given by the "top people" in Anglo-Saxon society' (1980, p. 39). While there are less accomplished versions of the more elaborate examples in a given region, as in Kent, the virtuosity of the buckle, shoulder clasps and purse from mound 1 at Sutton Hoo inevitably led Speake to talk of a Sutton Hoo master craftsman and a workshop; later pieces may have been produced by workers trained there. The style as a whole points to the continuing exchange of ideas between England and the Continent and also how at this social level in the first half of the seventh century the paramount members of society employed their own craftsmen to produce exotic display items demonstrating their success in leadership; it also reflects their success in exchange in acquiring the necessary raw materials in large quantities. Was it they who distributed the products of their workshops to the remainder of society?

Throughout the early Anglo-Saxon period the basis of the economy was the land and what it produced, and the efforts of those who farmed it. For many, life remained at a self-sufficient level in which food was produced with little need to create a surplus. Materials were found locally. During the sixth century, craftsmen were increasingly operating from workshops, employed by those who had made a greater success in the agricultural way of life and were able to support a greater number of specialists and farmworkers. At all times goods were being imported; in much of England the distribution patterns imply unequal access to such goods, the quantities falling off rapidly beyond the point of entry or greatest consumption. The exception is Kent, which not only imported a particular range of materials from the Continent, but also maintained a near monopoly over those goods. The overseas economy of Kent was the most developed in early Anglo-Saxon England; so strong is this overseas flavour of the Kentish economy and its society; that it can almost be seen as part of the Continent rather than the rest of England at this time. Outside Kent there are particular regions which reveal a high level of consumption of exotic goods imported from aboard. The observables, the exotic items of gold, amber, shell, garnet, pottery (and perhaps what it contained, for instance wine), glass, mercury, ivory, may give us a distorted image of the nature of exchange, but there is no reason for rejecting the acceptance of the pattern at face-value. It is considerably harder to characterise the form of exchange at a local level, although we may hypothesise about its nature on the basis of the organisation viewed through alternative forms of evidence.

The archaeological evidence is a kaleidoscope of numerous activities which differ from one area to the next through time. Certainly more obvious patterning can help in disentangling one strand from another, but until more research is aimed directly at such problems, our understanding will advance very slowly.

The archaeological evidence can be viewed as reflecting the activities of corporate groups making or strengthening relationships by the action of exchanging goods and of corporate leaders acquiring valuable things and relationships. By such means their position and power were enhanced and the material means were provided to set in motion community activities. As these activities became more intense a greater demand would have been placed on those who made it possible, the food-producers, who would have been under increasing pressure to maximise output. On the developmental road towards kingdom-states, alliance networks changed with events over time; the role of exchange in the making and breaking of such alliances cannot be ignored and we should be wary of hastening true commercialisation into Anglo-Saxon England too early, even though that was the inevitable result of this society's structure.

3

Elusive Craftsmen

The study of technology is important in its own right, but it also deepens our understanding of a society as a whole because it is intimately connected with the way in which people are organised and the structure of their economy. An understanding of technology is a critical step towards understanding a society. We may examine the technologies applied to the basic raw materials in early Anglo-Saxon society, wood, metal, clay, fibres and minerals, paying particular attention to aspects which are peculiar to the period and leaving the general matters of technology as understood. We must also give some consideration to composite commodities. Of equal importance are the source and nature of the raw materials and of the effort and organisation that lie behind the crafts and skills described.

The most prolific source for the study of Anglo-Saxon technology is the vast array of artefacts which have survived as grave-goods in burials. An examination of the results of early Anglo-Saxon craftsmanship point to the effort and organisation involved in procuring the raw materials. Detailed studies of particular artefacts direct attention to the varying complexity involved in manufacturing items, many of them designed for specific functions. Much of the variation in the items is indeed directly related to their use, but the variability in the design of objects destined for the same function may point to socio-cultural differences.

Complex Technology

There have been few detailed studies of the technology of

particular types of artefact, or products requiring tools in their manufacture. Rather, individual studies have been made of certain types in the reports on the excavation of cemeteries. Where such detailed studies have been made they tend towards the typological and shy away from the technological aspects. Similarly the sociological aspects are rarely dealt with. It is not surprising that the more complex, composite artefacts are more rare than those whose production is relatively straightforward. Despite the level of organisation required to bring together the materials and expertise to produce complex citems, it is still surprising how few have survived. Perhaps this may serve to emphasise the difficulties of actually manufacturing such items in the period.

An example of this are the disc and composite brooches of Kent (Avent 1975). They are found predominately in Kent and are believed to have been manufactured from *c*. 550 to *c*. 650 (ibid., p. 56–64). Leigh has suggested some refinements to the chronology and the sequence of development (1984b); 192 such brooches are known suggesting that the *minimum* output was a little under two per year. There are three main types of brooch: keystone garnet disc brooches, plated disc brooches and composite brooches, which in Avent's scheme overlap chronologically; each main type is dated AD 550–630, AD 600–630 and AD 610–50 respectively. Such phases may reflect the work of individual workshops, individual craftsmen breaking new ground, or the conservatism of the consumers once a type was fully developed. The greatest changes in the technology and style of the brooches in Kent occurred in the last quarter of the sixth century with the introduction of solid gold objects decorated with filigree and cloisonné work replacing gilded silver objects. It is strange that although this technology was known it was not used by Kentish craftsmen for nearly 50 years. A shortage of gold has been argued as a reason, emphasising the importance of the ability to procure the necessary raw materials.

The production of such brooches was a complex procedure, both in the gathering together of the raw materials as well as the actual production of the objects themselves. To manufacture a garnet disc brooch a two-piece mould would be made in clay from a model, in which would be cast the skeleton of the brooch in silver. This would include the rims, inner and outer, the central setting border, empty cells for the keystones, other settings and the outline, at least, of the animal ornament. The casting would then be cleaned up with a graver to remove residual material and to sharpen the outlines, and then polished. Then niello would be applied to the rim decoration, applied to the recesses as a powder, cast, ground and polished. Then the outer band of the rim would be fixed, probably with solder. Gilding, normally done by taking powered gold mixed with mercury to form an amalgam, was painted onto the surface and then heated so as to drive off the mercury. The settings would then be fixed, usually backed by gold foil (Avent and Leigh 1977; Meeks and Holmes 1985), which would most often be of garnet, but also glass, stone and shell. Finally the iron pin would be attached to the hinge fitting, pointed at the catch-plate and coiled at the other end to form a spring hinge.

It is known that some of the settings in such brooches are glass, but many, as in other types of brooch, especially in Kent, are of garnet. Garnet, as we have seen, is found in such places as Egypt, Britian, Scandinavia and many parts of Europe. The selected garnet had to be split and then shaped to fit the cells and patterns; alternatively, the cells may have been shaped to take the pre-cut garnets. Shaping the garnet could have been carried out by three methods (Arrhenius 1971). Slices can be cut using an abrasive wheel which results in a smoothly sloping, or facetted edge. Secondly, the shaping can be done by flaking or chipping. Lastly there is some evidence for a diamond, quartz or garnet-tipped point being used to cut a groove along which the garnet could be snapped into two. Visible garnet-edges tend to be smooth, which may suggest wheel-cutting, but if rougher methods were used the slices could be polished afterwards to remove any roughness (Bimson 1985). What is less clear is whether they were cut in Kent or imported ready cut. The Kentish examples tend to be simple shapes, discs and rectangles, which are equally common in Europe. Other shapes, square, diamond, triangles, lentoid, drop or half-disc, are much rarer and are found on the Continent in southern Germany, Hungary and south-east Europe in general. The question is difficult to answer especially when complicated by the possibility of re-use.

While this outlines the process of manufacture, each stage required a different combination of raw materials and tools which would in turn have had to be obtained and processed. Despite the quantities, at least of surviving examples, being small, the actual list of items required is quite daunting, including wood, charcoal, iron, silver, mercury, clay, lead, antimony, tallow, tin, gold, garnets and other stones, and abrasive. There are also the various tools required for casting, graving, cutting, bending and polishing. Despite the small scale of production the craftsmen would have needed considerable knowledge and skill to accumulate the equipment and materials to produce these brooches.

The range of craft skills in use during the early Anglo-Saxon period is well represented in the archaeological record, although unevenly studied. However, the survival of certain types of artefact is as much the result of various factors prior to burial as to post-depositional processes. The rarer survivals can add an altogether different dimension to our understanding of the period, and serve to sharpen our awareness of the difficulty of establishing precisely how rare certain items were in society at the time. A typical example are musical instruments, in particular lyres, which are known from four burials, Bergh Apton (Norfolk), Morningthorpe (Norfolk) the well-furnished barrow burials of Sutton Hoo mound 1 and Taplow (Bruce-Mitford 1970; Lawson 1978). Such stringed instruments were perhaps not so rare as their apparent survival would suggest; the Bergh Apton and Morningthorpe examples indicate that they are not the preserve of rich, perhaps royal, burials. The form of joinery used on such instruments implies 'able craftsmanship and an availability of at least small gouges and chisels' (Lawson 1978, p. 96). Considerable care was taken in constructing them, in hardwoods, and there is a conformity in the examples known which date from the fifth to eighth centuries.

The arch of the lyre was fixed by mortise and tenon joints, strengthened by metal plates, which carried six pegs holding the strings. The soundboard on the Bergh Apton example was similarly strengthened by a metal binding strip. To the outside of the frame were attached wrist straps making it possible to support the instrument and use both hands in a performance. The fittings were individually made for each example, with only a general standardisation.

We may compare the intricacy of the production of small objects, such as brooches and musical instruments which were both functional as well as objects of beauty, with craftsmanship at the opposite end of the scale which involved complex carpentry as well as considerable effort, for example boat building and house construction.

The Sutton Hoo lyre was deposited with many other possessions lying around the burial chamber in a ship, which remains one of the best examples of contemporary marine engineering. Such a survival is very important, for while we may be largely ignorant of the details of land travel, the role of ships in transporting men and goods across the waters to England is known to be great. The ship (Bruce-Mitford 1975) was an open rowing boat driven by 38 oarsmen, 80 feet long, 14 feet wide at the centre and the depth amidships 4 feet 6 inches, with the prow 12 feet 6 inches above the level of the keel plank amidships. It was clinker built without permanent decking and no evidence was found for a mast. The hull was stiffened with 26 ribs. It was probably steered over the stern by a large paddle. The ship and its contents in barrow 1 is one of three known boats, the others being from Sutton Hoo mound 2 and Snape on the River Alde 10 miles to the north-east. Unfortunately these were not recorded as well as the example from mound 1.

The principal limitation of the Sutton Hoo boat was that, in having a keel plank and not a keel, it would not have been able to support a sail; the slightly smaller boat from Kvalsund (Norway) dating to *c*. AD 700 was provided with an incipient keel and may have been able to bear the greater stresses of a sail. In the absence of a greater range of evidence it is difficult to be certain about how representative the Sutton Hoo mound 1 boat is of the range of ship types. There can be no doubt that crossings of the North Sea and the English Channel were being made; the fifth century migrations and the international trade of the sixth and seventh centuries are clear testimonies to such sea journeys. Experiments and modern calculations suggest that the Sutton Hoo type boat could average a speed of 3 knots for little more than six hours, so that a crossing of the North Sea from Holland to East Anglia could have been achieved in about 14 days, although if sails were available the time would be considerably less (Green 1963).

The need for houses, barns and byres constructed of timber was more common and fundamental to everyday life. The skills required were no less than for the intricate metalworking and jewelling skills of the Kentish craftsmen, but the effort and raw materials required were on an altogether different scale. A variety of building types are represented at Cowdery's Down, but building C12, the largest and possibly the most elaborate, may serve to demonstrate the skills required.

It has been estimated that to construct the rectangular timber building, C12, would have required the movement of *c*. 81 tonnes of topsoil, clay and chalk for the footings, and building materials such as timber, daub and thatch weighing 70 tonnes (Millett 1983, M5/02). Our ignorance of the methods makes if difficult to establish accurate estimates of the effort involved in carrying out the various tasks; we may at least gain some idea of the order of magnitude of the work. The foundations of C12 would involve the movement of about 45 m³ of material, which would take approximately 90 man-hours. The timber work presents more difficulty as we are even more uncertain about the methods and tools available. Millett takes the absence of large saws (1983, p. 198) literally and assumes timber would have been split radially; it must however be noted that tools are generally rare finds during the period and the absence of a surviving saw need not represent the real situation (Wilson 1968; Darrah 1982). If an adze was used, smaller trees might have been more practical so that one finished square might be one round long. We gain an impression of the quantities of oak involved from the estimates for the building; the 55 m³ would have been obtained from about 18 mature oaks. A conservative estimate suggests that the principal timber work would have required trees from 2 hectares of oak forest to construct the building, excluding the floorboards.

The probable sequence of events in erecting such a structure would begin with the excavation of the flat-bottomed wall-trenches dug into the chalk which, judging from the evidence of signs of pecking on the trench sides, were made with a pointed tool. Gaps were left for the doorways and the resulting trench would have measured 22.1 × 8.5 metres, although it was slightly wider at the middle of the long sides. Staggered vertical timbers were erected in the trench, probably with horizontal members between the verticals; stakes were placed in a line down the centre between the verticals to hold the intervening panels of daubed wattles. The most practical means of achieving this would be to partially construct the wall panels on the ground with the uprights and horizontals pegged together; the wattling would then be inserted and finally the wall plate. In the absence of internal roof supports, the wall was supported by two pairs of curving cruck blades supporting a horizontal carrying a king post to support the ridge. Rafters would be placed from the wall-plates to the ridge piece, probably supported on purlins. Millett (1983) also argues for a raised joist and plank floor. As the majority of the roof load, thatch or oak shingles, was placed on the wall plates, steeply inclined external raking timbers counteracted the thrust of the rafters.

The total man-hours required to construct such a building is impossible to estimate. The preparation of the foundations and the timbers alone would have required considerable time and although C12 is the largest building excavated at the site, the effort required to build many of the others would not have been much less.

Such timber buildings would have been built using the accumulated experience of the community and would not have seemed such an intricate task to those who regularly witnessed the activity. The spirit of true craftsmanship is, however, best seen in those items which, as far as is known, were unique in their time and which required all the craftsmen's skills to achieve. A fine example is the helmet from the Sutton Hoo burial in mound 1. One might imagine, perhaps wrongly, that there would have been few craftsmen who either alone or in a group would at any one time have been capable of producing such an item because of the variety of skills required in its production. It is possible that the helmet is a Swedish product, but whatever the source it exemplifies the strength of contemporary craftsmanship.

The framework of the helmet consists of an iron cap, almost hemispherical, which was beaten out of one piece of metal. Over this cap, from the front to the back is a strong iron crest, D-shaped in cross-section and hollow, riveted at its ends to the cap. The crest was of two parts, flat and U-sectioned, the former bottom plate fitting inside the latter. It must have been either forged or welded to the cap or fitted hot and allowed to cool into position. Attached to the lower edge of the cap are a face-mask, two cheek-pieces and a neckguard. The fact-mask was rigid and attached by rivets, the neckguard and cheek-pieces hinged by strips of leather strengthened by bronze bars and riveted. The neckguard was solid and beaten out of two sheets of metal and held to the cap by two riveted leather hinges with metal reinforcing bars. It is assumed that the interior of the cap was lined with soft leather. The heavy cheek-pieces would have enclosed the face completely. The surface of the helmet was almost totally covered with figural and interlaced ornament applied to the surface of the iron cap in the form of tinned bronze sheeting into which the ornament had been stamped with dies. The bronze sheeting was held to the cap, cheek-pieces, neckguard and mask by fluted strips of bronze riveted through the edges of the foil to the cap of the helmet. Some jewels were fitted to the surface; there was a line of square-cut flat garnets on the eyebrows, and dragon heads which form terminals to the crest have cabochan garnets for eyes. The iron crest and bronze eyebrows were inlaid with silver wire. Parts of the surface of the helmet were gilded, the boar, dragon heads, the nose and mouth of the face-mask, under surfaces of the eyebrows and the broad fluted strips flanking the crest. Fluted strips holding and framing the decorative panels were of tinned bronze (Bruce-Mitford 1978).

There can be no doubt that much time and skill would have been required to produce such an ornate and complex piece of metalwork; the investment required was no doubt matched by the importance of the person for whom it was made and with whom it was buried with coins dated AD 622–629 at Sutton Hoo (Brown 1981b). The production of an item such as the Sutton Hoo helmet was undoubtedly a great achievement, but there are cases where the complexity and skill involved in the manufacture of even the humbler items is surprising. This can be demonstrated by examining items made from different raw materials. There is no doubt that much remains to be learnt about the technology of the period, but the few specialist studies that have been made are enlightening.

Forging

Apart from the almost ubiquitous knife, iron was most extensively used in the production of weaponry. Typically for the period the quantity of finished products is far greater than the known examples of production sites. There is direct evidence for iron-smelting from Shakenoak (Oxfordshire), Wakerley (Northamptonshire) and Mucking. Shakenoak produced iron-working debris (Cleere 1972), whilst at Wakerley and Mucking there were shaft furnaces. That at Wakerley consisted of a clay-lined furnace set 2½ feet into the limestone bedrock. There was no means of tapping the slag, requiring the furnace to be broken after melting and then rebuilt (*Med. Arch.* 1971, p. 132). At Mucking (Jones 1980) blocks of slag were recovered, the largest weighing 24 kilograms, produced when either waste slag or cinder was dropped into the bottom of the shaft, cooling into such blocks. That slag was at some times tapped during the period is shown by the debris at Shakenoak, which was accompanied by the clay linings from four furnaces and forging hearths. Leeds noted that 'scoriae', cinders, were to be found on most of the surfaces within sunken buildings at the settlement at Sutton Courtenay, suggesting to him that 'every man may have been his own smith' (Leeds 1936, p. 24. Such waste was also found to be common at Catholme (Losco-Bradley 1977).

Spears and axes have utilitarian forms, the manufacture of which would have been within the abilities of anyone with basic smithing experience; both have sockets for handles/shafts which would have been created by beating the iron around a former. The heads of the spears are usually slightly lozenge-sectioned, as a result of beating out the edges, and the socket, normally split on one side, was riveted to the top of the shaft. There are hints of preferred shapes on a regional basis, but there is little distinct typological development discernible. Occasional specimens are decorated with inlaid copper wire (Swanton 1973; 1974).

The handles and shafts of these implements and weapons were normally of wood, which is frequently visible although replaced by corrosion. The handles of knives were frequently made of two pieces riveted together, but the alder-wood handle of a knife from Christchurch (Hampshire) was one piece of wood which had been forced over the pointed tang (Jarvis *et al.* 1983). From the hafts of spearheads, normally split to allow a firm fit of the shaft, we find the use of hazel and ash, both of which tend to grow straight when pollarded. There is archaeological evidence for such management of woodland at this time from Barton Court Farm (Oxfordshire) (Robinson 1981). The length of such shafts is difficult to determine except where there is an accompanying ferrule binding the foot. With such items we are dealing with a simple use of wood. More complex carpentry was used on this scale on shields.

Shields were probably circular, of wood with a central hole for the handle which was protected by an iron boss; it is the iron handle and boss which usually survive in graves where they are found. The impression of the wood grain is often preserved on the metal components where they came into contact. Early bosses were squat cone shaped with a slight carination, developing through the period into very tall examples with no carination, called sugar-loaf bosses (Evison 1963). The bosses were made from a single billet of soft iron (Härke and Salter 1984) and fixed to the face of the shield by means of 4 to 5 rivets whose flat round heads are occasionally tinned. The ends of the rivets were bent over at right angles on the back of the shield making it possible to calculate that the wooden boards of the complete circular shields were 0.5 to 1.5 cm thick. The handles were generally fixed first, also by plain rivets burred over on the shield's front, at right angles to the grain of the wood (Leeds and Shortt 1953, p. 56; Jarvis *et al.* 1983, p. 127) and were often mounted off-centre. At one cemetery all of the wood for the boards was alder, and it was argued that the boards were of multi-ply construction because of the various directions of grain represented.

The suggestion that the boards are of ply construction has been questioned by Härke (1981) who argues that such evidence is created by the use of a wooden grip in front of the iron handle; a series of possible reconstructions was offered (Figure 3.1). The face of the boards was occasionally covered with leather (Leeds and Shortt 1953, p. 56), and even more rarely metal decoration was also added. Examples of such metal appliqués are from Caenby (Lincolnshire) and Sutton Hoo (for a list of possible examples, see Baldwin Brown 1903–37, iii, p. 199ff.).

Swords were the rarest and most prestigious weapons in early Anglo-Saxon England (Davidson 1962). They were two-edged weapons, normally about 90 cm long. The various fittings associated with the handle rarely survive as they were presumably made from organic materials. The known metal examples of mounts and fittings therefore form the basis for a typology (Böhner 1958). The earliest examples have straight pommel bars and guards, the latter slightly broader than the heel of the blade, and capped by a mount in the shape of a cocked hat. The sword hilt offered scope for embellishment; sometimes the pommel and guard are decorated, inlaid or gilded, embellished with runes and given a loose ring (Hawkes and Page 1967; Evison 1967). The blades may also be decorated, by a method known as pattern welding, although this is rarely apparent from the corroded form in which they are found (Wilson 1976b, pp. 265–66; Anstee and Beik 1961; Hodges 1964, p. 47ff.). Pattern welding was achieved by a complex and skilled process. A channel was left on each face of the blade into which separate strips were laid. Such strips were themselves complex; an iron rod was carburised, piled and drawn down and the process repeated until a rod of laminated iron and steel was produced. The bars were then folded or twisted together and beaten out to form the central element of each face. The blade was then polished to emphasise the bands of iron and steel.

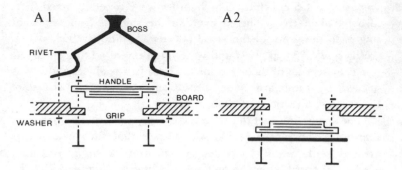

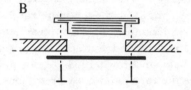

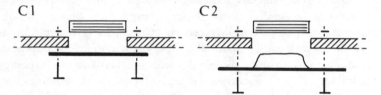

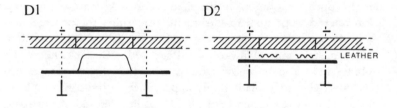

Figure 3.1: Possible reconstructions of early Anglo-Saxon shields (after Härke 1981, fig. 1). The evidence for the reconstructions comes from the iron fittings and indications of wood found on them

Casting

The apparent certainty of knowledge concerning the technology of sword and shield manufacture may all too easily divert attention away from the areas of greater doubt. In discussing the stages in the manufacture of the Kentish disc brooches considerable detail was omitted because of uncertainties regarding the actual methods of jewellery manufacture at the time. Understanding of these methods is critical to our appreciation of the technology employed and, as important, our knowledge of the organisation of metalworking; a lack of data makes resolution difficult. The existence in England, as on the Continent, of bronze models for the creation of the design in two-piece moulds has led to the suggestion that smiths were itinerant specialists (Werner 1970; Capelle and Vierck 1971). However, the models are not found in contexts reflecting their use, making the conclusion spurious. Certainly two- and multi-piece clay moulds were in use at Helgö, Sweden, a settlement which was a long-lived centre of metalworking. Much of the debate, particularly in Sweden, regarding the methods of manufacture of such metalwork stems from minor variations among moulds for the same design.

Variation between final products of a particular form of object may have been exaggerated by cleaning of the casts, especially if the castings were poor. Others believe that the degree of replication, despite small variation, can only have occurred if models were used, yet none have been found at Helgö. This has given rise to a series of, occasionally bizarre, arguments to account for the pattern. Secondary wax models may have been made from a durable master model (Holmqvist 1972, p. 24). Lamm argues that they were made of organic material, wood or bone, differences being introduced by the creation of a number of similar, but not identical, examples (Lamm 1973; 1980; Lamm and Lundström 1976). Another explanation would be that models were used once and then destroyed. There is a danger of losing the original problem in the search for models.

At Helgö it would appear that each mould was used for one casting only. When positive wax models are used they are extremely difficult to extract from the clay and they would have been destroyed in melting them out. Equally clay moulds may have been produced by carving in the negative directly onto the clay; while carving a negative is difficult it was achieved with success at other times, for instance in the medieval period with stone moulds. The degree of replication might be the same as that achieved by a traditional potter or modern cartoonist, but with slight variation. Models nevertheless existed in some parts of Europe and variation has been explained by the use of forms of the lost-wax or -lead process (Capelle and Vierck 1975; Vierck

1976; Arrhenius 1973; 1975; Dickinson 1982, pp. 21–2). A lead model for a square-headed brooch has been identified in Geneva (Bonnet and Martin 1982). The use of these various processes may have provided the vehicles for the transmission of decorative motifs, by copying.

The impact of any examination of variation between brooches in early Anglo-Saxon England is lessened by the near-absence of moulds, and few studies have been made. A study of a series of great square-headed brooches from southern England, of sixth century date, in which parts of the ornament are interchanged might at first argue for part-models being used to make up varying compound designs. The earliest in the series of brooches is thought to be that from the cemetery at Chessell Down; the various combinations of the design elements on the other examples in the series make it possible to suggest the sequence in which they were manufactured. While a superficial examination suggests that the same models might have been used, measurement reveals considerable differences; this may point, therefore, to straight-forward copying or replication from memory with or without a model.

Measurement has been used to examine the nature of variation between pairs of saucer brooches, particularly the ornament variation (Dickinson 1982); the study was based on 52 pairs of cast saucer brooches, but a number of problems were encountered with what might have seemed a straightforward piece of research (ibid. 22–3). Five types of ornament variation were classified which may be major or minor:

(1) No apparent variation
(2) Variations in size and alignment of individual elements
(3) Digital variation (where the number of elements in a motif varies)
(4) Form (where the form and execution of an element varies)
(5) Artistic quality

It was accepted that models were used to create all of the decoration required in the clay moulds, so that variation could occur in making the model, mould, casting or in any final cleaning. From one class of variation it was concluded that 'each brooch was made from its individual model' (ibid., p. 30). It was pointed out that this made the idea of an itinerant craftsman carrying durable models for each brooch pair a nonsense; the further possibility that each mould was individually carved was not entertained. It may be asked why it was necessary to go to the trouble of carving a model which by all accounts may only have been used once, when the same procedure, in fine clay would produce a mould directly. Wax as a modelling medium does certainly have the advantage of making sharp and fine decoration possible, but it could be argued that fine clay, at the right degree of plasticity, is more useful. The matter therefore hinges on whether carving directly onto clay in the negative is a skill easily acquired. Wax is the best alternative and which explains many of the observed variations.

Dickinson argues for a change in the organisation of the industry as chronologically earlier pairs show less variation than later examples; this may only be a change in ability and need not relate to changes in the medium used to make models. Some of the later pairs 'display a great variety and experimentation in the arrangement of motifs drawn from a widespread stock of artistic ideas' (ibid., p. 36); it is suggested that this may be the result of craftsmen working together in a workshop. Equally it may depend on the social factors that may have determined the decoration used; the earlier brooches may be designed to satisfy a society in which there is less variation in social identity than later. Workshops may have existed, as Dickinson suggests, from the later sixth century, but this need not affect any argument regarding the method of manufacture. Indeed the durable models from England listed by Capelle and Vierck (1971; 1975) are mostly later in the period, and may signify a period when larger scale replication was possible; put the other way, a time when individual designs were no longer necessary, and the functional aspect was becoming more important.

This type of debate applies to the manufacture of all cast metalwork, brooches and buckles being the most common, although it is obviously most easily studied in those types with decorative variation. Until more work of this type is carried out, variation between brooches will remain an art-historical subject rather than carrying implications also for social and manufacturing organisation and, at the foundation, the history of technology.

Containers

The technologies considered so far have been those relating to large-scale carpentry and items worn or carried, especially brooches and weaponry. A different range of skills was required for producing containers, be they 'buckets', glassware, turned wooden vessels or pottery.

Early Anglo-Saxon buckets (Stamper 1978) are of metal-bound stave construction. These should not be confused with pails which are cylindrical, handled containers made entirely of metal, mostly imported into England (Richards 1986). Buckets are most usually bronze or iron bound, straight sided and on average 10 cm high and broad; it is their smallness which makes the term 'bucket' inappropriate. A few taper to the top, such as the example from the cemetery at Berinsfield (Oxfordshire); some tapering vessels are bound with bronze, for example that from Droxford (Hampshire), others may be of mixed construction such as those from Harwell (Oxfordshire). Perhaps the greatest variation is in the form of the type of mount, or escutcheon, for the handle. The principal types are those with bifurcated beaked heads, mounts with zoomorphic or anthropomorphic heads, plate escutcheons with ring suspension loops or inverted triangular openwork mounts. Some have handles without mounts, or none at all. Those with bifurcated head mounts show varying degrees of debasement, one of the earliest being that from Little Wilbraham (Cambridgeshire).

The most notable group with plate escutcheon mounts are those with arcade and dot decoration in *repoussé*, which are allied to an extensive Continental group, although the English examples vary slightly (Arnold 1982a, pp. 58–9) and are concentrated in central southern England. Others may be kidney shaped or triangular sometimes having holes drilled for decoration. Two have ring suspension loops attached to the upper band, from Portsdown (Hampshire) and Mucking (Jones and Jones 1975, p. 178); the type is more common on the Continent. A common type of bucket mount on the Continent is that with openwork triangular mounts, although the only definite English example is from Gilton in Kent. Others may be in a Celtic tradition, such as one from Twyford (Leicestershire) with a moulded ox-head on the escutcheon (Hawkes and Smith 1957), and that from Souldern (Oxfordshire) (Kennett 1975) whose stylised anthropomorphic face is reminiscent of the late prehistoric bucket from Aylesford (Kent) (Evans 1890, p. 363).

The handles themselves are most commonly formed of a plain bronze strip, pierced at the end and riveted through the escutcheon or upper binding strip, allowing the handle to swivel.

They may also be decorated with dots, arcs, circles, triangles, stamped, notched or bear incised lines. Some have ends which are hooked passing through a mount or through opposed holes in the vertical bands.

The bindings consist of various combinations; there may be 3 or 4 horizontal bands and 2 or 4 vertical stays, normally held together by rivets. Bronze bound buckets were probably manufactured cold as the metal is unsuitable for shrinking onto wooden staves, unlike iron. Iron bound buckets tend not to have vertical stays, the bindings being both broad iron bands and rod-like hoops. Some of the more ornate buckets have sheet bronze triangular mounts suspended from the top band; the most ornate show a bearded human face in relief *repoussé* work and are known in Essex (Great Chesterford and Mucking) and Kent (Eastry, Sandgate and Howletts). Others have suspended pendants decorated with circle and dot designs.

The majority of buckets found in early Anglo-Saxon graves are of stave construction, bound with bronze and whose construction requires the same control over materials as a cooper. Generally the staves forming the bucket have constant height and thickness, but vary considerably in their width; an example from grave 60 Petersfinger (Wiltshire) has staves varying from 2 to 5 cm wide and 0.35 cm thick (Table 3.1).

Unfortunately there are few certain identifications noted of the species of wood used. Yew is noted from Luton (Bedfordshire) grave 32, Portsdown, Harwell grave 9, Welbeck Hill (Lincolnshire), Roundway Down (Wiltshire) and buckets 2 and 5 from Sutton Hoo. Other species represented are pine or fir at Stowting (Kent) and Ashton Valley (Wiltshire); oak at Higham (Kent) and ash at Mucking (grave 600). One surviving base is that from North Luffenham, made of a circular piece of wood cut with the grain, 0.2 cm thick, slotted into a groove at the bottom of the staves; such a method of fixing is common. Turned wooden vessels were amongst the grave-goods in the ship burial of Sutton Hoo mound 1.

Table 3.1: Dimensions of staves on early Anglo-Saxon buckets

	width	thickness	(cm.)
North Luffenham (Rutland)	4	0.5	
Louth (Lincolnshire)	4	0.5	
Hillersham (Cambridgeshire)	4	0.4	
Sleaford (Lincolnshire)	4	0.2	

Glass vessels are the product of an entirely different technology, and again most research has been directed towards their typology (Harden 1956b; 1978). There has been considerable debate about the origins of the glassware found in Anglo-Saxon cemeteries; some are Roman survivals, and a proportion was imported from glass-houses in the Rhineland and northern Gaul. Yet the very large concentrations at Faversham (Harden 1956b, pp. 146–7) and the fact that some supposed European types are more common in England than on the Continent, for instance the Kempston type cone beakers (Evison 1972) and bag beakers (Harden 1978, p. 2), encourage a view that some at least may have been made in England. Unfortunately the evidence for their production is limited as glass-houses leave little archaeological evidence when all of the waste can be re-cycled.

Harden's type-series (1956b, pp. 139–43) divided the total assemblage into a number of distinct categories, beakers with stems or claws, bell, bag or cone-shaped, with the related horns, pouch bottles, squat jars, bottles, palm cups and bowls, to which has been added a bucket-shaped vessel from the cemetery of Westgarth Gardens, Bury St Edmunds (Suffolk); slight variations have been made to the original typology (Harden 1978, pp. 2–6).

Attempts to characterise glass with a view to understanding its technology and source have been made, but glass is a difficult material to work with in this way because of compositional irregularities (Sanderson and Hunter 1980; Hunter 1985). There are, for instance, no apparent compositional differences between Roman and Anglo-Saxon glass vessels (Sanderson, Hunter and Warren 1984) although there are marked changes in appearance; this may be the result of a decrease in technological ability. Anglo-Saxon glass displays a variety of colours, especially brown, ochre, yellow, blue and green, which are probably brought about by a lack of control of the furnace conditions rather than by deliberate colouring.

Much of the craftsmanship and its relevant technologies considered so far is in marked contrast to the most common of artefacts, pottery. Clay was used to make a range of items ranging from loom-weights to the unique clay figure from Spong Hill (Hills 1980a), but pottery vessels are the most frequent. Brisbane (1981) has suggested three modes of production for pottery in early Anglo-Saxon England; vessels for domestic use were made on settlements; specialised vessels were made for funerary use, both as a grave-good with inhumation burials and for containing cremated remains; and a relatively small quantity of imported wares. Very little research has been carried out on domestic wares and it remains far from clear to what extent the domestic and funerary pottery production can be separated.

The only known or suspected production sites are at Elsham in Lincolnshire comprising concentrations of burnt material and sherds of pottery (which have not been excavated and which may represent the remains of funeral pyres), the excavated kiln (?) at Cassington (Arthur and Jope 1963) and possibly Sutton Courtenay (Leeds 1936, p. 28). The settlement at West Stow has produced indirect evidence for manufacture in the form of large quantities of pottery, antler pot dies and 'a reserved area of clay' (West 1985, p. 129). The general absence of kilns has normally been accepted as negative evidence for the use of bonfires for firing pottery during the period.

A certain, if unknown, quantity of the pottery was coil made, and the decorated pottery tends to be finer and thinner-walled than the undecorated. A typology of the forms of cremation vessels has been produced by Myres (1969; 1977) and a simplified version by Hurst (1976). Research on the shape of cremation vessels incorporating measurement indicates that a more logical means of sub-dividing the material is possible. Richards created a method of defining vessel shape (1982) using a fixed set of rules; the profile of vessels is recorded and normalised to a standard height, a parameter which does not seem to be relevant to the definition of forms. The plotting of frequency distributions of particular size ratios provides peaks which represent preferred forms. It has been shown that particular shapes tend to be correlated, in the case of cremation pottery, with particular grave-goods, the sex of the individual which the vessels contain and the decoration on the vessel (Richards 1982). Other systems lack such precision and, therefore, such correlations.

The decoration is most frequently made by incised lines, wide or narrow, close-set or widely spaced, produced by small hand tools; in its most extreme form the surface can be corrugated. Much of the ceramic material in eastern England, less so in the south, is stamped, that is decorated by pressing a carved die or naturally occurring object into the surface. Few of these tools have been found; definite examples of dies (Briscoe 1981) are known from West Stow (X4), Lackford and Little Eriswell (Suffolk), Shakenoak and Illington, mostly made of antler, but bone was also used. Their rarity has led to the suggestion by Briscoe that the majority were made of a less durable material such as wood or even a soft stone such as chalk. Linear decoration is often combined with bosses, where the walls of the pot are pushed up from inside into rounded or oval knobs.

When so little is known about the firing technology it is difficult to generalise; the Cassington kiln was a type of updraught kiln similar to Roman types. A variety of tempers were used as additives to clays; whether the choice was conscious or not has yet to be studied, although it has already been observed that the same clay was used with different tempers in certain places. The most striking temper used was that of vegetable matter, known as grass- or chaff-tempering, perhaps added as a water-absorbing agent (Brisbane 1983, p. 254). Brown has argued that the material is animal dung which would be in accordance with Brisbane's suggestion that the domestic wares are a farmyard product (Brown 1976). Other tempers are chalk, limestone or shell, various localised stone such as flint, ground pottery (grog) and sand.

Textiles and Dress

In our consideration of technology and the production of particular artefacts we have been considering portable items which would have been of assistance to everyday life, some more so than others. One fundamental product which we have not examined is clothing, essential for warmth and protection. The production of textiles appears to have been a widespread craft which is probably the best represented in the archaeological record. Both the tools used in its manufacture, such as combs, beaters and loom-weights, and the finished products are well attested from both cemeteries and settlements.

Combs are often found as grave-goods with cremations — Hills has noted a correlation with female burials (1981a) — and often survive in sunken buildings associated with weaving equipment. They were often made from bone and antler, although wood may have been used more often than is now apparent because it rarely survives. Combs were made by cutting the tines on the edge, or edges if double-sided, of a flat sheet of bone, which was normally strengthened by one or two ribs fixed along the edge or centre by iron rivets. Some of the more elaborate types have barred cases to carry the comb (Hills 1981a). They were decorated both before and after assembly, with incised lines, compass drawn circles and ring-and-dot motifs. It is not easy to be sure of their function or functions. They may be multi-purpose, for combing hair as well as in the weaving process. It is generally felt that the tines are too close together to be used for carding wool, although some simpler combs which may be wool-combs are known. They may have had a function in aiding the picking out of broken threads on the loom. Nevertheless an assemblage of tools is often found together comprising shears, combs and spindle whorls for spinning. Looms are most frequently indicated by loom-weights, annular in form, for weighing down the warp threads on upright looms; they are occasionally found in rows in the base of sunken buildings where they may have fallen or been taken off the loom, or originally stacked in a column. Whether the length of such rows represents the width of the material has been debated. Parallel rows of clay rings found at Grimstone End (Suffolk) (Brown *et al.* 1957) were 2.4 m long and 0.22 m apart. A row of 43 found at Old Erringham (Sussex) was 1.5 m long; experiments have shown that 0.5 m of warp thread would require 14 loom-weights; 1.5 m would there-fore require 42. A 'loom' found at Bourton-on-the-Water (Gloucestershire) (Dunning 1932) was represented by postholes 2.3 m apart, suggesting a maximum width of about 2 m of cloth. This type of evidence assumes greater importance when assessing the nature of early Anglo-Saxon dress. Such looms may have been present in every household.

Another weaving tool is the weaving batten, of bone or iron, used for beating up the weft. They are most commonly found in women's graves of the sixth century accompanied by a relatively large quantity of grave-goods. Also used were pin beaters, long pieces of bone with a central swelling and pointed ends for beating down individual threads. Some of the best collections of these tools have been found in sunken buildings at Swindon (Wiltshire) which were accompanied by small bone pins and various iron instruments.

The textiles themselves are normally known as a result of being preserved by corrosion, where they have been in contact with metal objects in graves; wood and leather are often preserved in the same manner. Such corrosion deposits are frequently referred to by names implying that the textile is replaced by corrosion products. In fact what is usually observed are negative casts around the original structure which may be studied by scanning electron microscopy (Janaway 1985). The end result is an impression of the surface of the fabric, now disintegrated, maintained in the form of a metal compound which results from the chemical composition of the adjacent object. Occasionally actual textile survives adhering to metal. The majority of weaves preserved in these ways are plain, with a variety of twills, especially broken diamond twill; braids are also known (Crowfoot and Hawkes 1967).

Much of the cloth was made up into clothing. It is possible to reconstruct some of the clothing in part through the textile remains in graves, but mostly using the position of dress fasteners such as brooches and buckles (Cook 1974; Bell 1981). Some analysts have made considerable use of pictorial, literary and archaeological evidence from the Continent. It is perhaps unreasonable to expect Continental evidence to represent accurately the styles of dress worn in early Anglo-Saxon England. The safer approach is to start with that evidence which is directly relevant. More work of this type could be carried out to isolate culturally determined variation in both dress and the manner in which artefacts were worn (Vierck 1978a; 1978b; 1978c).

Women's clothes show about eight variations in the position of dress-fasteners, with one, two or three brooches being worn in varying position on the shoulders and chest, sometimes with sleeve fasteners (frequently referred to as 'wrist clasps') particularly in eastern England. Men's dress fastening is limited to buckles and sleeve fasteners; three possible combinations are found. The principal problem in reconstructing clothing from this evidence is that the range of dress-fastenings need not only be dictated by dress; social identity and/or display may enter here. The evidence suggests that the female costume comprised various combinations of a number of elemental garments; a dress, undergarment, cloak and a veil. The dresses were secured at either one or both shoulders, with brooches, pins or possibly stitches. They may have been open-fronted, the borders of the open seam being either fastened together or pinned back at the breast, again with brooches and pins. Such dresses may have been worn over a sleeved under-dress which generally received no fastenings, with some exceptions which were secured at the wrist with a clasp which may carry evidence of braid (Crowfoot 1952). Some women wore a cloak fastened at the shoulder or breast, and some gathered clothing in at the waist with a girdle, usually secured with a buckle. Clearly the more elaborate the dress, the more dress-fasteners required, although there is here the danger of a circular argument.

Wear on square-headed brooches has been examined by Leigh as a means of understanding how they were used to fasten clothing (1980, p. 487ff.; 1985). The majority of single brooches examined were found to be more abraded on the top left corner than the top right. A slightly larger percentage of pairs of brooches were more abraded on the top right than the top left corner. This may indicate that the brooches were consistently worn in a particular position, but not in the same way. Single brooches were generally worn with the headplates pointing to the left and pairs with their headplates pointing to the right, and parallel. Leigh argues that the wear arises more on the corner of the headplate because they were worn pointing downwards, and at a slight angle so that one corner was lower down. He suggests that they were worn for display only, rather than as a dress-fastening, being heavily abraded from contact with coarse outer clothing. However, even outer clothing must have required fastening and such wear would also have arisen if they were worn on undergarments in such a way as to come into contact with the inner face of the coarse outer garments; such extreme wear is perhaps more likely to have occurred in this way than on the outside.

Male dress presents a greater problem; sleeve-fasteners imply a sleeved upper garment, either inner or outer, and buckles suggest a belt, but there are difficulties in going beyond this. Buckles and strap-ends, for instance, need not be associated with clothing. The fact that many people were buried without durable dress-fasteners may imply that organic materials were often used, either on their own or in conjunction with metal fasteners; a few bone buttons are known.

Function

Clothing was the principal function of textiles, just as the principal function of buckles, sleeve-fasteners, pins and brooches was to hold the clothing together. Such metalwork and fabric may have been decorated in a way which conveyed meaning to the wearer and the viewer, but all of the artefacts whose technology we have considered had, first and foremost a function to their owners. In certain instances these functions seem obvious to us, yet at times they are less so.

Vessels may have been used for eating, drinking, containing and carrying liquids, but each type may have had a specific function such as the use of open bowls as lamps. Glass vessels are normally interpreted as for drinking. Some, especially cone beakers, will not stand in an upright position, suggesting a degree of ceremony involved in imbibing. 'Buckets' have a very similar capacity, one which seems too small for them to be practical for fetching water to the house; indeed it should be noted that durable containers for the bulk carrying and storage of liquids and solids are rare, except for the large metal cauldrons, dishes and buckets from rich seventh-century burials like that of Sutton Hoo mound 1. The various cups and horns in graves may have been for the consumption of alcoholic liquid, including *beor*, *ealu*, *medu* and *win* (Fell 1975). Small buckets and bowls may also be associated with drinking.

The range of drink-associated items buried as grave-goods may be symbolic of an individual's role in society in the same way that pieces of weaving equipment in durable materials are found in richly accompanied women's graves. Containers are strongly associated with male-rich graves, while perforated spoons found in a few female graves may have been used as strainers in connection with the serving of drink. The capacities of such vessels may offer clues to their function. The majority of 'buckets' measure about 10 × 10 cm, with a capacity of about 0.7 litres, others are larger. The larger vessels tend to be found with richer burials perhaps reflecting conspicuous consumption by leaders and a role in storage and distribution. Glass vessels also vary in size, but cone-beakers, generally *c.* 25 cm high and *c.* 9 cm diameter at the mouth, had a capacity of about 0.3 litres.

The function of early Anglo-Saxon pottery seems at first glance to be obvious. Much of it was used to contain cremations or as accessory vessels in inhumation graves; it is the funerary pottery that has attracted the most attention. Very little research has been carried out on the functions of domestic pottery; there must have been a variety of functions which, glibly, can be placed under the headings of cooking and storage, but behind such distinctions there is little clarity. It remains unclear whether the types of vessel so commonly found in cremation cemeteries were also used domestically; the evidence of the settlement of West Stow where stamped vessels of a type found in cremation cemeteries were present amongst other rubbish and which may have been made there, is ambiguous. Cremation urns tend to have a greater volume than those accompanying inhumations predominantly in southern England. This may imply that in cremating areas the vessels were made a certain size for the specific function of containing the ashes, whereas in areas practising inhumation there may not have been such specialised production, the vessels being drawn from the domestic stock. Hence their smaller size reflects domestic use and they are of a similar size to those found on settlements. Yet precisely what are the vessels found on settlement sites used for?

Published reports rarely comment on evidence for the function of domestic pottery, and unlike studies of later medieval pottery the presence or absence of sooting on the vessels' surfaces is not always commented on. Large domestic pots at West Stow had been given a thin coating of clay on the outside after they had been fired; this layer is usually slightly reddened as a result of partial firing (West 1985, p. 129). Leeds described coarse vessels, many tempered with organic material, found within sunken buildings at Sutton Courtenay as 'cooking-pots', which were associated with fire-reddened pebbles. While the association may not be relevant to the function of the pottery, he interpreted the stones as pot-boilers (1936, p. 24). Hearths are a fairly common feature in a proportion of such buildings and Leeds also describes some pits as being for cooking. Sooting was noted on vessels at Bishopstone (Bell 1977, pp. 229–33). But as Hurst has emphasised (1976, pp. 292) such pottery 'presents a serious problem' for it is often so fragmentary or 'unstratified', so as to make study difficult; he also describes them as 'cooking-pots'. They actually range from small globular vessels to larger storage vessels, as found at Sutton Courtenay; some have a few or numerous perforations in the walls of the vessel. Such colander-type vessels are known from Mucking, West Stow and Sutton Courtenay (Jones and Jones 1975, fig. 54.6; West 1985, fig. 152; Leeds 1927, pp. 72–3).

The discussion of early Anglo-Saxon pottery in Myres (1969) has little direct comment on the uses of pottery, except that many were used in mortuary rituals. Indirectly, the titles given to various types imply that distinctions were considered possible. All decorated pottery was described as a subset of all cremation wares. Yet the undecorated vessels were given a variety of titles, despite the majority having also come from cemeteries; biconical and globular vessels were labelled 'urns', squat vessels as 'plain bowls', and a variety of shapes that could not be fitted easily into the typological scheme were labelled domestic wares, 'crude accessories', 'wide-mouthed cook-pots' and 'cook-pots with lugs' (ibid., pp. 26–9, pp. 148–70). Myres also emphasised the

117

difficulties faced in categorising these wares because of their crude and formless nature. However he noted that his category of wide-mouthed cook-pots are often smoke-blackened on the outer surface. More direct indications of function come with small groups of vessels having three solid or horizontally pierced lugs for suspension by a cord or thong; these were designed primarily as household utensils. Horizontally pierced lugs on the rim as well as perforation in the necks of vessels are quite commonly found on settlements of the period, for instance Bishopstone (Bell 1977, p. 235) and Mucking (Jones and Jones 1975, p. 159).

We can but guess at the extent of the use of wood or leather containers for storage, cooking, serving, eating and drinking. The existence of small wooden vessels is demonstrated by those which were strengthened by metal parts, like buckets and the small silver rimmed cups from Chessell Down (Arnold 1982a, p. 59). If glass vessels *were* prestigious drinking vessels, one might expect their cheaper equivalents to appear in the ceramic assemblage; true skeuomorphs are not present amongst the pottery, although there is a strong similarity between the turned wooden vessels with metal rims from the Sutton Hoo mound 1 ship burial and the squat jars of Harden's type VIII (1956b; 1978). In form alone there are similarities between certain glass bowls and plain ceramic bowls, but it is difficult to find ceramic equivalents of distinctive glass forms, suggesting that any social and economic symbolism conveyed by the shape and function of such vessels was conveyed equally by the material used, and that there were rigid boundaries between them; there was not, for instance, a poor man's version of the glass cone beaker.

The function of certain artefacts is less open to interpretation. Swords, spears and shields are taken to be weapons of warfare, defensive and offensive, and there is nothing to suggest that they were used in any way other than conventional modes (Alcock 1978; Davidson 1962; Swanton 1973). The questionable relation-ship between assemblages of grave-goods and life is emphasised by the often curious combinations of weaponry found (Figure 3.2), which can at times seem quite impracticable; this need not deny that the presence, for instance, of a shield alone may symbolise something. Such weaponry may have been designed principally for warfare and combat, yet the existence of wild animal bones on settlements, especially deer, points to hunting being a means of supplementing the diet; yet what was used to bring down such game? The use of spears is possible yet arguably a hazardous

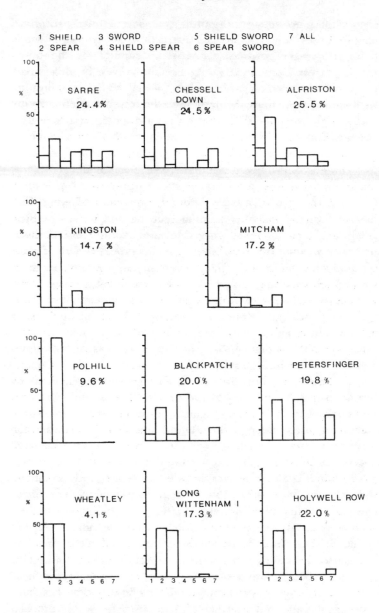

Figure 3.2: Histograms illustrating the frequencies of weapon combinations in early
Anglo-Saxon cemeteries and the percentages of graves with weapons. The regular
pattern of the sixth century may be compared with that found in seventh century
cemeteries which reveal a reduction in the number of combinations and the proportion
of graves with weapons. There are also regional differences

occupation more suited to hunting as a sport. Hunting may well have been seen as a pleasurable distraction, but from a practical point of view the bow and arrow is more useful. Yet bows and arrows are very rare in early Anglo-Saxon graves. From an argument based on such negative evidence it may be that as a hunting weapon they were more common than the record suggests, having such a high use-value that they were not disposed of at burial; if accepted this would also say something of the use-value of weaponry. Support for this view is found in the general rarity of tools in graves. Many tools may have been made of organic materials but some, for instance wood-working tools, were of metal. These are occasionally found, conventional types with normal functions such as planing, cutting and boring (Wilson 1968). On the Continent a curved form of axe, the *franscisca*, was used as a weapon by throwing it, but this type and conventional forms of axe are rare in England, even though it would have been a basic tool for cutting timber. The same argument, that tools with a high use-value were not placed in graves, applies to tools associated with most crafts, such as agriculture, metal-working and textile manufacture, although the last-named is well-represented on settlements. This may be contrasted with items associated with dress (Table 3.2).

The absence of brooches, or other dress-fasteners, in many female graves, might lead to the conclusion that they were not necessary items, or that organic materials may have been commonly used. Despite their being one of the most common types of artefact in female graves, they may have been considered a personal luxury. This may actually apply to all of the grave-goods found, beads, brooches, buckles, weaponry and containers; they may all be luxury items with little use-value. The major exception is the ubiquitous iron knife, perhaps so common and such a personal item that it was felt to be expendable. Knives would obviously have been the most common tool in everyday life, being useful for numerous functions. This may well indicate a great deal about concepts of value in early Anglo-Saxon England.

There are other less common artefacts whose possible functions have been considered elsewhere. There are some whose function has stimulated considerable debate such as 'purse-mounts' (Brown 1977) and 'needle-cases' (ibid., 1974). Others have stimulated less comment such as tweezers found in male graves; if it were accepted that they were primarily depilatory we must consider their role in the alteration of the physical appearance of

Table 3.2: *Ranges of artefacts, sub-divided by category, buried as grave-goods in six early Anglo-Saxon cemeteries*

Category	Artefact	Collingbourne Ducis, Wiltshire	Lyminge, Kent	Alfriston, Sussex	Petersfinger, Wiltshire	Polhill, Kent	Winnall II, Hampshire
Tools	Whetstone				X		
	Brush	X		X	X		
	Needles	X			X	X	
	Spindle Whorl	X				X	
	Comb	X	X			X	
Prestige/luxury	Crystal ball		X				
	Spoon			X	X		
	Purse			X	X		
	Bucket	X		X	X		
	Tweezers		X	X	X		
	Glass	X	X	X	X	X	
Dress/ornaments	Ring	X	X	X	X	X	X
	Bead	X	X	X	X	X	X
	Pin	X	X	X	X	X	X
	Brooch	X	X	X	X	X	X
Weapons	Sword	X		X	X		
	Shield	X	X	X	X		
	Spear	X	X	X	X	X	
Miscellaneous	Pottery	X	X	X	X	X	X
	Key	X	X	X	X	X	X
	Strap-end	X	X	X		X	X
	Buckle	X	X	X	X	X	X
	Knife	X	X	X	X	X	X

men and women as a cultural trait. Although rather intangible, such possibilities must be borne in mind when considering dress and the decoration of artefacts as there are other media for the expression of design and meaning. It is difficult to gauge the extent to which cosmetics, leather working, paint and carving were used as surviving examples are rare or non-existent. We are forced to perceive early Anglo-Saxon society through those durable artefacts which have survived, whose functions and meanings are often poorly understood, and there is the danger that our image of the society is seriously distorted.

4

The Topography of Belief

In the absence of contemporary, or near-contemporary, written evidence we have no direct source for a study of pagan Anglo-Saxon religion. Even the details of early Christian worship are obscure (Owen 1981). The maintenance of the secular structure of society is aided by ritual. The symbolic content of material aspects of ritual fall within the scope of archaeological research. Within one symbolic form may be condensed numerous aspects or meanings of the world, such as the unity and continuity of social groups, primary and associational, domestic and political. It has been proposed that there is a symbolic content in the grave-goods buried with the deceased which reflect social identity and status on either side of the boundary between life and death, but little work has been carried out on the remaining elements of the burial ritual.

The evidence for paganism contained in place-names such as *Thunreslau* (Essex), containing the name of the pagan god *Thunor*, may indicate places of worship (Gelling 1978, pp. 158–61). However, there is no evidence that pagan religious practices took place at specified places and there is, at present, no archaeological evidence that such 'sites' formed a part of pagan beliefs, and some may have no religious significance.

The place-name elements that have been considered at length by many writers are normally divided into two groups, those containing the name of a god or goddess such as *Thunor*, and those which may mean a sacred place (Wilson 1985). Both types are evenly distributed from the Humber to the south coast of England, although Norfolk is notably blank (Gelling 1978, fig. 11). The question of whether there is a relationship between the location of names indicative of a sacred place and topography, especially prehistoric and Roman routeways, is marred by the absence of any consideration of the possible coincidence of topographic factors determining the position of the roads and of archaeological features which may be contemporary with paganism of this type. However Wilson has observed that there is a noticeable difference in the location of names with *hearg*, and with *wēoh* and *wīh*, the former being on high ground not close to such roads, the latter on low ground and, perhaps inevitably, closer to old routes. It is argued that *hearg* sites are temples belonging to large groups or individuals, whereas *wēoh* may be roadside shrines.

There is the hope that aerial photography will in due course confirm the existence of structures at such places, but at present the only known building which has been interpreted as a place of pagan worship is building D2 at Yeavering (Northumberland) although this need not be the type of structure to which 'pagan' place-names refer. The first timber building was left standing when enclosed by a large structure which may even be Christian. The nine successive deposits of ox-skulls heaped against a wall led to the suggestion of sacrifice and feasting.

There are a few ways in which we may gain some insight to the pagan Anglo-Saxon belief system; for instance, runic inscriptions, the decoration on artefacts and cemeteries. Runes and the runic alphabet are interpreted as being connected with magic (Page 1973). Runic letters and inscriptions have been identified on a number of objects of metal, ceramic and bone found in early Anglo-Saxon cemeteries (Figure 4.1), for instance that carved on the astragalus of a deer found in a cremation urn at Caistor-by-Norwich, or the h-rune on a sixth-century brooch from Wakerley. The greatest problem arises from the interpretation of the inscriptions for there is 'no recorded context of thought to help us understand an inscription' (Page 1973, p. 12). There are examples of 't'-like runic forms on weaponry, for instance a sword-pommel from Gilton and a spear-blade from Holborough (Kent) which may refer to *Tiw* as a war-god; it occurs also on some cremation urns from Caistor-by-Norwich and Loveden Hill. Few of the inscriptions on early Anglo-Saxon objects have been interpreted. Some were put onto the object at the manufacturing stage, such as that on a cremation urn from Loveden Hill or that on the Holborough spear which is inlaid in contrasting metal. Others were probably added after manufacture such as the sword mount and Byzantine pail from Chessell Down (Arnold 1982a).

The occurrence of such inscriptions is rare, which may imply

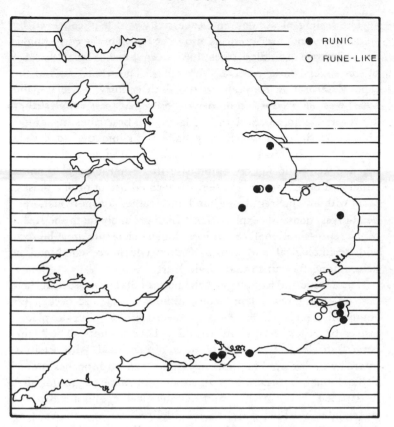

Figure 4.1: The distribution of runic and rune-like inscriptions in early Anglo-Saxon England (after Page 1973, fig. 6, with additions). Examples of inscriptions are concentrated in Kent, the Isle of Wight and the east Midlands

that the right or ability to produce and own objects bearing runic letters was limited to a small group in a society which was otherwise illiterate; we may allow for many such inscriptions having been on organic materials such as wood which has perished, but this would be an argument *in silentio*. There is no need for the owner of a runic inscription to have understood it, but their rarity does suggest some form of exclusion. The geographic distribution is also uneven, there being concentrations in Kent, the Isle of Wight and the region around the Wash from the Humber to Norfolk. The remainder of the country is without them in the period up to *c*. AD 650, but it cannot be said that they were runeless regions.

The feeling of secrecy and exclusivity which is conveyed by runic letters and inscriptions is also to be found in the early Anglo-Saxon interest in riddles. These have been noted in the decoration of some metalwork, especially brooches. The whole basis of the type of decoration common in the sixth century, Style I (Salin 1904) was the production of visual riddles. At their simplest they are reversible human and animal faces. On bracteates, metamorphoses are depicted which may have been intended to have a mythical or religious symbolism. Leigh (1980) suggests that dancing and acrobatic figures emphasise that some type of shaman ritual and belief may be implied: 'Repeated use of profile masks, often with an apparent head-band and feathers or more elaborate head-dress, demands explanation which probably lie in the realm of the representational'. Such iconological elements must be seen with technological and artistic factors which are combined in determining the outcome of Style I art.

The artistic and iconological elements of Style I are seen at their best on square-headed brooches, although they also occur, less commonly, on such artefacts as sword-fittings, buckle plates, saucer brooches, clasps and drinking horn mounts. The 'chip-carved' Style I ornament is three-dimensional with exciting interplay of design. The shape of square-headed brooches cannot be functional, but there is a consistency of shape suggesting that it satisfied both artistic and iconological requirements; the rectangular head-plate and rhomboidal foot allowed the exciting mixture of symmetry and asymmetry. Each area is laterally symmetrical providing room for the pairing of animals or other motifs in mirror images suitable for any narrative or iconographic scheme concerned with pairs of creatures. The varying pattern of upraised bands provided a variety of fields for such designs. Leigh believes that such brooches were modelled in wax, an ideal 'medium for the communication or representation of iconological ideas, even if, for the present, we are ill-equipped fully to appreciate these intentions' (1980, p. 428).

A primary requirement in such decorative schemes appears to have been that of ambiguity (Leigh 1984a); an animal had to be interpretable as human, for instance when an animal mask is inverted or turned through 90° it becomes a human mask and vice versa. By these tricks the designs are full of visual surprises. In addition the fragmentation of forms permitted disguise and deception as originally pointed out by Bakka (1958, p. 5). Like the runes we may well ask what proportion of society could understand such decoration, noting that the metalwork with this degree of decoration is relatively rare. In *later* Germanic mythology smiths are depicted as the repositories of wisdom, masters of runes and of magic songs (Turville Petrie 1964, p. 233). Leigh suggests that the Style I art is a facet of Anglo-Saxon society seen previously only in poetry; the decoration can be viewed as graphic poetry based on metaphor and alliteration, often in the form of riddles (1984a).

The overlapping and succeeding decorative system, Style II, also contains a variety of combinations of animals and humans, especially the boar, bird and serpent (Speake 1980, pp. 76–92). The written evidence concerned with Germanic myth and belief, and certain artefacts, indicate that such animals had particular associations; the boar, for instance, may have had associations with kingship, although the situation is complicated by each possibly having multiple symbolic association and being used for both magical and decorative reasons. The potential symbolism of a wider range of artefacts has been explored by Meaney (1981).

Cemeteries can be used to reconstruct aspects of belief systems through the study of the variables such as grave-good position, the grave-goods themselves, body position, funerary urn decoration, orientation, the grave construction and associated structures and physical anthropology. The absence of communal places of pagan worship might suggest that religion was a personal activity, but at death the individual was most likely to be buried in a communal cemetery.

The majority of cemetery excavations concentrate on the graves themselves, the edge of the excavation being determined by their extent. There is now a greater interest in the whole cemetery, brought about in part by the adoption of open-area methods of excavation, which is more likely to reveal additional structures, such as buildings and markers, which may also be connected with belief. The few examples of structures in cemeteries suggest that they may be more common than is apparent; aerial photography of a cemetery in Kent, at Updown near Eastry, suggests the cemetery was bounded by a ditch for much of its life, perhaps spilling outside when it was believed to be fully used. At Bishopstone in Sussex, adjacent to the cemetery whose nucleus was a bronze age barrow, were a number of postholes, some of which assumed a trapeziodal shape. It measured '6.15 m long and 2.15 m wide at the narrow end, in the centre of which was a large posthole; the other end was 2.76 m wide without an intermediate posthole, but with an additional flanking posthole externally at either side' (Bell

1977, p. 195). Similar posthole 'structures' have been excavated at Compton Appledown (Sussex), a cemetery with mixed burial rites. There were four-post arrangements varying in size; one was over a grave but few were actually associated with graves. The excavator suggests they might be roofed structures or timber revetted barrows. Round and rectangular ditched enclosures were also present which, possibly like the four-post arrangement, appear to have covered burials on or close to the ground surface. Ring-ditches of this type have been widely reported and were first discussed in detail by Hogarth (1973), and more recently possible reconstructions have been considered by Hedges and Buckley (1985).

Although there is a wide range of structural evidence it unfortunately rarely allows reconstruction. The graves themselves vary in their shape, being sub-rectangular or more ovoid, but rarely in the past were details of the shape in three dimensions recorded. Sockets are found, usually in opposing pairs on each of the long sides of the grave in varying combinations, 2 to 8 in number; their shapes suggest use for vertical and horizontal timbers. In a few examples from east Kent the sockets were angled as though the graves had been covered with a pitched structure with the members angled at 30°. Posts set in a four-post array may be found about 1 m from the edge of the grave. Sometimes they are misaligned suggesting that they may be associated with the grave but are not strictly contemporary. Ledges may be found around all or part of the mouth of the grave-pit; some may be intended to support lids to the grave, or they may be a slightly more complex way of achieving the same result as with sockets but using a ground plate rather than earth-fast timbers; sockets and ledges are also found together.

Individual sockets for free-standing posts have been located at some cemeteries, and they may also occur with other structures, ditches and kerb-slots. Ditches, 6 to 7 m diameter around a grave may have a causeway, sometimes containing a relatively large posthole, or may be a complete ring. Their vertical sides suggest they are not purely quarries for a barrow mound, and the evidence of holes for upright timbers suggests a fence. St Peters, Broadstairs produced an example with a rectangular slot in which had stood sandstone slabs, forming a kerb, acting either as a boundary or purely to retain soil in a platform. One would need to know the original depth that such slabs were inserted into the ground to determine whether they could retain soil; certainly the penannular ditched structures *imply* an 'entrance' through the fence which would obviate a soil filling although, as suggested for the Orsett (Essex) cemetery, there may only have been a low mound over the grave. Individual posts at the foot of a grave, or in such a gap, may be seen as short grave markers or perhaps as relatively tall posts capable of carrying far greater symbolism.

As many of these marked graves were aligned east to west and had no grave-goods there has been a tendency to view them as lying within a Christian context and dating to the later seventh and eighth centuries. This might raise many problems for it is an argument *in silentio*. Greater problems are raised by the discovery at Tandderwen (Clwyd) of ditched graves, of varying sizes with entrances; one was dated by C14 to AD 510 ± 60 (pers. comm. K. Brassil). Other examples are known from Anglesey, Scotland and the Continent and it is difficult to disentangle the questions of cultural affinity with the practical response to the varying needs of construction, protection and veneration of a grave. In Kent such graves tend to lie near the edges of cemeteries, which is therefore taken to indicate a late date as though the cemetery spread outwards from an original nucleus. A problem is that the presence of such ditches need not imply a barrow but their absence need not necessarily imply that there was no barrow; indeed the wide spacing of some graves in cemeteries almost suggests the existence of barrows, albeit without other structural evidence.

Occasionally the excavation of cemeteries reveals preserved examples of complex graves. An annular ditch at Spong Hill contained a wooden lined grave of great complexity which appeared to have been robbed in antiquity. The floor was planked and the walls, probably also built of horizontal planks, had regular corners although there was no trace of nails or clamps; traces of a lid were located. Such timber chambered graves with rich and varied grave-goods are known elsewhere in England and on the Continent (for a survey of examples see Hills 1977a, pp. 172–3), and it is argued that the elaborate construction of this grave befitted a person of high rank.

The two basic forms of burial in early Anglo-Saxon England were by inhumation and cremation. Both forms may occur in cemeteries in varying proportions, but the basic difference in belief governing the choice is not known. Inhumation and cremation appear to have been practised simultaneously by some communities, whereas in others there may be a shift in emphasis with time, with inhumation being more strongly represented latterly. Timber structures are almost exclusively associated with inhumation burials which is the most common burial rite in early Anglo-Saxon England. The bodies, occasionally covered by stones, are normally extended or lightly flexed, most frequently without grave-goods. Where they do occur they may be personal items which, at least in life, would be attached to clothing such as knives, jewellery, actual dress items, strapends, buckles, pins, with additional items such as weaponry and vessels of various materials. There was a degree of regularity about the position of the artefacts in the graves, especially within individual cemeteries, as though such positions were considered most appropriate.

Re-use of prehistoric barrows is known in most areas of England, for both inhumations and cremations, but the frequency of primary barrow burial is less clear. Later agricultural activity can easily remove low barrows, but the existence of various sized barrows over graves are attested in many counties. Such elaborate forms of burial occur towards the end of the pagan period, at first as a component of a cemetery, or as a wholly barrow cemetery and later with often rich 'isolated' barrows, although their isolation may be more apparent than real. It may be argued that elaborate and visible forms of burial occur at times when individuals are asserting their power roles and at times of stress in society, although the nature of the stress during the phases of barrow building is unlikely to be the same. Stress may be caused during earlier periods by the effects of migration and colonisation, by the turbulent political and economic state of affairs in the latter. On the other hand, Shephard suggested that isolated barrows of the early seventh century onwards, symbolised a stability in the social system through the emergence of paramount rank, and that the earlier barrow cemeteries reflect a system regulated by a higher degree of organisation than the flat-grave cemeteries. Shephard did not consider the earliest phase of barrow use (1979).

Cemeteries in which cremation was the predominant rite are located in eastern and Midland England. Wells (1960) produced evidence that suggested cremation took place on the ground with the fuel heaped over the body. Just as the burial of horses and dogs (note that these are not the animals most commonly incorporated in iconography) as well as joints of meat is attested in some inhumation cemeteries, there is also evidence for animal bones associated with cremation. At Illington in Norfolk Wells noted a pattern of pigs being found with adolescents, oxen with adults and horses with adult males. Some of the cremated bone and grave-goods may be placed directly into the ground, although burial in a decorated or undecorated vessel is the most common practice. Both inhumations and cremations can be covered with stones, or even small cairns. The objects accompanying cremations may be burial items such as jewellery, playing-pieces or unburnt toilet sets and miniature versions of household items, such as combs and shears. Some urns have a hole deliberately made in them, in rare instances fitted with a piece of glass. There is also a relatively small group of inhumation graves where fires have been lit in the grave before or after the body has been inserted.

Beneath the basic distinctions in burial rite a considerable amount of variability is found, of which there has been little detailed research. One problem which is frequently encountered with the data, is the extent to which the variability is determined by ritual and belief rather than other factors. On the Isle of Wight, for instance, the largest cemeteries occur at the lowest altitudes, whereas the re-use of prehistoric burial mounds occurs at heights greater than 350 feet; the latter observation is governed by the distribution of the prehistoric barrows, the former is not, but neither need be a response to ritual. A pattern of this type may reflect changes or variability in the settlement pattern.

Considering the data from the Isle of Wight in more detail we find that nearly all of the possible permutations of cremation, inhumation, under visible barrows as primary or secondary deposits, or in flat-grave cemeteries are to be found. We may learn something from the fact that some of the permutations do not occur. (Figure 4.2) As we have seen, flat-grave cemeteries are not found at the higher altitudes, nor are barrow burials apparently found at low altitudes. In some cemeteries primary Anglo-Saxon burials under barrows occur alongside secondary deposits in prehistoric mounds.

Here again there are problems as the absence of visible burial mounds at any location may only be a reflection of the succeeding land-use pattern. Subsequent ploughing can easily have caused the destruction of smaller barrows especially on the more consistently cultivated low-lying arable land. The available evidence (Arnold 1982a) does suggest that more elaborate forms of burial, cremation and barrows, are found at higher altitudes in smaller cemeteries. The dating of those downland cemeteries on the Isle of Wight in which barrows are used and dating is possible, is consistently late fifth and early sixth century.

The majority of burials in early Anglo-Saxon England conform

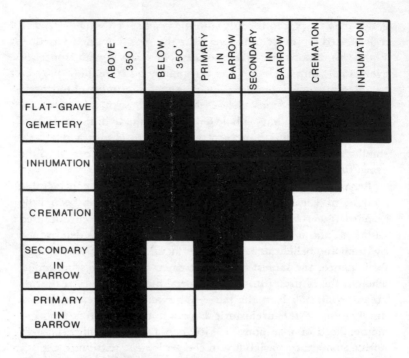

Figure 4.2: Matrix indicating correlations between cemetery location and mortuary data on the Isle of Wight. Positive correlations are shown in black

to the basic types and can yet reveal a great deal about ritual and belief when the most common associations of traits have been identified. They are, however, normally silent about the cause and circumstances of death despite the advances in 'forensic' archaeology. One, as yet uncatalogued, group of burials may be of greater use in understanding the rituals of belief.

There are a number of examples of individuals thought to have been buried alive, as at Sewerby (Yorkshire) and possibly Worthy Park (Hampshire), and many where there are unusual burial positions and grave-goods such as the claimed 'ploughman' at Sutton Hoo revealed as a three-dimensional soil stain in recent excavations. There are many more examples of skeletons buried either without the head, or with the decapitated head placed elsewhere in the grave. Here we face a problem caused by the overlap between cause of death, crime and punishment, and ritual; in some circumstances these might be quite separate factors, but they can also be strongly interrelated. At Sewerby the burial of a contorted old woman above that of another suggested an execution. At Worthy Park grave 43 was of a woman lying on her back, her face crushed on the floor of the grave, arms bent behind the chest, knees bent to the left with the feet together. The unaccompanied 16-year-old girl in grave 78 was found lying in a similar position. Osteological examination suggested that she had been raped. There is little direct evidence regarding attitudes to crime and punishment in pre-Christian England, but the attempts of the early Christian kings, from Aethelberht onwards, to replace the blood feud with a system of financial compensation suggest that previously crimes were avenged with violence. It has been suggested that the examples from Worthy Park may reflect this degree of violence (Hawkes and Wells 1975).

One means by which pagan Anglo-Saxon beliefs may be identified and better understood is by determining those aspects which were transferred to a Christian milieu following the conversion and those that became redundant. Unfortunately this suggestion is tinged with much optimism; it is, for instance, very difficult to distinguish a pagan from a Christian grave, and even when a grave might be ascribed to one of these notional categories, it tells us little about the actual beliefs held by the interred person or the funeral party. Much of our knowledge of the conversion of England is contained within Bede's *Ecclesiastical History of the English People* and the *Anglo-Saxon Chronicle*, in which the progress of missionaries and the conversion of leaders is documented. This policy of converting the head of a socio-political group in the belief that the remainder of the population would follow was often very effective, but there were political benefits to be gained by appearing to accept the new religion although a reversion to paganism is documented in a number of areas, such as Kent. It would be useful to know how the conversion of such figures affected the form of their burial. Bede tells us of the burial of royalty in major churches in the seventh century but no such grave has been excavated intact under anything approaching controlled archaeological conditions.

Attempts have been made to chart the conversion to Christianity through late cemeteries, but the problem is that graves without grave-goods orientated east to west and which might be accepted as Christian after a notional date in the seventh century, are also known before the seventh century. The question of the development of churchyard burial is therefore very difficult as factors which are applied to the definition of Christian burial often apply equally to pagan ones, and elements of pagan ritual may have persisted many generations after a nominal conversion to Christianity.

It is suggested that in England during the late seventh and early eighth centuries, cemeteries were abandoned in favour of new sites, and that such secondary, and possibly Christian, cemeteries were in turn abandoned in preference for a graveyard which would lie within a Christian village (Hyslop 1963; Meaney and Hawkes 1970). Whether the mobility of the cemeteries was matched by that of the settlements, or whether a Christian village with its churchyard might be expected to overlie its pagan predecessor are rarely discussed although Baldwin Brown argued that the graveyard would owe its existence to the presence of a secular church (1903, pp. 262–3). The archaeological evidence indicates that the majority of pagan cemeteries were adjacent to their settlements, although artefacts deemed appropriate to a pre-Christian context have been recovered within churchyards and later villages, albeit relatively rarely. It should be noted that the principal distinction between pagan and Christian burial is the presence or absence of grave-goods. This distinction gives rise to many problems; unaccompanied graves in cemeteries where grave-goods are present, are interpreted as the pagan 'poor' whereas graves in cemeteries with no grave-goods are Christian (social status indeterminable) and graves within graveyards, even with grave-goods, are Christian. Such assumptions may greatly mislead and the dangers are the same as arise when using the orientation of a grave alone as a guide to belief, as pointed out by Rahtz (1978).

The process of conversion should not automatically be expected to reveal itself in the material manifestation of religious activity. The subject should not be treated as though a limited number of models is favourable when the factors determining the location of pre-Christian and Christian cemeteries and settlements will be varied and numerous (Morris 1983). Despite this the study of the latest 'pagan' Anglo-Saxon graves/cemeteries has introduced a seemingly strong argument regarding the conversion to Christianity. The example of Sancton in Yorkshire is instructive (Faull 1976). There a large cremation cemetery existed on the light soils of the downland (Myres and Southern 1973). Its size, like that of a number of cremation cemeteries in eastern and Midland England, suggests it was a centralised crematorium serving a wide geographical area. In the sixth century a smaller and predominantly inhumation cemetery came into existence close to the present village in the valley bottom and which Faull suggests was for the 'local Sancton settlement'. Sancton II is adjacent to the medieval churchyard and suggests that one is a continuation of the other. The limited study of Middle-Saxon settlements, and especially the manner in which beliefs about nucleation and stability of settlement have come under attack (Foard 1978; Taylor 1977; 1978) should encourage caution in the search for uniform models.

The problem with studies made of 'double cemeteries', that is where an earlier one, often larger and with greater numbers of grave-goods, overlaps with or is superceded by a nearby smaller example with fewer grave-goods (examples discussed by Morris 1983, p. 54ff.), is the uncertainty of whether such changing patterns reflect belief, the failure or multiplication of settlements or both. Equally it is generally assumed that the reduction in the volume of grave-goods is purely a factor of religious beliefs, whereas economic considerations may be as pertinent (Arnold 1982b). Warnings about relying too heavily on the question of belief have been given by Morris:

> There is virtually no archaeological evidence to confirm that cemeteries like Winnall II or Polhill were being operated under Christian influence, or that the material culture displayed within them was in any way due to the impact of Christian ideas. (Morris 1983, p. 54)

Obviously what is not in doubt is the fact that conversion to Christianity did take place, yet our problem lies in comprehending the material correlates of that process and of filtering out those factors which are independent of it and those which are connected. Morris (ibid., pp. 59–62), concerned about the dangers of seeking all-embracing explanations, has listed those medieval churchyards which appear to be located wholly or partly over pagan cemeteries. While the number may be larger than the examples of so-called 'Final-phase' cemeteries, it still needs to be demonstrated that this coincidence is significant in terms of the conversion and is not a factor of statistical probability given changing settlement location preferences and the multiplication of settlement loci, a feature which Morris is also keen to emphasise (ibid., p. 62).

In analysing such questions it is the gaps in knowledge which continually frustrate. However adequately one element in a case may have been excavated, the uncertainty about remaining elements precludes straightforward interpretation. At Barton-on-Humber, for instance, Rodwell's excavation of the church of St Peter and areas of the churchyard suggest that the latter came into existence in the Middle-Saxon period and that the church was built in the cemetery in the tenth century. This arrangement was preceded by a seventh-century cemetery some 400 m to the south-west. But uncertainty about the location of the settlement(s) contemporary with the cemeteries makes detailed discussion difficult (Rodwell 1984, p. 17).

The difficulties in determining the nature of pagan Anglo-Saxon belief systems are the same even with overtly Christian evidence. It is because there is always a wide range of factors determining the form of religious activity and belief, that doubt can always be cast on our conclusions. There is no evidence that the Christian Church continued to function in south-east England beyond the period AD 425–50. It remains a possibility that throughout the sixth century some interest in cult sites was main-tained, or that they remained sufficiently identifiable to act as foci for later churches (ibid.).

At the time of Augustine's mission to England in AD 597 British churches already existed. Nearly 100 seventh-century churches are known from archaeological, architectural and writ-ten evidence, although we only have a complete plan of that at Yeavering. It is only in recent years that investigators' eyes have turned from the plan to the elevation where there may be as much, if not more, evidence.

The important early churches which were sited in a limited range of locations have been listed by Morris (1983, p. 40). Ease of communication may have been an important consideration, and, even allowing for bias in the written sources, it appears that many churches were established at either centres of royal authority or in juxtaposition with them; Canterbury, for example, was a royal *civitas* in Bede's eyes. It was apparently usual practice to found churches at royal centres in the seventh and eighth centuries and this led to the pattern of minsters at royal *tún* (Williams 1984). As power was often divided between various members of a royal family, acting as sub-kings to an overlord, there was considerable scope for the proliferation of churches and to some extent the distribution of churches in the seventh century may reflect the centres of spiritual and secular power and wealth. The early dioceses reflected kingdoms and kingship and their centres were generally areas with concentrations of pagan Anglo-Saxon cemeteries — that is, centres of population. The fact that a majority of churches were established in former Roman towns suggests a greater concern for 'pastoral and political factors' (Biddle 1976, p. 119), and also perhaps practical, than for concern with the past.

The connection between Christianity and kingship is hardly surprising when missionaries and bishops could only operate with the support of secular leaders and it was the royalty and nobility who provided the land and resources which were necessary for the erection and maintenance of ecclesiastical centres. Thus Morris suggests that 'the mechanisms which enabled the spread and consolidation of Christianity in the 7th century were basically political' (1983, p. 46), and he cites numerous examples and various forms which this association could take.

Little recorded building took place in England prior to AD 650, and that which did is confined to Kent, with lesser efforts in East Anglia and Wessex. There was a short and premature flurry in Deira in the 620s, and in Northumbria there was an almost continuous building programme from the middle of the century. But it was in the 670s and 680s that most church building activity was taking place, possibly during a period of relative peace after the turbulence preceding AD 660. The turbulence took the form of warfare between kingdoms, normally aimed at the acquisition of territory. In the middle years of the seventh century, Northumbria fought seven wars while Mercia was almost continually seeking to expand its frontiers, possibly because of a desire to seek coastal areas and take a more direct part in overseas trade. By the early eighth century Mercia had acquired London and tolls were being exacted in Kentish ports by the 730s. It is often overlooked that Mercian aggression towards the West Saxons on three occasions in the seventh century as late as the 660s may in part have been to secure suitable ports; in *Hamwic*, as in Kent, there are early eighth-century silver coins of Mercian origin suggesting that the River Itchen, irrespective of the extent of the development of the trading centre, may have been a port for the Midlands.

But the lull in warfare during the second half of the seventh century provided an environment in which nine sees could be founded in 25 years, compared with 7 during the previous 50 years, many of them in areas of Mercia or Mercian political influence; Mercia also led the field in the establishment of monastic sites.

The coincidence of centres of royal and ecclesiastical power is a reasonably clear pattern. London was a bishop's see from AD 604 and Kentish kings had a hall there by AD 675 (Biddle 1976, p. 116). Paulinus was bishop of York in 627 and it has been argued that it was also a royal centre (Addyman 1977, p. 500). The same coincidence is found at Canterbury, Winchester, Hereford and Worcester. Such foundations should not necessarily be taken to indicate political stability, for as we have seen, the expansionist policies of kingdoms, especially Mercia, involved the continuous ebb and flow of frontiers, at times incorporating centres which had been created by competitors.

The important aspect is the manner in which the protection of people's souls and the spread of Christian belief went hand-in-hand with commerce and administration. Some centres may have earlier, albeit presently obscure, origins given the sixth-century burials in Northampton, Worcester and St Paul-in-the-Bail, Lincoln. While the important royal and ecclesiastical centres and what may be subordinate royal seats played a major role in founding a structure for Christian worship, we know far less about its organisation and, indeed, about the buildings themselves. About 90 churches are known from this formative period, but few have been excavated by archaeologists. The putative church at Yeavering could easily be translated to a rural settlement and look at home because its plan is very similar to that of domestic buildings. This raises various questions about the origins of church form in England, but it also warns of the difficulties in identifying early timber churches. The same layout is to be found at St Paul-in-the-Bail, but there remains doubt about the dating of the first two phases. The early Kentish and Northumbrian churches are better known, but even here there are many question marks.

The dates given in the written sources for the first conversion of kingdoms, ignoring the relapses into paganism, offer an indication of the topography of the conversion of England (Figure 4.3). The initial conversion of Kent was followed by a rapid movement northwards along the east coast into Yorkshire and beyond, but progress westwards was slow. The known foundation dates of seventh-century churches in England, when plotted in 25 year periods (Figure 4.4), show a similar pattern of early churches in Kent followed by a rapid extension along the east coast. During the period AD 651–675 there was a multiplication of churches in these areas, as well as a gradual expansion westwards.

It may be relatively easy to carry out an investigation of

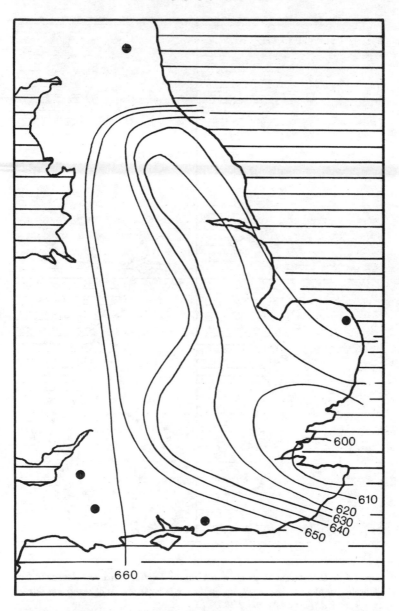

Figure 4.3: Trend surface diagram showing the process of English conversion to Christianity based on written sources and the location of British monastic foundations. The contours, in years, emphasise how the initial conversion of Kent was followed by a rapid spread of Christianity northwards along the east coast. British foundations (black dots) are found on the edges of the area converted to Christianity between AD 590 and AD 660

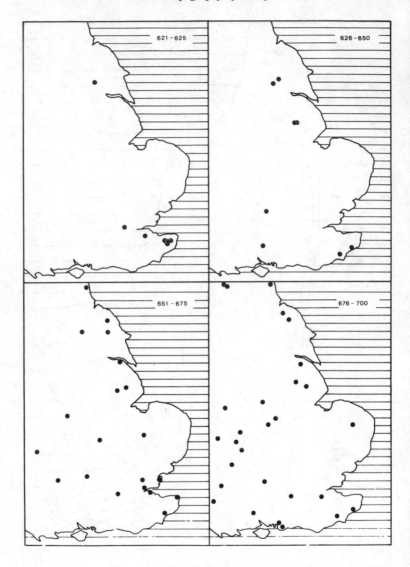

Figure 4.4: Distribution maps of seventh-century English church foundations in four chronological phases. The developing pattern reflects the process of conversion defined in Figure 4.3. (Data: Morris 1983.)

churches in terms of structures, but whether we consider paganism or Christianity, it is harder to see the workings and activities of such religions. Similarly it is difficult to appreciate both the extent to which paganism remained popular during the seventh century and of the effects of Christianity on the people at that time. It is one thing to view the conversion of royalty and the construction of churches, but an altogether different matter to view the beliefs of the remainder of the population.

5

Mighty Kinsmen

Status and Identity

The subject of the social organisation of human communities has only been researched in detail by archaeologists since the beginning of the 1970s. Despite the early Anglo-Saxon period having, potentially, some of the best data for such studies, it is in the prehistoric period that most research has been carried out. Historians of the Anglo-Saxon period have tackled the subject and, being predominantly concerned with the origin of institutions, much of their attention has been focused on the earliest law-codes. For the archaeologist, interest is in the social organisation of society at all levels, the status of the individual, the structure of the group and the formation of the kingdoms. During the period prior to the laws being written down, the greatest resource must be the 25,000 or so Anglo-Saxon graves which have been excavated. These may be examined using their orientation, the character of the grave and the interment. Comments have been made regarding the social standing of individuals, principally on the basis of the wealth of their grave-goods, but attempts to apply the same theory on a rigorous basis incorporating a broader spectrum of variables have provoked as many reactions as the variety of results.

Previous approaches to variation in early Anglo-Saxon grave form have been especially ethno-historical (Leeds 1913, p. 26) and while individual variables such as grave orientation have been considered (Russell 1976; Faull 1977, pp. 5–8; Wells and Green 1973; Hawkes 1977; Rahtz 1978) it is classes of object that have aroused most comment (see for instance: Davidson 1962, pp. 9–11; Chadwick 1958, p. 32; Hawkes 1973, p. 145). Such a

statement as 'a very rich grave may give an idea of the social structure . . . of a particular person' (Wilson 1976a, p. 3), while not
necessarily false, indicates the manner in which such observations
have been limited to particular classes of grave, with no
comprehensive study being made. Thus, whilst the equation of
many grave-goods with wealth is accepted by numerous scholars,
there is a reluctance to apply the principal right across the board.
Wealthy graves are taken to indicate a particular social identity.
It is possible that all graves have the identity of the individual
encoded in the mortuary ritual, but the lack of distinctive classes
amongst the majority of graves dissuades writers from speculating
about the identities of the remainder. It should be pointed out that
most often the study of graves extends no further than the
examination of 'grave-groups', noteworthy associations of
artefacts in individual graves, thereby ignoring the other
variables. Obviously graves are part of a funeral ritual and should
not be treated simply as sources for the study of particular types
of artefact.

The form of a burial may reflect, to a varying extent, ritual, the
funeral, a person's life, and his relationship to other people. It is
assumed that a grave and its contents are the result of a conscious
selection and deposition. Thus the organisation of the dead in
cemeteries has often been taken to reflect the organisation of the
living society. Any study of the social organisation of early Anglo-
Saxon society using the cemetery evidence must make a number
of assumptions because of the very special circumstances which
surround the disposal of the dead with grave-goods. Rituals may
wholly, or in part, reflect religious beliefs and have little or no
bearing on daily life. If, however, the manner in which the dead
are disposed of reflects an individual's social standing, it must be
remembered that the funeral was conducted by friends and
relatives, and therefore a whole series of additional factors may be
introduced. If the accompanying grave-goods are accepted as an
indicator of the deceased's social identity, should the quantity of
grave-goods be taken as an indicator of, for instance, position in
an hierarchical scale, or is the particular combination to be taken
as symbolising a person's role? It should never be forgotten that,
in life, it is not merely access to resources, but the use of those
resources that is important.

The problems of using burials to reconstruct social organisation
extend beyond those of mortuary ritual. As Richards observes *if*
'material culture does not merely passively reflect social relations,

but is actively used to articulate them, a simple relationship between artefacts and social status is denied' and therefore 'we cannot assume that status is directly mirrored in the wealth of grave-goods, and by assigning "wealth scores" to artefacts arrive at the hierarchical structure of society' (1984, p. 42). It is necessary to demonstrate that grave-goods were used to mark social identity, which is extremely difficult to prove, and also to show which artefacts were actively chosen. At least amongst inhumation burials there are various combinations of grave-goods made up from a limited range of types of artefact. Whilst there are favoured combinations there are a few unusual ones which may indicate someone whose role may have been unusual and specialised.

The subject of social organisation can be approached from a number of different levels. Early Anglo-Saxon society formed itself into a series of kingdom-states and a different form of organisation must be envisaged as preceding them. Within such changing socio-political units we may explore the subjects of class, lineage, achieved or prescribed status. The development of such groupings and the concepts of leadership are very much bound up with the subject of population densities. Graves are not the only route to studying social organisation, yet the alternatives, for instance the settlements of the period, have their own problems. A variety of methods have been employed, but little comparison of the results has taken place despite there being a considerable degree of apparent uniformity between them. Attribute analysis of inhumation and cremation cemeteries may be compared with methods based on various assessments of the quantity of grave-goods.

The social structure of early Anglo-Saxon England is a subject which has for long been confined to historians and social anthropologists. Such studies have depended on limited amounts of documentary evidence, particularly the laws and the charters, which are frequently difficult to reconcile with each other (Chadwick 1905; Seebohm 1911; Bullough 1965). Information regarding early Anglo-Saxon social structures has often been extrapolated from these documents which all tend to belong to the latter half of the period or later. The view has been expressed that the task is made more difficult because much of the earlier structure of society may have been suppressed by the power of later lordship and Christian kingship (Loyn 1974, p. 209). From the laws, especially those of Aethelberht of Kent, it emerges that there were a number of classes of person, ranging from the slave (*theow*) to the governor of the shire (*ealdorman*), and including the *ceorl*, unfree or half-free cottagers, freedmen occupying farms and rent-paying tenants (*gafolgelda*), and also the free farmer (*frigman*) and landed nobleman (*gesith*). It is notable that in this hierarchical system distinctions were made in terms of *property holding* and this is reflected in the fines paid by each class for specific crimes. As a relative scale of position this is probably as close as it can be defined. This data provides one of the major hypotheses derived from the written sources which may be testable by archaeology.

Studies of kinship in Anglo-Saxon society (Lancaster 1958; Loyn 1974) suggest that society was seen as being descended from a common ancestor and was non-unilineal. The limits of the kin group are not given in the sources, probably because they were common knowledge and unquestionably adhered to. It is not possible to discern the patterns of residence, but there are hints of a predominantly virilocal system. Anglo-Saxon poetry suggests that emotional identification with the kin was very close. The system, however, was by no means rigid and the circle of effective kin, small. A lack of descent groups is thought to be probable despite the patrilateral bias.

While the laws, charters and poetry allow such generalisations to be made they remain very distant from the nature of the archaeological data for the period, notably the cremation and inhumation cemeteries. Material symbolism pervades all societies being an integral part of culture. To explore such symbolism through the archaeological data, in this case the early Anglo-Saxon cemeteries, the first task is the division of the graves into groups on some logical basis, followed by the application of insights gained in studies of other cultures to understand the actual relationship between material symbolism and social relations which underlies the archaeological patterning.

In an attempt to integrate the written and archaeological data Alcock compared the range of grave-goods in Northumbrian male graves with a three-fold division of society based on the document-ary evidence for *thegns* or noble-warriors, *ceorls* or free warriors, and the unfree. The graves were graded into three classes on the basis of weaponry: those with a sword, scabbard and fittings, spear and shield; those with spear and perhaps also a shield; and those with no weaponry at all who may be buried with knife and perhaps a buckle. In general terms such intuitive divisions are useful, although if articles buried with a person do symbolise the social *persona* type, there may be greater subtleties involved in the other grave-goods accompanying such burials (Alcock 1981). We should ask how the variation in female graves relates to this male pattern.

Cemeteries from various parts of England have been examined and it is useful to compare the results, although comparison is made difficult when neither the quality of the data used nor the methodologies are uniform.

The inhumation cemetery at Holywell Row, Suffolk, has been examined by Pader (1980; 1982) for which there was information regarding age, sex, the grave-goods and skeletal position. However, the excavation was not complete and the graves had been found by trenching and probing (Lethbridge 1931, p. 1). Here, as with all such work using statistical techniques of analysis there is a 'fundamental difference between statistical association and archaeologically meaningful association' (Doran and Hodson 1975, p. 169) which should be borne in mind at all times. Analysis of the attributes of the graves showed that particular artefacts were related to age and sex (Table 5.1). Four classes of artefact were only found with females, irrespective of their age, whereas with males only the shield and spear were male-linked; only the shield was age-linked. Males and females were buried with two items, whereas knives were not only found with both sexes, but especially with adults. It can be seen that there was the least restriction in the selection of artefacts for females, or there may have been a wider choice of artefact types associated with females to choose from. The flexed skeletal position was primarily a female attribute.

A comparative study of the cemetery at Westgarth Gardens, Bury St Edmunds, showed that the artefacts there were more strongly constrained by age. In addition to differentiation in classes of object and skeletal position on an age and/or sex basis, spatial variation was found to account for the presence or absence of artefacts and their position in the grave was related to skeletal position. Comparison of female graves in two areas of the cemetery showed clear differences (Table 5.2).

Similar differences were found with male graves; in one area knives and buckles were always on the left and all other grave-goods at the head, usually to the left. Elsewhere in the cemetery spears were found on the right and shield bosses not at the head, but by the feet or on the chest.

These patterns led to the suggestion that there 'is a closer

Table 5.1: Relationship between attributes of graves at Holywell Row, Suffolk (after Pader 1980)

Object Type	Sex	Age
brooch	F	NS
implement holder	F	NS
beads	F	NS
sleeve fasteners	F	NS
knife	NS	ADULT CHILD
belt	M > F	NS
vessel	M > F	NS
spear	M	ADULT CHILD
shield	M	ADULT
extended skeleton	NS	ADULT CHILD
flexed skeleton	F > M	CHILD ADULT

M = male, F = female, NS = not significant

Table 5.2: Differences in position of grave-goods in female graves in the cemetery of Westgarth Gardens, Bury St Edmunds, Suffolk (after Pader 1980)

Sector	Knife and implement holder	Shoulder ornament	Sleeve fastener
1	right	left and right or just left	flexed — yes extended — no
2	left	left, right and centre	no

relationship between females and children than between adult males and either adult females or children' (Pader 1980, p. 155). As young children had items which they must have been given, it seems more likely that they indicate ascribed status, although Pader feels that it could also indicate achieved status; it was suggested that the burial programme related to 'attitude' towards children as a group and did not necessarily represent the distribution of their own power or wealth so much as reflect the adult situation. The most obvious conclusion which emerges from the study, and all others, is that the sex of the individual is strongly reflected in the accompanying grave-goods, when they are present. Furthermore, females often seem to be buried with a greater number of artefacts and need, Pader suggests, to be analysed using different scales. It is another means by which the 'principle governing the different social positions of each sex are emphasised'. Pader feels that a scoring system alone, whether the sexes are mixed or not, is simplistic and quotes examples where in 'sectors' of the cemeteries analysed, one sex may appear to be much wealthier than another. However such a pattern would be revealed even with a scoring system. The greatest problem with this research is that the whole cemetery was not excavated and the sectors are determined on the basis of age, sex, artefact and skeletal positioning, which are also the factors being interpreted.

The majority of inhumation cemeteries, particularly in southern England, were excavated before the development of modern, more rigorous, excavation and recording techniques. For most cemeteries the only reliable data is precisely which objects came from which grave; skeletal reports, if present, are often general and are rarely consistent, thereby denying direct comparison; plans, if made at all, may be little better than sketches. Despite these obvious difficulties attempts have been made to isolate the most common combinations of artefact divided by sex where possible. This exercise has been carried out for eight cemeteries spread over six counties in southern England (Arnold 1980) using a monothetic divisive technique (Peebles 1972; Doran and Hodson 1975, pp. 177–80; Tainter 1975; pp. 9–11), which is a measure of the gregariousness of types of grave-good combination, a technique which is suitable when the variables are limited. The method divides the population into groups on the basis of the presence or absence of the most common attribute at the point where a division is to be made. Very common objects, for instance knives and buckles, were omitted as they cause a higher number of small sub-divisions than, subjectively, seems acceptable.

The principle result of the technique is that it divides the graves into clusters by sex, emphasising how this factor dominates the grave-goods, but there are serious limitations imposed on interpretation when age is not admissible. A number of the differences between cemeteries are attributable to time, a factor which must be taken into consideration in any such study, because not all classes of object or combination were current throughout the period. Four cemeteries which are broadly contemporary may usefully be compared: Sarre (Kent), Alfriston (Sussex), Chessell Down (Isle of Wight) and Long Wittenham I (Berkshire). A number of combinations comprising up to two artefacts are found to be common to a number of the cemeteries. Where unique combinations are found it is the result of particular types of object being found commonly at only one of the four, particularly with female graves; pins at Long Wittenham and tweezers at Chessell Down are cases in point. This again emphasises how there is more

Table 5.3: Comparison of monothetic divisive groupings of grave-goods in four early Anglo-Saxon cemeteries

SARRE, Kent	LONG WITTENHAM I, Berkshire	ALFRISTON, Sussex	CHESSELL DOWN, Isle of Wight
brooch	brooch	brooch	brooch
beads	beads	beads	beads
beads/brooch	beads/brooch	beads/brooch	beads/brooch
pin	pin		
key		key	
beads/pin	beads/pin		
	brooch/key	brooch/key	brooch/beads/pin
	brooch/pin	brooch/pin	
beads/key/brooch	brooch/beads/pin		brooch/beads/pin/tweezers
	brooch/beads/key	brooch/beads/chatelaine	tweezers
beads/key		beads/chatelaine	brooch/tweezers
			brooch/ball/spoon
sword	sword	sword	sword
spear/shield	spear/shield	spear/shield	spear/shield
spear	spear	spear	spear
shield		shield	shield
shield/sword		shield/sword	
shield/spear/sword			shield/spear/sword
shield/spear/sword/bucket	spear/shield/bucket-bowl	spear/sword	spear/shield/sword/bucket
			spear/shield/bucket
	spear/tweezers	shield/sword/bucket	spear/sword
	spear/key	spear/bucket	
		spear/pottery	
		pottery	
spear brooch			
shield/beads			

variety in female symbols than male. Tweezers at Chessell Down are most strongly associated with females, yet at Long Wittenham are accompanied by spears, not usually found with women. At Sarre the combination of spear-brooch, shield-beads are found emphasising that for certain categories, items normally associated with particular sexes can be mixed. Keys, beads and brooches are as strongly correlated with females, as weaponry is with males (Table 5.3), although the sex of the individuals is, here, assumed.

Research carried out on early Anglo-Saxon Sussex may also emphasise, particularly with inhumations, that certain types of artefact reflect social identity, although Welch placed more emphasis on regional and tribal identities (1983, p. 163ff.). For instance, a particular range of brooch types were observed as being characteristic of particular regions and Sussex was, thereby, shown to belong to a province bounded by Surrey, west Kent, Essex, the north of the Thames valley, Gloucestershire, Wiltshire and Hampshire. Saucer brooches worn as pairs on the shoulders could be combined in richer burials with square-headed brooches on the chest, with poorer equivalents of these types, the cast disc brooch and the small long brooch, being commonly found.

The 'identity' which Welch revealed in central southern England is in marked contrast to the patterns found to the east in Kent and west in the Isle of Wight. The apparently large number of shared traits in material culture between these two areas has tempted some to view the link as a result of the Jutish/Kentish settlement of the island documented in the written sources. The problem is that we do not actually know how or whether a Jute would symbolise membership of that identity group, if indeed the Jutes were considered to be one at the time the settlement of the Isle of Wight was supposed to have occurred. If such an interpretation is to be accepted we would be justified in examining the archaeological basis for it.

The fifth-century material with a Kentish link from the island is very slight and is found in association with a bizarre mixture of burial rites. About 13 per cent of the total graves at Chessell Down (Isle of Wight) have sixth-century material which would conventionally be described as 'Kentish'. The significance of that figure can only be measured by some consideration of the proportion of female graves with such diagnostic artefacts in broadly contemporary cemeteries in Kent. The published data from three such cemeteries reveals 5 per cent at Lyminge, Sarre 4 per cent and it is only at Bifrons, with 12 per cent that we come at all close to the Chessell Down figure.

These types of analysis can be compared with similar research carried out on cremation burials (Richards 1984; 1987). If the different methods of disposal are based on belief, then such a comparison may make it possible to isolate those other parts of the burial ritual which are not. Cremation cemeteries have a distinct advantage over those where inhumation was the predominant rite as the sample size is often large, and the cremation urns, which contain the, albeit burnt, burial are often recorded in far greater detail than the graves which contain inhumation burials. The data from the excavation of two cremation cemeteries in the east of England were compared, Spong Hill in Norfolk and Elsham in Lincolnshire. The comparison was to determine whether urn size, shape and decoration might, in combination or alone, be used to symbolise an identity group. The combination of particular variables may have been desired if the urns were for particular individuals or selected to cultural criteria. Whilst both cemeteries have similar proportions of decorative classes, the motifs appear to have been used differently, suggesting perhaps local differences in funerary symbolism, or chronological differences. Most of the hypothesised identity groups based on shape and size of vessel, grave-goods and sex were found to be correlated with the type of urn decoration, whereas other decorative motifs were used to represent identity groups which were not reflected in the form of the urns. Certainly, some groups appear to have been more heavily symbolised than others. At both sites, groups marked by the presence of toilet sets and the 'male' groups are each distinguished both in the form and decoration of the urns. However, only a few types of decoration indicate 'femaleness' which is never reflected in urn form. The female grave-goods are the direct equivalent of those found in inhumations. However, toilet sets and the male grave-good groups found in cremations occur less frequently in inhumations, and the symbolism was more highly developed in the elaboration of pot form and decoration. Richards suggests that these social identities are being treated differently in cremation; it may be that the obvious difficulties of incorporating the large and heavy weaponry in male cremation urns resulted in over compensation in other areas where symbolism was possible. Similarly the lower degree of distinctiveness in female pots may be the result of the symbolism being overt in the grave-goods. Some of the correlations were found at both of the sites studied, others at only one, suggesting that there is both an 'Anglian culture' and local funerary symbolism, and whilst chronological factors may be equally potent, they were not considered by the writer for very few such graves can be accurately dated.

In a selected analysis Richards has examined the significance of cremation pottery shape. Certain decorative motifs were found to be more 'appropriate' to certain shapes, at times running counter to the supposed chronology. Similarly certain artefacts are found more commonly in certain shaped vessels, and a social explanation is favoured: that is, the grave-goods and vessels reflect the age, sex or social status of the deceased, and that there was a 'collective conception of the urn form that was appropriate for the burial of a person from a particular social mileu'.

Symbolism of this type may not be limited to the decoration on the vessel; many artefacts are decorated but research has yet to be extended beyond the classification of such styles and motifs. The most recent research into Style I ornament (Leigh 1980) has suggested that ambiguity was a common feature of this art and that its use may extend beyond mere ornamental function. The hidden meaning in such ornament emphasises how, when it is used on relatively few artefacts, it is an instrument of exclusion used by a limited number of people to maintain an elite position. The rarity of runic inscriptions, both magical and secret, perhaps performed a similar role. We have already seen that there are distinctive groups of cremation pottery often ascribed to potters or workshops. But these may also indicate membership of a particular social group. The combinations of motifs on brooches, for instance the distinct groups of great square-headed brooches identified by Hines (1984), might point in the same direction. The manner in which particular motifs are interchanged and new ones occasionally added, on both the pottery and metalwork might, for instance, reflect a form of heraldry denoting individual descent groups. We can but dream of the possibility of colour and carving being used on timber in a similar way, for instance on houses. It is important to note that when 'mass-production' of artefacts takes over from the more personalised form of manufacture, it may be reflecting the ascension of political over social identity.

The studies considered so far all emphasise the potential for examining the relationship between social identities and the form of burials, and assume that those burying the dead, whether by cremation or inhumation, used such markers as were most appropriate for the deceased. The type of social identities being consciously marked are thought to be based on various combinations of such factors as age, sex, ethnic affiliation, family, or other social groupings. All of the studies tend to emphasise particular points; the different manner in which males, females and children are buried, and the greater variation in female inhumations. It is evident that it is the sex of the individual, and to a lesser extent the age, that is most strongly indicated.

Early Anglo-Saxon cemeteries, a number of writers suggest, are more likely to reflect identity groups than status, yet there seems no insurmountable problem in *both* being represented in the burial of the individual. This might be achieved by the actual quantity of the grave-goods and their symbolic content. Status may be just as important an aspect of social identity as age and sex, etc. In studies that have been carried out it has been assumed that status and the wealth of the individual are reflected in the quantity of grave-goods buried. Much of this type of research was carried out with a view to increasing the degree of objectivity in cemetery studies; the literature is full of such comments as 'rich graves', 'high wealth', but by establishing systems for measuring such 'wealth', it allowed that wealth to be put into perspective, within and between cemeteries, and to extend such statements to all graves. The same problems exist in studying status as with social identity, because we do not actually know on what basis the form of burial was selected; it is one thing to reveal statistically significant correlations, but quite another to determine their meaning. In studies of social identity it is assumed that the nature of the burial is determined by a set of conscious rules and would be appropriate for the deceased irrespective of whether the grave-goods belonged to them. In studies of status it is similarly assumed that the quantity and quality of the goods are appropriate for the degree of power which the individual wielded; they may have belonged to that individual, they may all be gifts, but this does not prevent them representing the same thing. It is noticeable that in studies of symbolism the manner in which quality of grave-goods co-varies with other factors is rarely considered and significant relationships are sought in a limited number of variables.

It remains to be seen what happens if such grave-goods are broken down into groups on the basis of their quantity and quality. Pader observed how in one 'sector' of the cemetery at Holywell Row there were certain unifying characteristics but they were differentiated by artefact style; on the females particular brooches were found, they had a uniform body position and this extended to the 'richest' of the graves in the cemetery, grave 11 (Pader 1980, p. 150). It was observed that in one 'sector', females had 'average' quality and quantity of artefacts and the males were not 'exceptional' and that this surely cannot indicate that the females were of higher rank, wealth or power than the males. Yet this ignores the possibility that the manner in which rank was symbolised in the graves is not uniform for males and females; other studies have shown clearly that a common characteristic of female graves is that they generally contain a greater number and variety of grave-goods than male. This may be a direct reflection of the superior role of women in Anglo-Saxon society or may, for instance, result from women being viewed as property and a means of demonstrating the power/wealth of males. There is no reason why social identity cannot be reflected at the same time.

The most obvious example for demonstrating that status is reflected in at least some graves is the limited number of graves which display great wealth; the nature of the objects buried may well symbolise the person's identity in terms of age, sex, ethnic identity, etc., but at the same time it is the person's wealth and indirectly the power commanded to acquire that wealth which is also being displayed. Such symbolism extends beyond the grave-goods and includes the form of burial as well; that is, there is an appropriate form of burial for wealthy individuals. Thus there are reasonable grounds for believing that social identity and status, horizontal and vertical relationships, are communicated in burials.

Studies of wealth and status have been carried out on inhumation cemeteries in southern England and at Sleaford in Lincolnshire (Brenan 1985). These are better suited to this form of analysis than cremation or mixed rite cemeteries where the factors determining the survival of grave-goods appear, at least, to be more complex. The emphasis placed on the grave-goods in such studies, to the exclusion of other factors, is the inevitable result of a general lack of data on, for instance, age, sex and body position. However, the growing number of modern, well-recorded, cemetery excavations provides hope that the type of multi-variate analysis that is possible for inhumation cemeteries will soon be carried out (Huggett forthcoming). The different variables which can be recorded for cremations have encouraged studies geared towards symbolism of a different nature.

The social structure of the cemetery of Alfriston has been considered by Welch (1983, p. 211), although typically the skeletal data is absent and the sex of the individuals had to be assumed on the basis of the grave-goods where possible; the result is that not all of the individuals can be sexed, thereby placing greater emphasis on those graves with sexually diagnostic grave-goods. In the first three-quarters of the sixth century 'the female population was headed by six rich women, representing one, or, at the most, two families' (ibid., p. 199). There were similarities in the type of ornaments worn on the body, suggesting to Welch that this symbolised membership of particular families. Their counterparts within the male population are identified with ten men buried with a greater quantity of weaponry. In spatial terms it was noted that the richest females of the sixth century occurred in pairs and there was, in overall terms a tendency for graves of the same sex to cluster together.

This analysis, like so many comments on status, was purely subjective in as much as the significance of these statements was not assessed, and there was an inevitable concentration on the richer graves. The nature of burials may reflect, as suggested above, a combination of factors, such as descent and kinship, sex and age, manner and place of death, as well as wealth and status. In a ranked society it follows that increased relative ranking of status positions in a social system will positively co-vary with an increased number of persons recognising duty status relationships with individuals holding such status positions. The status symbols should be more esoteric in form as their value and rarity increase.

Two methods of analysis have been applied to a large number of early Anglo-Saxon, predominantly, inhumation cemeteries in southern England (Arnold 1980; 1982b). The first ascribed 'wealth-scores' to the complete range of artefact types found in the cemeteries on the basis of their rarity making it possible to ascribe overall scores to each grave. There are a number of problems with such a method, for instance, the grave-goods from all of the cemeteries in the sample had to be scaled according to frequency before the graves could be analysed for ranking, which may obscure social groups. It may be argued that rather than assess objects in terms of their labour-value, it should be achieved by use-value. Unfortunately the range of uses of many of the objects is unclear which may distort our interpretation. However, the general result of assessing grave-goods by their use-value is generally a reversal of the pattern produced by labour-value. This is a particularly strong ideological distinction, but one which becomes most difficult to maintain when assessing the use-value of tools and brooches. Very few tools, which may have a very high use-value, are found in graves, but many brooches, which have a certain use-value, are not functionally absolutely necessary, but may convey more in meaning through their shape and decoration. The wealthier members of society may have been able to afford elaborate non-utilitarian items whilst the poor may have used and been buried with alternatives made of organic materials, which would create a different order, but tools are no more common in the richer than the poorer graves.

The second method examined the number of types of object in each grave, thereby being more an assessment of the ability to acquire a variety of objects rather than pure quantity. Where the sex of the skeleton was recorded, this permitted the data to be divided. It was observed that female graves, with few exceptions, have on average a greater degree of wealth than males, although when assessed by the number of types of object per grave, this difference is less apparent; females display a greater multiplicity of objects rather than a variety, which cannot only be because of the need to fasten clothing as many female graves have no dress-fastener; the male and female scales are clearly not the same. Little evidence was found for an increase in the numbers of wealth positions through time, there being an average of six in the whole study area. The number in individual cemeteries varies from four to eight, with two to four groups clustering at the lower end of the scale, the remaining, richer groups being positions with small membership. It is difficult to disentangle the complex relationship between the size of a cemetery, the length of time during which it was used, the number of status grades observable and the overall status of the community using it. It would seem that very rich graves tend to be found in larger cemeteries, which might be correlated, if the interpretation proposed by James *et al.* (1984) is correct, with the type of settlement with larger sized halls. Any developments through time in the structure are not so much in the number of ranks as in the degree of wealth possessed by them. The average number of rankings in the cemeteries, observed when analysing the wealth scores, are 7 for Kent, Sussex and the Isle of Wight, 6 in the upper Thames valley and 5.3 in central southern England. The number of wealth positions in the graphs for those cemeteries where both sexes are combined may distort and exaggerate the distribution, in varying degrees, as male wealth is displayed in a different manner to female. While many of the groups observed on the graphs sub-divided by sex may be associated, they have different positions on the graph. Thus on the overall distributions there may be up to twice as many social positions as actually existed. Where it is possible to take the sex of the individuals into account there are more female groups than male, but this is as likely to be caused by the greater range of female wealth dispersing the information across the graphs, than by any other factor.

The average wealth scores (Table 5.4) for the whole area studied is 30, and within individual cemeteries varied from 15.5 to 40.7 points. In Kent and the upper Thames valley the value is 28, in central southern English counties 24; in Sussex and the Isle of Wight (where only single figures are available) the scores are 40.7 and 33.4 respectively.

A very similar variation is found in the average number of types of object in the cemeteries. The overall average is 1.8 types and in individual cemeteries varies from 1 to 3.1 types. For Kent, Sussex and the Isle of Wight the average figure is 2, but in the upper Thames valley and central southern counties the value is below average at 1.6 types.

The distribution of wealth in male graves is always more uneven than in female. In the female graves in the upper Thames valley and central southern England, the wealth scores and number of types per grave are uniformly distributed. Unaccompanied graves are least common in Kent and Sussex, the highest figures being in the later cemeteries of the upper Thames valley and the counties to the south. The distinction between the coastal regions and those inland are very apparent. Where there are similarities between areas these need not imply that the same developments were taking place at the same time. However, because such similarity is also found in the written and other archaeological sources, it is probable that they are no mere coincidences.

In general, there is a development from the earlier cemeteries examined where the majority of graves are grouped at the lower end of the scale, through a stage with one or two separate groups, to the final pattern of one with very rich graves removed from the lower groups. The change is taking place from about the middle of the sixth century onwards and reaches a climax with male, rich graves under barrows from *c*. 600 AD. This latter form of exclusive burial is more common in central southern England and the upper Thames valley, possibly because the burial rite was in use longer as a result of the late conversion to Christianity, or

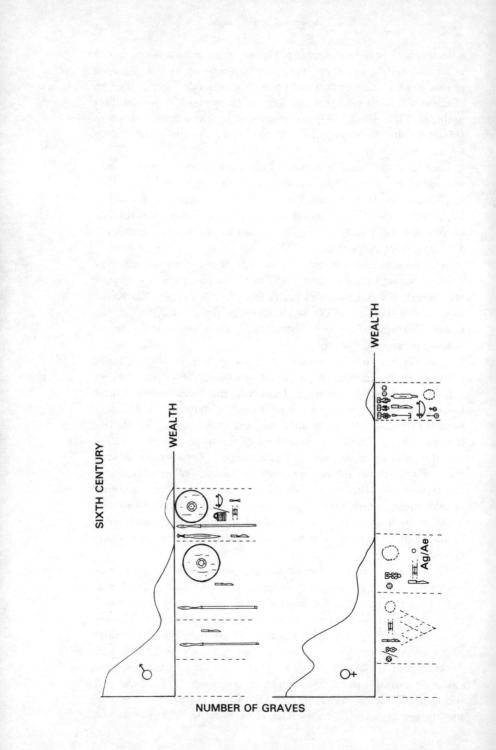

SIXTH CENTURY

WEALTH

WEALTH

Ag/Ae

NUMBER OF GRAVES

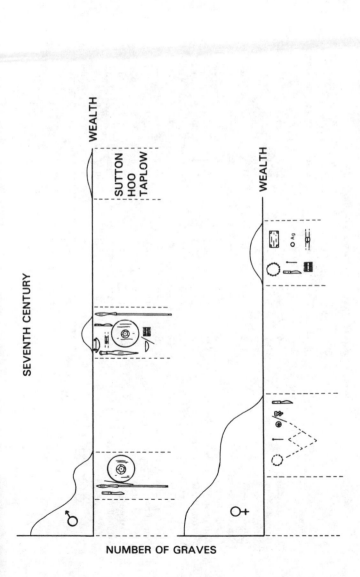

Figure 5.1: Schematic graphs summarising the frequency of particular grave-good associations in sixth- and seventh-century England. Changes are revealed in the nature and quantity of grave-goods amongst both sexes

Table 5.4: Synthesis of data concerning analysis of cemeteries in southern England

	No. of graves			Wealth scores			No. of types		
	Total	% male	% female	average, all graves	average, male	average, female	average, all graves	average, male	average, female
Lyminge, Kent	44	40.8	40.8	28.3	26.8	25.3	1.7	2.0	1.4
Bifrons, Kent	97	–	–	34.4	–	–	2.5	–	–
Sarre, Kent	192	–	–	29.8	–	–	1.9	–	–
Gilton, Kent	113	–	–	31.2	–	–	2.6	–	–
Kingston, Kent	297	–	–	22.5	–	–	1.5	–	–
Polhill, Kent	125	33.6	20.0	20.2	22.5	33.6	1.4	1.7	2.0
Abingdon, Berkshire	122	45.8	40.1	37.0	16.4	69.8	1.8	1.2	3.0
Berinsfield, Oxfordshire	95	28.4	26.3	28.4	30.4	54.1	2.1	2.5	3.0
Long Wittenham I, Berkshire	230	23.8	39.0	24.8	29.1	41.3	1.4	3.1	2.1
Wheatley, Oxfordshire	47	–	–	22.1	–	–	1.3	–	–
Harnham Hill, Wiltshire	76	–	–	17.0	–	–	1.0	–	–
Petersfinger, Wiltshire	63	34.7	26.8	37.4	32.7	81.8	3.1	2.5	1.5
Blackpatch, Wiltshire	95	12.6	18.9	28.6	34.8	65.3	2.1	2.7	3.4
Worthy Park, Hampshire	140	14.2	11.3	21.6	39.7	43.8	1.0	2.8	4.0
Winnall II, Hampshire	45	33.3	37.7	15.5	8.6	25.9	2.0	0.5	1.4
Alfriston, Sussex	129	–	–	40.7	–	–	2.0	–	–
Chessell Down, Isle of Wight	110	–	–	33.4	–	–	2.0	–	–

because of multiple leadership in those areas increasing the number of people for whom such burial was considered appropriate.

Most studies of social organisation have been based on grave-goods and skeletal information. Shephard (1979) has studied barrow burials as a special form, but because barrows over graves may be more common than was realised due to the variable preservation of the barrow structure, he may have studied an anomalous cross-section of cemetery data. The form of the grave would certainly be another way of examining variation; it is notable that richer graves tend to have the more complex forms and, as at Finglesham (Kent), are often robbed (Chadwick 1958) as though they could be clearly identified from their form. With cremation burials there would appear to have been very little variation in grave form on the surface, but with the inhumation burials there is considerable variation with plank-lined graves at Spong Hill (Hills 1977a; 1984) stone-lined cists at Loveden Hill (Vierck 1972) and a very wide range of types documented in Kent.

The analysis of social organisation need not be confined to cemeteries, despite their holding the greatest potential; the large number of settlements that have been excavated should be comparable, although many of the possible details concerning the buildings escape recovery at present; for instance, functional details such as the position of windows and, in some cases, door-ways, and any social differentiation that might be expressed in the degree of elaboration in, for instance, carving. Where settlements and their adjacent cemeteries have been excavated there is never-theless great potential for research. However the few examples where this data has been recovered have not been published, for instance Bishopstone and Mucking. Many of the settlements that have been excavated have inadequate stratigraphic detail to allow the sequence to be established, and rarely is it possible to deter-mine the function of the buildings.

Such uncertainties that exist at the moment about settlements seriously constrain the questions that one might ask of the data. At Cowdrey's Down the degree of preservation was unusually high; the settlement comprised three phases of three, six and ten major buildings respectively some of which were contained within two fenced compounds in each phase. Similar layouts have been observed at Chalton and Thirlings (Northumberland). The excavator of Cowdery's Down did not believe that this recurring pattern reflected agricultural needs so much as 'a more fundamental

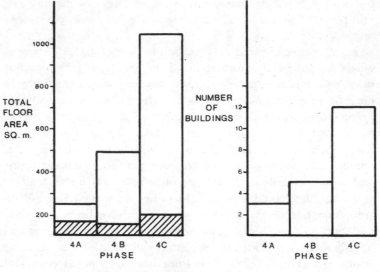

(LARGEST BUILDINGS SHADED)

Figure 5.2: Histograms showing the total available floor area and the number of buildings by phase at the settlement of Cowdery's Down (Hampshire), showing how both increase through time

division into social units, whether according to kinship, sex or status' (Millett 1983, p. 247). Each phase had a major building close to, but outside, the enclosures which may represent either a communal or a leader's house. The settlement itself is smaller than most that have been examined (although few have such a refined phasing and may be of longer duration) and the buildings are generally larger than elsewhere; they are however comparable in size with those of Yeavering which may indicate high social status. Each phase sees increasing differentiation in the quality and size of buildings (Figure 5.2) which Millett suggests may be linked to increasing social stratification. This involved not only a progressive increase in the number of buildings, but also of their floor area. We have already seen that a few settlements have quite different clusterings of building size compared with the majority, which may be linked with status.

The Kingdoms

The indication of increasing social stratification in early Anglo-Saxon society through the sixth and seventh centuries has a much wider implication for the development of the documented Anglo-Saxon kingdoms. The development of ranked societies in post-Roman England forms part of a transition period culminating in the formation of states, in this instance the English state. The early Anglo-Saxon period is one of increasing cohesion in political units. Most theories concerned with the formation of such societies (see, for instance, Service 1978; Claessen and Skalnik 1978; Webb 1975) emphasise the role of conflict between and within societies, and of integrative processes whereby the benefits of public works, redistribution, military organisation, etc., inevitably lead to the growth in power of a few members of society. The principal factors involved are population growth and pressure, war, conquest and the influence of previously existing states (Arnold 1980; 1984a). The early undeveloped state is viewed as a society in which:

> . . . kinship, family and community ties still dominate relations in the political field; where full-time specialists are rare; where taxation systems are only primitive and *ad hoc* taxes are frequent; and where such differences are offset by reciprocity and close contacts between the rulers and the ruled. (Claessen and Skalnik 1978, p. 23.)

Claessen views the kingdom or early state as:

> A centralised socio-political organisation for the regularization of social relations in a complex stratified society divided into at least two basic strata, or emergent social classes - viz. the rulers and the ruled -, whose relations are characterised by political dominance of the former and tributary obligations of the latter, legitimized by a common ideology of which reciprocity is the basic principle. (Claessen 1978, p. 640.)

England provides a useful laboratory for the study of social evolution in the centuries after the migrations. The written sources indicate that seven principal kingdoms were in the process of formation soon after the migrations. These were Kent, the East,

South and West Saxons, the East Angles, Mercia and Northumbria, often referred to as the Heptarchy. The rate of political and social change during these centuries rapidly accelerated as groups consolidated their positions; the seventh century in England is a particularly remarkable period of change, which has been viewed in terms of endogenous factors (Arnold 1982b).

A number of factors deemed to be relevant to the control of the emergence of complex ranked societies in early Anglo-Saxon England can be examined using the archaeological data. These may be summarised as: increasing specialisation in procurement and production; increasing access to resources, producing an exploitive elite and authoritarian leadership; trade or limited vengeance warfare, increasing to warfare for resource acquisition. Thus the type of structural hierarchy under examination appears as a function of the interrelation of population and activity-agglomerates, movement minimisation and differential accessibility, often emerging in clusters under conditions of mutual competition.

The identification of early Anglo-Saxon population aggregates has been achieved in the past by the combination of a number of forms of evidence — archaeological, documentary and the allied study of place-names (Ekwall 1936; Leeds 1913, p. 39, map 4; Collingwood and Myres 1937, p. 353, map VI; Davies and Vierck 1974). The distribution of pagan Anglo-Saxon graves gives an immediate, if potentially misleading, impression of population densities when presented as a trend surface diagram (Figure 5.3). There is clear evidence for population agglomeration, especially in Kent, Essex, Norfolk, Lincolnshire and South Humberside, with confined, lesser agglomerations, or dispersed population, elsewhere.

Anglo-Saxon politics, with its numerous royal associations, joint kingships and the possible implications for territorial division, are extremely complex. While the particularism of historians of the period has resulted in an understanding of much of the structure of institutions and the sequence of events, no attempt has been made to understand the causal processes. Whether or not one considers a king's responsibility as being over a group of people and/or territory, the isolation of the population aggregates permits the minimum areas of the developing kingdoms to be identified geographically with some degree of certainty. One means of increasing wealth is to increase the size of the family or group, and hence reproductive competition is an important factor in

Figure 5.3: Trend surface map of early Anglo-Saxon graves by grid generalisation. Lowest contour 50 graves per 25 sq km, thereafter 100, 200 etc. The distribution may also indicate the distribution of population, revealing dense concentrations in particular areas

Table 5.5: Average population figures represented by early Anglo-Saxon cemeteries

Cemetery	No. of graves (p)	Approx. time (t)	p × 30 / t
Lyminge, Kent	44	90	14.6
Bifrons, Kent	97	110	26.4
Sarre, Kent	192	160	36.0
Gilton, Kent	113	100	33.9
Abingdon, Berkshire	122	120	30.5
Berinsfield, Oxfordshire	95	110	25.9
Long Wittenham I, Berkshire	230	180	38.3
Harnham Hill, Wiltshire	76	70	32.5
Petersfinger, Wiltshire	63	100	18.9
Blackpatch, Wiltshire	95	80	35.6
Worthy Park, Hampshire	140	160	26.2
Alfriston, Sussex	129	150	25.8
Chessell Down, Isle of Wight	110	120	27.5

economic competition. On this basis we may expect to find that wealthier graves should be located in cemeteries of above-average wealth in the heart of emerging kingdoms.

A diagram showing the density of early Anglo-Saxon graves in England may seem a major step forward, yet it remains rather static, being an aggregation of about 300 years of human occupation. To introduce any detail and depth into such a diagram presents difficulties. The total number of graves represented is in the order of 25,000, a figure which stands as a minimum basis for determining the population of early Anglo-Saxon England. Naturally, levels of population must have fluctuated at both a national and local level although it tends to be assumed that population was on a generally rising track. At a local level the population of individual cemeteries can give a pointer to the size of the communities using the cemeteries, although it is impossible to prove over what distance the dead might be carried for burial. The greatest difficulty arises in dating the length of use of a cemetery, based as it must be on the chronologically diagnostic grave-goods. Nevertheless calculations (Table 5.5) show that the average size of such communities at any one time varied considerably, most falling within the range 20 to 40 individuals. There are grounds for believing that in some areas, for instance East Anglia, the dead were brought from much further afield than in, for instance, southern England, where cemeteries served individual communities (Arnold 1981, pp. 246–7).

The written sources indicate that before the end of the seventh century there were ten separate royal families ruling simultaneously in England, eight south of the River Humber if one includes Sussex and the Isle of Wight. Before the end of the seventh century a series of political events had caused the lesser kingdoms to disappear, such as when Caedwalla, King of Wessex, exterminated the dynasty which once ruled the Isle of Wight. Such political activities may have been necessary for the acquisition of resources. The two main processes by which resources, scarce or non-existent within a territory, may be obtained are by aggression or by some form of peaceful exchange; the absence of a raw material in a particular territory, but its presence in graves, implies that such processes were operating. Little is known about attitudes towards territories and their boundaries and even though many classes of artefact can be assigned to a general production area, information about both can at present only be gleaned from the distribution of the artefacts themselves; that is, from the graves.

Emerging complex societies often developed in close proximity to each other and the competition for land and resources frequently lead to aggression and the annexation of smaller groups within the larger. The *Anglo-Saxon Chronicle* provides a generalised impression of aggressive activities during the period, although problems with the earlier entries (Harrison 1976) and the possibility of bias on the part of the compilers cannot be overlooked. It is nevertheless possible to chart the confrontations recorded as having taken place between AD 550–700 (Figure 5.4). Rarely is the place given or identifiable and the earlier entries must be excluded from the discussion because of the unsatisfactory nature of the earliest part of the *Chronicle*. The period that follows reveals a pattern of predominantly 'West Saxon' aggression, not only against the 'Britons' in defence and expansion of their territory, but also against Kent from AD 568 and the South Saxons in AD 607. Problems with their northern frontier with 'Mercia' in the middle years of the seventh century mark the beginning of a decline in the fortunes of the West Saxon kingdom, yet their aggression continues, being directed towards Kent and the Isle of Wight, which from the evidence of the grave-goods from cemeteries in those areas, were at various times two of the richest maritime kingdoms. This was also the occasion of the annexation of the Isle of Wight by the West Saxons. In the absence of any indication of a land shortage we might conclude that a primary consideration was the acquisition of raw materials, which may be defined broadly.

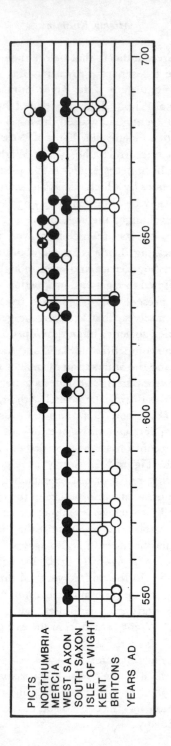

Figure 5.4: Diagram illustrating the incidence of warfare in early Anglo-Saxon England recorded in the Anglo-Saxon Chronicle, AD 550–700. The black dots are the recorded aggressors. The diagram emphasises how the seventh century was a particularly turbulent period in the development of the kingdoms

Such aggression is almost inevitable in societies with primitive exchange systems; warfare, trade and marriage meant external relationships of hostility and alliance, relations of antagonism and dependence, the opposite of isolation and self-sufficiency seen earlier in the period. Warfare, raiding, revenge and feud were probably major preoccupations entailing the extermination of lineages, capturing women and children, and slavery. This level of aggression gradually gave way to the political incorporation of the defeated. The nature of the aggression was not so regular and institutionalised to have encouraged the construction of defensive structures which do not appear until the ninth century.

Large quantities of weaponry are found as grave-goods in early Anglo-Saxon cemeteries which might provide another means of studying aggression. One study involved the quantification of weaponry in various areas (Arnold 1980, pp. 86–90). Arguably, societies which had most need for aggression for resource acquisition would have had a lower level of armament due to their relative poverty. Alternatively, poorer societies may have used a disproportionately higher volume of resources to manufacture weapons and may have been less willing to use them as grave-goods. Three principal weapons were utilised during this period, the sword (Davidson 1962; Anstee and Biek 1961), the spear (Swanton 1973; 1974) and the shield (Atkinson 1953; Härke 1981; Jarvis *et al.* 1983, pp. 127–8). It is possible to identify the combinations that occur most frequently, the percentage of armed males in each cemetery, and how such patterns change through time. It has been suggested that particular weapon types symbolise social identify, but in this analysis it must be remembered that the graves represent the result of a funeral and it is difficult to distinguish between those aspects which were peculiar to that ritual and those reflecting life.

The analysis suggests that in the earlier cemeteries there was a more equal distribution of the favoured weapon combinations, with a higher proportion of weapon graves; both are reduced with time. While the quality of the data may not be uniform and it is difficult to calibrate the figures using the number of female graves present, it should not pass unnoticed that there is a strong similarity between the sixty-century cemeteries of Kent, Sussex and the Isle of Wight for instance. Elsewhere in Wiltshire and the upper Thames Valley there is a different emphasis on particular weapons, fewer weapon graves on average, and certain classes of weapon, notably the sword, are poorly represented. It might be argued that this is symptomatic of the 'West Saxons' need for aggression towards the better provided-for areas elsewhere in southern England. This form of analysis helps to clarify the relationships between cemeteries and regions. The supposedly high levels of weaponry in Kent has been commented on:

> Sarre . . . is set apart from the majority by virtue of a high proportion of male burials with weapons, including numerous swords, far in excess of what is normal even in aristocratic cemeteries such as Bifrons. The only truly comparable case in Kent is the cemetery at Buckland, behind Dover. Here then, we have two unusually well-armed communities in strategic positions close to known albeit later ports. (Hawkes 1969, p. 191.)

An examination of the figures reveals that although Sarre has more weapon graves than Bifrons, the proportion of graves with swords is very similar. There are other cemeteries with a far higher proportion of weapon graves and especially graves with swords. The cemeteries at Alfriston and Chessell Down show a uniform pattern with Sarre (percentages of weapon graves are: Sarre 24.4; Alfriston 25.5; Chessell Down 24.5). Chessell Down has a higher proportion of well-armed males than these other cemeteries (Sarre 14.8; Alfriston 3.3; Chessell Down 18.5), the last only superseded in the sample by Petersfinger (23). If the well-armed male is to be taken as an indication of commerce or incipient ports of trade, Sarre and Buckland are not alone in this respect. However, the pattern may equally reflect similarities in social organisation of males in the respective regions.

Analyses of this type, where historical data may be compared with documentary sources, emphasise a problem which underlies the whole study of the development of the Anglo-Saxon kingdoms. The problem of integrating the two types of data has been discussed elsewhere (e.g. Driscoll and Nieke 1987) especially the particular problems pertaining to this period (Arnold 1987). In any attempt at integration there has to be some form of framework to which the data can be related. In the case of the development of the kingdoms, the documents may give us the names of king-doms and kings, even dates, but this information lies in a vacuum without additional information, such as the spatial controls. If the leaders and territories of the sixth and seventh centuries could be isolated using the archaeological data, placing the patterns in a long-run time series, a direct comparison could be made with generalisations derived from the written sources.

A number of models have been proposed for the nature of the development of the early Anglo-Saxon kingdoms (Arnold 1980; 1982b; 1984b; Hodges 1978; 1982a). The archaeological data have been examined to determine the various factors which controlled the development of large political units resulting from the amalgamation of smaller ones. Such work is necessarily at a generalised level, one which is compatible with a level of abstraction employed by many historians. A general model for the earliest phase of political development has been put forward by Dumville:

> There may have been a general lack of tribal homogeneity, each major group comprising the leader and his immediate relatives with a motley rag-bag of racially mixed followers. (1977, p. 78, n. 39.)

Wallace-Hadrill (1971, pp. 15–16) considered it necessary to distinguish between various levels of leadership, *dux* and *rex*, although he was not proposing an evolutionary model; rather a pattern which Hodges describes as 'cyclical' leadership (1982a, p. 27). Sawyer uses a similar model in suggesting that some or all of the kingdoms of the Heptarchy had been

> . . . created by the fusion of smaller kingdoms which preserved traces of their former independent status in still being described as kingdoms or sub-kingdoms under the rule of *reges*, *reguli* or *subreguli*. (1978, p. 21.)

Much of the confusion in the written sources over the earliest leaders (see Dumville 1977, p. 101) may have arisen, as Sawyer suggests, because a later kingdom originated by the amalgamation of smaller groups each with their own leader.

Leaders are named in the early medieval written sources but the nature of their leadership is rarely defined; the labels used do not necessarily imply a particular form of leadership at the given time. Leaders are generally only observed in the archaeological data as the result of making a number of assumptions, which emerge in the literature as 'royal palaces' or 'high wealth'. This correlation between wealth and status is frequently made (Alcock

1981, pp. 175–7; Crowfoot and Hawkes 1967, 65–6; Dickinson 1974, p. 35; Evison 1963, p. 61; Hills 1980c, p. 92; Wilson 1976a, p. 3) and there is the benefit of support from the written sources (Cramp 1957). As discussed above the existence of high status positions may not be in doubt, but it is less clear how they may be translated and symbolised in the archaeological record. If the written sources are to be utilised to emphasise how social identity is symbolised at burial (see, for instance, Richards 1984, p. 43), the indications that status is also symbolised cannot be ignored. The correlation between rich graves and high status is, however, a limited one, as it tells us nothing of the means of acquiring power or wealth, nor anything of what that wealth symbolised to contemporaries.

The existence of a developing form of kingly leadership by the seventh century, has led to a search for a settlement type befitting persons of such status. A problem arises in the choice of factors which should be used for the identification of such 'palaces'. Initial, perhaps premature, excitement following the identification of a type of large hall from aerial photographs (Rahtz 1976, pp. 65–8; Sawyer 1983b) has been tempered by the discovery, from excavation, that the form and size of these buildings is present on many, otherwise ordinary, rural settlements; in one instance excavation showed that they were medieval rabbit warrens (Clark, Hampton and Hughes 1983). Many writers have taken building size as an indication of high social status. This may be a useful guide to status but it is fraught with problems. The range of sizes of buildings at Cowdery's Down is above the norm, and the largest are comparable with buildings described as 'palaces' elsewhere in England. There is no reason why the Cowdery's Down examples should not be stately residences, but does size alone make any of these structures the principal residence of a king?

The problem is exemplified by two sites, at Northampton and Yeavering in Northumberland. To the east of a series of minster churches in Northampton, dating from the Middle Saxon period onwards, was a rectangular stone hall with an internal floor area of 315 m^2 which has been dated to the eighth century. Mortar mixers stood beside it. The building is interpreted as the centre of secular power on the royal estate in the same way that the minster was the seat of ecclesiastical authority (Williams, Shaw and Denham 1985). Below the stone building was a large timber hall of the seventh century with a floor area of 252 m^2, consisting of a rectangular centre with square annexes at either end, which appears to have been a highly sophisticated, possibly bayed, structure, which was set out extremely precisely, a conclusion now frequently reached about most early Anglo-Saxon halls. In contexts associated with the eighth-century minster and 'palace' were a bronze shrine fitting, a bronze stylus, glass vessels and a decorated pin; all are relatively unusual items. Yet no such artefacts were associated with the timber predecessor. We are left with the problem of whether the timber structure and the stone building which replaced it were used by persons of a similar status for the same functions. Or was the erection of the stone palace and church a reflection of a change or an extension in the status of the site, from unexceptional rural settlement to 'palace'. The timber building was certainly large, being 35 m^2 larger than the largest at Cowdery's Down. It may be that the position at Northampton points to a change that occurred in the seventh century; prior to that date leaders' status was symbolised not in buildings but through other media, for instance burial, and that with conversion of the country to Christianity and the changes in burial rite that followed, there were commensurate changes in the means of symbolising status.

The problems of interpretation surrounding Yeavering are of an altogether different nature (Hope-Taylor 1977). The settlement is identified with Bede's *Gefrin* which was graced with royal visits and of Paulinus who preached and baptised there in AD 627. The site was abandoned in the early eighth century in favour of *Maelmin*, according to Bede, which has been identified, a few kilometres away, from aerial photographs. Hope-Taylor's interpretation promotes the settlement as a British folk-centre with religious foci and a 'cattle corral' which became the palace of the Anglo-Saxon kings of seventh-century Bernicia, an administrative centre with great halls for king and court. The post-Roman development consisted of wooden buildings and a great enclosure, with a square enclosure of wooden building on the site of a prehistoric stone circle, around which were inhumation burials. This was followed by the construction of major halls, a temple and a 'grandstand'. At the settlement's height the grandstand was enlarged, the great enclosure rebuilt, and a great hall (A4) was built. Under its threshold was a grave associated with an object identified as a surveyor's *groma*, or as a ceremonial standard. When Paulinus visited in the 620s, the temple was altered and reconsecrated and is associated with the final phase of a cemetery in the western part of the settlement. The settlement itself was deliberately burned in the seventh century followed by a relapse into paganism, the phase marked by numerous posts, the foci for graves, and which may have carried 'totemic and zoomorphic emblems of the tribe'. There then followed the building of a church with a churchyard contemporary with the abandonment of the western cemetery in favour of orderly rows of graves at the church. The grandstand was replaced and new halls built. This settlement was also destroyed by fire, but the significance of the site is indicated by four new buildings before a final decline and abandonment (Hope-Taylor 1977).

It is impossible to do justice, in summary, to the magnificent timber structures which were excavated, especially the grand-stand, halls and pagan temple and the details should be sought in the excavator's report. However, a paradox arises again when we contrast the magnificence of contemporary 'royal' burials and the apparent material poverty of Yeavering. Hope-Taylor emphasises that the *potential* magnificence of the buildings cannot only be measured by postholes, as the timber and plaster may have been ideal media for decoration by carving and painting. But over and above an acceptance of the identification of Yeavering as Bede's *Gefrin*, the principal factors used to emphasise the settlement's status are the size and nature of the buildings; we must be wary, at present, of being overawed by the range of archaeology at Yeavering when there is so little to compare it with in northern England. The great hall had a floor area of 336 m^2, but comparison of size between this example and large timber buildings further south becomes increasingly meaningless when the factors determining their size were probably varied and numerous.

The development of the early Anglo-Saxon kingdoms and leadership might have been symbolised by palatial central places. Contenders for this position have been argued on their individual merits, in the case of Northampton by site continuity and context, and in the case of Yeavering by historical evidence, and the scale and type of the structures. There are obvious dangers of labelling every large building excavated a 'palace', especially when there are no factors to assist. High status settlements may be expected at major centres, particularly those that achieved ecclesiastical and commercial prominence in the seventh and eighth centuries, such as Canterbury (Kent). We should, perhaps, be wary of imposing such status on other settlements too readily (Hawkes 1979; Arnold

1982c); to do so makes great assumptions about early Anglo-Saxon society and especially about how authority was held, dispensed and symbolised in the material world. Within the pagan world, as exemplified by the rich seventh-century burials, power may have been demonstrated in visible moveable wealth. The construction of magnificent buildings as appropriate housing for such individuals may only have arisen following the establishment of Christianity; the power and authority of the church was demonstrated in buildings and secular lords may have felt it necessary to make their position felt in the same manner.

Broadly speaking the richly accompanied graves of the period belong to three types which fall into three chronological phases:-

(a) mid to late sixth century.
(b) early to seventh century.
(c) later seventh century.

Defining the relative wealth of such graves in any more detail than 'rich' or 'very rich' poses problems and, so far, objective assessments have had to be content with techniques of analysis based on quantity rather than quality. Subjective as it may be, it is generally true that the quality of the grave-goods in pagan Anglo-Saxon graves increases with quantity.

Male-rich graves of the sixth century cannot yet be dated as accurately as the female because there are fewer grave-goods and, in particular, fewer that are dateable. It would be dangerous to assume that they both represent the same phase of social and political development, but given the observation by all researchers that there is generally greater variation in female graves, the differences may not concern us here. The male-rich graves are characterised (Table 5.6) by an extensive array of grave-goods, always including weapons and some form of container. There is nothing in these graves that is obviously non-utilitarian, but the frequency of the association distinguishes the graves from the remainder of the population. The sixth-century women's, rich graves (Table 5.7) form an equally clear group in most, but not all, areas. They are characterised by richly decorated dress ornaments, as common to this group as weapons are to the men, in most cases by a key and a coin, and in a few cases by perforated spoons and crystal balls. That the same type of grave may be found not only in areas with other links, such as Kent and the Isle of Wight, but also in other parts of England as far north as Leicestershire carries a number of important implications. One is

Table 5.6: The contents of male-rich graves of the later sixth century

	earscoop	ring	game	musical inst.	comb	shears	tweezers	knife	horn (vessels)	glass	ceramic	metal	wooden	arrow (weapons)	axe	buckle	shield	spear	sword
Petersfinger, Wiltshire, 21	X						X	X					X				X	X	X
Blackpatch, Wiltshire, 47							X	X					X		X	X	X	X	X
Sarre, Kent, 39								X					X			X	X	X	X
Alfriston, Sussex, 86								X			X		X		X	X		X	X
Mucking, Essex, 600													X				X	X	X
Spong Hill, Norfolk, 40													X			X	X	X	X
Holywell Row, Suffolk, 29								X					X				X	X	X
North Luffenham, Rutland							X	X			X		X	X			X	X	X
Chessell Down, Isle of Wight, 26								X				X	X			X	X	X	X
Sarre, Kent, 54						X		X											X

Table 5.7: The contents of female-rich graves of the later sixth century

	Sarre, Kent, 4	Chessell Down, Isle of Wight, 45	Bifrons, Kent, 42	Bifrons, Kent, 21	Bifrons, Kent, 29	Bifrons, Kent, 41	Alfriston, Sussex, 62	Alfriston, Sussex, 43	Lyminge, Kent, 44	Petersfinger, Wiltshire, 25	Abingdon, Berkshire, 61	Worthy Park, Hampshire, 10	Long Wittenham I, Berkshire, 71	Holywell Row, Suffolk, 11	Spong Hill, Norfolk, 24	Empingham II, Rutland, 73
coin	X	X		X	X		X		X							
glass vess.	X				X	X										
ceramic vess.																
metal/wooden vess.	X	X		X						X	X				X	X
comb	X								X							
chatelaine																
weaving batten	X	X												X	X	X
key	X	X	X	X	X	X					X		X	X	X	X
knife	X	X	X	X	X	X					X	X	X		X	X
crystal ball	X	X	X					X								
spoon	X	X	X				X		X							
pin	X					X				X						
ring	X	X	X	X	X	X	X			X	X	X	X	X	?	X
gold thread	X	X		X	X	X			X				X			X
buckle	X	X	X		X	X		X			X	X	X	X		
necklace	X	X	X	X	X	X	X	X	X	X	X	X	X	X		X
brooch	X	X	X	X	X	X	X	X	X	X		X	X	X	X	X

that the items associated with this very distinctive form of female, rich burial were used in everyday life in a similar manner to which they are found as grave-goods, for how else would a social norm such as this be transmitted over such a wide geographical area, unless attendance at state funerals was a necessary duty?! Another possibility is that such women came from a limited number of identity groups, for instance Kent, and were married into elite families as part of the formation of alliances with distant political groups.

A non-utilitarian aspect may be seen in some of the items; we might note that orbs surmounted by a cross were used as royal symbols on the Continent in the sixth century. Minimally a key, like the males' containers, is a tool, but the frequency of the association may imply much more, for instance, the leader of the household, the privilege of privacy and the protection of self and property. Poorer graves which nevertheless have some of the range of items found in the richer examples — for instance, Winterbourne Gunner (Wiltshire), grave 7 (Musty and Stratton 1964, pp. 91–3) and Alfriston, grave 62 (Griffith and Salzmann 1914, pp. 44–5) — may represent emulation of the elite in richer areas. Alternatively, they may represent scales of leadership on an hierarchical basis within or between areas.

In the later sixth and early seventh centuries the male graves reveal more variety than the earlier examples (Table 5.8) and the group is dominated by the rich three: Taplow, Broomfield and Sutton Hoo mound 1, which share so many characteristics of context, arrangement and grave-goods. The major difference between these graves and the earlier examples is that they are under mounds. It remains less clear whether such graves represent deposition in a formal burial area reserved for the exclusive use of the elite (in their time) with perhaps close associates or family. The only site of this type which has seen extensive excavation around the burial mound(s) is Sutton Hoo. There a flat-grave cemetery exists, although its extent is unclear. In this respect it will be of interest, when the data becomes available, to consider whether such a cemetery is in any way different to those without such rich barrow burials. Whether Sutton Hoo is unusual in this respect is unclear. Degrees of emulation may also be observable here as a number of such graves contain only what we might think were the more available of the items associated with the elite, or are much cruder pieces; for instance, Lowbury Hill, (Berkshire) (Atkinson 1916). Again this may represent the extension of the

Table 5.8: The contents of male-rich graves of the early seventh century

	Cuddesdon, Oxfordshire	Coombe Bissett, Wiltshire	Alton, Hampshire, 16	Taplow, Buckinghamshire	Broomfield, Essex	Oliver's Battery, Hampshire	Coombe, Kent	Sutton Hoo mound I, Suffolk
earscoop								
ring		X						
game				X				
musical inst.				X				X
comb								
shears								
tweezers								
knife				X	X	X	X	X
vessels								
horn					X			X
glass	X	X			X	X	X	
ceramic						X		X
metal		X	X		X	X	X	X
wooden				X	X	X		X
weapons								
arrows								
axe								X
buckle		X	X	X	X		X	
shield		X	X	X	X		X	
spear		X	X	X	X	X	X	X
sword	X	X	X	X	X	X	X	X

Table 5.9: The contents of female-rich graves of the early seventh century

	Gilton, Kent, 81	Kingston, Kent, 299	Swallowcliffe, Wiltshire	Sarre, Kent
coin			X	X
glass vess.			X	
ceramic vess.				
metal/wooden vess.		X	X	X
comb		X	X	X
chatelaine	X	X		
weaving batten				X
key		X	X	
knife		X	X	X
crystal ball				
spoon			X	
pin				X
ring	X	X		
gold thread				
buckle		X	X	
necklace	X	X	X	
brooch	X	X	X	X

hierarchy, or the necessary extension of the range of symbols of leadership by the uppermost echelons in certain areas because of emulation. There is, therefore, the possibility of grades of leadership, but we should also not overlook the, albeit unknown, circumstances of death, and the interesting but difficult possibility that items may be deliberately excluded from burial. Here also we find a consistency in weapons and containers amongst the males, but rarely anything potentially symbolising leadership, except the particular combination itself. Sutton Hoo mound 1 and the female grave at Swallowcliffe (Wiltshire) are the notable exceptions in having a number of non-utilitarian items in addition to their great wealth. The women's rich graves of this phase (Table 5.9) are not only difficult to find, they also lack consistency. Graves of this general type also occur throughout England, and their associated grave-goods have been examined in a comparative fashion by Vierck (1972).

The rarity of rich graves, both male and female, as the seventh century proceeds (Table 5.10) has been viewed as a reflection of the increasing frequency of Christian burial for the elite, as reported by Bede at Canterbury (HE I 33) and which archaeology is beginning to demonstrate as the pace of church archaeology increases. While it has been suggested that there may be a symbolic function in the combination of the artefacts, there are some utilitarian objects which might, subjectively, seem out of place in the hands of such people, and others which are more obviously non-utilitarian. In the former category could be placed weaving equipment and in the latter so-called 'regalia'.

Some of the items from Sutton Hoo mound 1 were labelled regalia very soon after their discovery and presumably the implications of insignia of office and, more precisely, insignia used by royalty at coronations, were fully appreciated. The sixth and seventh centuries are prehistoric as far as the details of inauguration rituals are concerned and we may have to be content with the probable identification of such symbols. It would help to have an understanding of the meaning behind the symbols of office, but, as Nelson (1977) has shown, the sources are principally concerned with rites, especially anointing. A greater problem here is that the written sources connected with inauguration rituals are inevitably concerned with the *installation* of leaders, whereas the archaeological data are concerned with their *funerals*. It remains interesting that heirlooms, relics and regalia are rarely absent from installation ceremonies in anthropological studies that have

Table 5.10: The contents of male- (above) and female- (below) rich graves of the later seventh century

Male graves

	Item	Rodmead, Wiltshire	Ford, Wiltshire	Galley Hills, Surrey	Lowbury Hill, Berkshire
	earscoop				
	ring				
	game				
	musical inst.				
	comb			X	
	shears				
	tweezers				
	knife		X	X	X
vessels	horn				
	glass				
	ceramic				
	metal		X	X	X
	wooden	X			
weapons	arrows				
	axe				
	buckle	X	X	X	X
	shield	X	X	X	X
	spear	X	X	X	X
	sword	X	X		X

Female graves

Item	Winchester, Hampshire, 23	Roundway Down II, Wiltshire
coin		X
glass vess.		
ceramic vess.		X
metal/wooden vess.		X
comb		
chatelaine		
weaving batten		
key		
knife		
crystal ball		
spoon		
pin	X	
ring		X
gold thread		
buckle		
necklace	X	X
brooch		

been made (Fortes 1968) and the possession of such objects as vehicles for the continuity of office is common; after each generation the rites may be redefined, but for periods they may remain fixed. If the objects being buried in rich graves of the sixth and seventh centuries are complete sets of items symbolising leadership, it is very important to note that they *were* being buried with individuals. Those mound burials with few lavish items might, in this light, be seen as those in which the 'regalia' was passed on. The problem here is the question of completeness, which cannot be demonstrated in either case.

The written sources do throw some light on the symbols of leadership. Nelson (1977) points out that the date at which a fixed inauguration ritual was introduced is unknown, but a case can be made for elements of West Saxon usage, *ante* AD 856, being preserved in later forms, and 'the relatively early introduction of a fixed rite in England may be explained in terms of the precocious [*sic*] political and ecclesiastical centralisation already achieved by the eighth century' (Nelson 1980, p. 48). Nelson's research has brought to our attention 'the sceptres of the Saxons, Mercians and Northumbrians' included in a fourteenth-century coronation out of respect, it is argued, for earlier ritual tradition (Nelson 1975, p. 45; 1977, p. 56). The use of a helmet rather than a crown until *c*. AD 900 (1980, p. 45) and weapons generally, is common (1975, p. 59) and Bede describes how Edwin set up bronze drinking cups for the refreshment of travellers beside highways; his majesty was such that banners (*vexilla*) were carried before him in battle, in peacetime his progress was preceded by a standard-bearer, and when walking along roads a standard (*thuf*) was carried before him (HE II 16; Bruce-Mitford 1974, pp. 7–17; Deanesley 1943). An important distinction emerges between earlier and later Anglo-Saxon leadership:

> . . . the significance, political and symbolic, of inauguration rituals arose largely from the fact that no early medieval King succeeded to his kingdom as a matter of course . . . In no kingdom of the early Medieval west was there quickly established a very restrictive norm of royal succession. (Nelson 1977, p. 51.)

Without forcing a connection too strongly, for the reasons already given, we are again reminded that symbolic items were buried in some graves; this could be taken to suggest that the nature of leadership was changing rapidly and/or there was at times a lack of hereditary succession. The more worrying alternative is that we may more frequently be dealing with heirlooms at this level of society, in the funerary context, than can ever be demonstrated, despite a number of writers' suspicions. It is only where there is a great quantity of diagnostic items that the objects which were antique when buried can be isolated.

The rich pagan graves do not belong to a long time-span, perhaps 150 years at the most. If there was a continuous succession of leaders in any single area, they may only represent five generations at the most. It is interesting that Dumville suggested that in the royal genealogies that survive from this period 'only that extent (perhaps four or five generations) which is essential to the smooth running of the social structure will be remembered, while more distant ancestors . . . are not recalled in the context of exact genealogical relationships' (1977, p. 87). Perhaps they only go back to a point at which those societies' forms of leadership could be identified or existed, prior to which the genealogy is a figment. The genealogies were recorded in the seventh century, within a Christian *milieu*, which would suggest that the accurate elements begin in the second half of the sixth century, which can be confirmed by the archaeological evidence. Of equal relevance to the sequence of rich graves is Dumville's observation that 'there comes a superior limit of immediate credibility and in each case this is somewhere in the second half of the sixth century', and more precisely 550 × 575. This is also fully in agreement with the archaeological data as it is then that the sequence of rich graves begins, and, by the same set of assumptions, the earliest stage at which leaders are represented in the archaeological record. Leaders may have existed before, but at this time it was felt appropriate to represent a person's status in an observable (and durable) form at death.

A case can, therefore, be put forward that early Anglo-Saxon archaeology gives us leaders in the form of richer burials; the historical sources give us the names of leaders and their territories; given the changing configurations of the early kingdoms, the names applied to regions in the sixth century need not be the same areas in the seventh. While a link can rarely, if ever, be made between the two data sets, there is one element in which they could at least be seen to overlap, that is with boundaries.

In the introduction to the Ordnance Survey's map of *Britain in the Dark Ages* (1966) it was explained that ' the names of large regions and provinces have been written across the areas covered, but the precise boundaries have not been shown because they are rarely if ever known, and because they were constantly changing through the period' (1966, p. 33). There we have three important elements: the boundaries, the areas bounded and time. We need not dwell on how we know that boundaries were constantly changing when they are rarely known (!), but it is important to note that various writers have followed the same procedure as the Ordnance Survey, while a few have been bold enough to draw lines representing the boundaries between the kingdoms. The one course of action is perhaps an acceptable level of generalisation, the other requires more justification. Whether actual boundaries are marked or not, both practices fossilise 200 or 300 years of political development in one image, when they are thought to be 'constantly changing'.

If the model for political development in the sixth and seventh centuries is to be tested we need to see not only the political territories but also to know the manner in which they were changing through time. This may be achieved experimentally by reconstructing the frontiers using unweighted Theissen Polygons, created by drawing perpendiculars at the mid-points between the rich graves. Time is being telescoped and a number of assumptions need to be made which may reduce the expectation that the resulting maps will reflect the general pattern of political development and, in particular, will demonstrate the merger of small groups into larger ones. The data is very unlikely to be strictly contemporary, but each phase is up to 50 years duration; given the necessity in prehistoric studies of considering material which may span hundreds of years as though it were contemporary, this lapse of methodology seems comparatively minor. The funerals of the members of the societies in question would not have occurred at the same time, but the periods over which the locations/graves were venerated would be more likely to overlap.

Some rich graves no doubt await discovery but it may be argued that they are more likely to be found in those areas which already possess them, than in new areas. Some areas of England already do possess more than one such grave in the same time bracket, but at what distance they have to be apart before they should be separated by a boundary is arbitrary; in this analysis the distance has been fixed as 5 km. Centricity of burials may seem logical on the basis of veneration of the dead, residence patterns and security, yet it must be noted that we know little of the decision-making processes that governed the choice of site for burial of an individual. Reconstructing such territories also tells us nothing of the details of the organisation of the society within them, which is perhaps the more important aspect. That such graves represent a uniform social plane is assumed from the outset in dividing the rich graves from the remainder of the population and treating them as a specific social persona type. The method assumes maximum political control of the landscape, and all the maps suffer from the 'boundary effect' caused by the edge of the study area.

The results of the experiment can be briefly described (Figure 5.5). During the mid to later sixth century a number of regions of roughly equal size are created. Many of the hypothetical territory edges correspond with natural features, particularly rivers. By the late sixth and early seventh centuries there has been a marked change. The Kent region, for instance, has lost ground on its north-west frontier, but expanded westwards; Essex appears as a distinct zone, incorporating part of the area south of the Thames; Sussex remains as a separate unit extending further westwards, with a new region to the north lying astride the Thames. The Hampshire zone now incorporates the Isle of Wight. Wiltshire and the upper Thames valley remain divided into small units. Finally in the later seventh century Kent, Sussex and Surrey are now one with the region to the north; one region remains in the upper Thames valley looking northwards, leaving a large zone comprising Hampshire and the Isle of Wight and, again, the smaller regions in Wiltshire, now extending further westwards.

In the second and third phases the territorial frontiers correspond less with possible natural examples, and it is more likely that as the political map of southern England became more artificial, there would be a greater need to construct artificial boundaries, such as linear earthworks (Figure 5.6). Few such earthworks are closely dated, although a few are demonstrably post-Roman. A number have been seen as reflecting early Anglo-Saxon period political history; for instance, the eastern section of Wansdyke (Fox and Fox 1958), the east Hampshire complex (Coffin 1975), Bokerley Dyke (Rahtz 1961) and those on the borders of Surrey and Kent near Westerham (Clark 1960) and Crayford (Hogg 1941). The absence of close dating tends to leave such testimonies of human territoriality floating amongst the details of political history and it is of little value to correlate them speculatively with either historical events or with the hypothetical frontiers generated

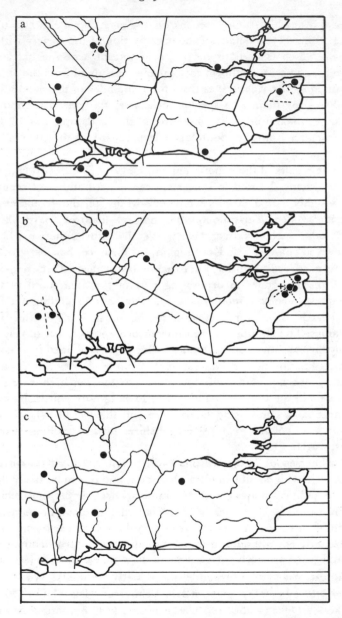

Figure 5.5: Three chronological phases of rich graves in early Anglo-Saxon southern England, acting as centres of territories defined by Theissen Polygons: (a) mid-late sixth century; (b) early seventh century; (c) later seventh century. The changing configurations reflect the manner in which territories were annexed and merged to form larger units, especially by Mercia to the north. The graves incorporated in the maps are listed in Tables 5.6 to 5.10

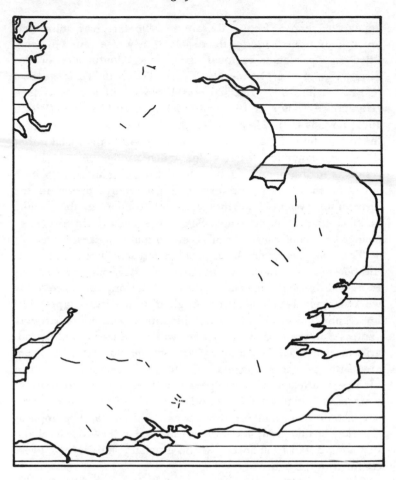

Figure 5.6: The location of possible early Anglo-Saxon linear earthworks in England. Note their absence from the Midlands.

here, despite there being a number of apparent matches; far worse would be to use such correlations to date the earthworks (see, for example, Wheeler 1934)! The linear earthworks are, at least, a reflection of the existence of territories. An area for further research may be those zones which appear to be frequently disputed, that is frontier zones which appear to be areas of regional groups. Clear evidence for extensive exchange networks in diagnostic metalwork between regions and which might have produced a mixing of two regions' artefact types on a frontier, is largely absent. Cemeteries located close to such zones which appear to change frequently are notable for their indistinct, amorphous nature, and for the problems they have posed in being fitted to a particular regional assemblage. Contenders for this category might be Orpington (Kent) (Tester 1968), Portsdown (Corney *et al.* 1967; Bradley and Lewis 1968) and Horndean (Hampshire) (Knocker 1957) and Ocklynge Hill (Sussex) (Welch 1983, pp. 334–40). They may emphasise that the mechanism for the distribution of diagnostic artefacts lay within the social rather than the economic structure for much of the period. Those residents in frontier zones may have had allegiances with both sides, or may have been excluded from participation in the distribution system. The movement of frontiers in the volatile political state of early Anglo-Saxon England would also have changed the configurations of access to material possessions.

There has been very little detailed research directed towards the question of how far group identity, at varying levels, was expressed through artefact styles and decoration since early workers applied such labels as 'Anglian' to particular types. The impression gained is that such identities were more strongly expressed in the sixth century after which the more rigid bound-aries of such socially formative years became more blurred. There are certainly various layers of artefact distribution in which 'domestic' artefacts have a separate and fairly rigid distribution, whereas elaborate artefacts found especially in rich graves cross-cut such divisions and are found over a wider area. The implica-tion may be that group identity was stressed at the lower level and that long-distance alliances, within England and beyond, were confined to the elite.

These maps are not the material for a history of the English kingdoms, just as a correlation with Bede and the *Anglo-Saxon Chronicle* would be very dubious when they rarely mention bound-aries. At a general level it could be claimed that the results support the original hypothesis; at the specific level of historical detail the maps are at least stimulating. It is interesting that it is the regions that are generated by this method for the sixth century whose names are most commonly placed on maps of Dark Age Britain and which form the vocabulary of the early kingdoms. The altera-tions to the pattern appear to reflect a demand for control of the coastline which may relate to a desire to control emerging ports of trade. It should be noted that it is the more northerly and landlocked kingdoms that are most belligerent in the second half of the sixth and seventh centuries, attacking the southern groups and annexing them into larger territories.

At the level of more specific historical interpretation we may observe, for instance, that the East Saxons are interpreted as having relieved Kent of the London area by the early seventh century (HE II 3), but eventually lost it to Mercian control before AD 700 (HE III 7). The political history of Sussex is not at all clear, but it is generally agreed that its independence was under threat by both the Mercians and the West Saxons. For the Isle of Wight and the Meonware to have been given to the south Saxons by Mercia in the seventh century has interesting strategic implications *vis à vis* the position of the West Saxons. In the late seventh century Kent was apparently very unsettled as it was disputed by the West Saxons and Mercia, the latter being the dominant force by the middle of the seventh century.

At such a level there is perhaps no problem and it comes as something of a relief to find some agreement. To attempt to go further would be to fall into the trap that has been so carefully laid by historians: 'Many texts that archaeologists cite with great confidence are the subject of debate' (Sawyer 1983a, p. 46). It is, however, informative that it is only when we come to a very detailed level of integration that problems arise. Some of the changes observed in this analysis are occurring before the earliest suggestion that they were taking place in the documentary sources. In part this will be due to the inevitable imprecision of archaeological dating, 'missing' pieces of evidence, and the various problems that can be found with the historical sources. To say that would imply acceptance of a correlation between the two types of evidence at even the most general level. A typical example is that of Sussex and the Isle of Wight which are to be seen as disappearing as independent units on the basis of the archaeological analysis in *c.* AD 600 and have little or no seventh-century archaeology. Historically they are described as being annexed in the second half of the seventh century in conflicting accounts by Bede and the *Anglo-Saxon Chronicle*.

The method of analysis offers a very useful integration between the archaeological data and the written sources and is the only obvious way of achieving this. Whether integrated or left as a purely archaeological analysis, its rejection leaves the scope for understanding the development of the kingdoms very limited. One area which may, in part, bring together the questions of leadership and territories is the burial of supposed symbols of leadership. The majority of cases where such items are present are female graves of the sixth and early seventh centuries, the notable male example being Sutton Hoo mound 1 with its set of regalia. Attention has been drawn to Edwin's 'standard' of AD 632 which has been compared with the Sutton Hoo mound 1 iron stand (Bruce-Mitford 1978, pp. 403–31). The Roman world has been raked through for similar paraphernalia, but attention might also be drawn to the 'six pronged instrument of iron, in shape much like an ordinary hay-fork' from Benty Grange (Derbyshire) (Bateman 1861, p. 31); the pronged, almost rune-like, symbol beside the diademed portrait on the obverse of the seventh-century WITMEN gold coinage and its copies (Sutherland 1948, 46–50, pp. 88–94). This is more convincing than the crosses held by the figures on the reverse of the early *sceatta* coinage (Bruce-Mitford 1974, pp. 11–17). The important grave under the threshold of the large hall (A4) at the royal site at Yeavering, contained a similar iron object. A ceremonial significance has also been attached to the whetstone which Bruce-Mitford describes as 'an emblem of kingly office' (*ibid.*, p. 6), and which most commentators refer to as a sceptre, linked with other examples from cemeteries (Bruce-Mitford 1978, pp. 311–93; Evison 1975; Reynolds 1980). Helmets are especially rare symbols, examples belonging to this period are known from Sutton Hoo and Benty Grange, with fragments of metal decorated in a similar fashion to those on the former also being known from Caenby.

If it was assumed that symbols of office such as these always existed once this form of leadership had become formalised, their almost total absence from male graves might imply that they were passed on through the male line but not through the female. In terms of succession, whether hereditary or not, this is easy to understand when the effective, documented, leaders of the sixth century were male. The absence of such items from the majority of the wealthier graves might also indicate the increasing number of ranks in society, in which those sub-leaders were able to emulate the elite in many personal items, but not the symbolic. If it were also assumed that symbols of office were buried at a point of dislocation in a line of leaders, and given male succession, it may be significant that they are present in female graves of the sixth century.

Whatever the merits of considering grave assemblages in this way, the one cemetery where these ideas could be particularly germane is Sutton Hoo. It has been argued that despite mounds 2 and 4 having been looted they were not rich deposits in the first place (Arrhenius 1978, p. 194). Yet if the site is a royal cemetery why does mound 1 contain such a rich array of supposed regalia compared with the others? Does this represent a dislocation, permanent or temporary, in a royal line? Bruce-Mitford offers two reasons for the deposition of the sceptre: that it was not the sceptre of the East Anglian royal house and did not require to be handed on; and that its pagan associations were unacceptable to a Christian kingdom (Bruce-Mitford 1978, p. 377).

If the assumptions concerning the identification of symbols of leadership are valid, it may be permissible to suggest that during the sixth century wealthy males were buried with a regular assemblage of items, none of them overtly non-utilitarian, whereas females were accompanied by such items. During the seventh century there are fewer richly accompanied burials and there is a higher probability of males being accompanied by symbolic items.

The foregoing analysis concentrates on southern England because the principal written sources which may be used for comparison display a similar bias and the most extensive set of inhumation burials are also found predominantly to the south of the Midlands. Undoubtedly one of the most important kingdoms in the seventh century was Mercia, about which we know relatively little as it lies outside the scope of the written sources until the early seventh century, only entering the written record when the kingdom imposed itself, often violently, on its southern neighbours. Despite this obscurity there are strong similarities with the developments which have been noted elsewhere.

By the eighth century this Midland kingdom (Dornier 1977) incorporated the river systems of the Warwickshire Avon, Trent and Severn. The southern border lay on the edge of the Chilterns, to the east lay the Fens, beyond which lay other English territories. To the north lay Northumbria, the frontier possibly protected by a series of linear earthworks near Sheffield (Blair 1948, pp. 120–3). The centre of this territory is normally seen as the upper Trent valley in the eastern part of the Midlands, which is in accordance with the historical tradition of relatively late English settlement in the Midlands from East Anglia in the early sixth century (Davies 1977). The archaeological evidence indicates settlement in the Middle Trent and the upper Warwickshire Avon by this time and some types of metalwork, like the pottery, point to a strong connection with East Anglian styles; by the later sixth and seventh century there appears what may be called a Midlands

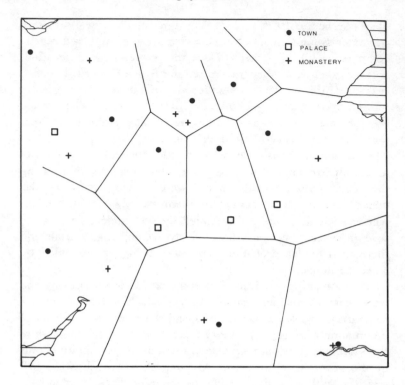

Figure 5.7: The kingdom of Mercia defined by Theissen Polygons drawn around early towns and also showing the location of monasteries and suggested 'royal palaces'. The kingdom expanded by annexing territory to the east and south. (Data: Dornier 1977.)

style of metalwork (Leeds and Pocock 1971, p. 34; Eagles 1979).

Rich graves of the type better known further south are to be found in the east Midlands at Empingham II (Rutland) burial 73, dating to the later sixth century (Clough, Dornier and Rutland 1975, p. 3), and the later barrow burial of Benty Grange further west (Bateman 1861, pp. 28–33). The condition of Mercia in the seventh century has been viewed through an obscure text known as the *Tribal Hidage* (Davies and Vierck 1974); its date is difficult to establish, but the contents are consistent with a developed kingdom which had united smaller tribal groupings in its formation and had expanded outwards. It is the very process of uniting smaller groups which creates the obscurity of this kingdom and difficulties arise as there are undoubtedly many focal points within its boundaries. Within Mercia there are sites revealed by aerial photography containing large halls, amongst other buildings, which have been compared in form and function with Yeavering; Atcham, near Shrewsbury (Shropshire) has not been excavated, but one building at Hatton Rock, near Stratford, indicated a date from the late seventh century onwards. During the seventh and early eighth century the secular and ecclesiastical organisation of the heartland of Mercia had been consolidated, providing the base for its outward expansion (Figure 5.7).

The development of the Anglo-Saxon kingdoms has been considered in terms of a number of related themes; changes in the structure of society; levels and distribution of wealth; administrative organisation; aggression between groups. Levels of decision making may manifest themselves in settlement patterns and which may also have strongly influenced the pattern of the economy, especially in terms of subsistence and exchange. Certain aspects have tended to figure largely in the literature concerned with the exchange of goods and the provision of services including administration. One of the most important aspects is the proposed change from exchange between kins and territories to that of market exchange.

6

Summary

The very absence of information and the lack of patterning in the sparse physical remains in fifth-century England (Arnold 1984a) emphasises how it was a time of recovery for society. Through the later fifth and early sixth centuries small-scale societies with low population densities and small cohesive political units are envisaged; as such identities became stronger some groups may have expanded through warfare whilst other weaker groups may have become linked to others. Within such a framework necessities which were not available locally could be procured through alliances and exchange; the giving of valuables may have been a means of contracting alliances and weaker groups may have tried to arrange marriages 'upwards'. The most important means of livelihood and protection would have been an individual's lineage and clan; such descent groups were tribal segments, which may have controlled marriage and defence, material wealth as well as intangible property. As the sixth century unfolded leadership appears as an office symbolised at burial, but such big men were not necessarily the heads of any form of centralised government. Leadership in such stateless societies must have entailed internal and external roles, with political leaders having superior access to ordinary goods, women and valuables through ceremonial exchange. Their position is more likely to have been achieved, not determined by birth. The position was won by demonstrating superior abilities, achievements and luck in oratory, dispute and peace settlements, war prowess and success in ceremonial exchange. Success in these fields had a double effect, enhancing the position of the successful leader as well as the reputation and power of the descent groups leading to leadership by birth. It is the last process which may

194

underlie the process of change which occurred in the seventh century and which is reflected in so many aspects of early Anglo-Saxon archaeology. Much of this picture remains a model; while much of it has already been tested against the available data, there remains much to do; some aspects may remain untestable.

The most commonly recurring pattern in the rural settlements of early Anglo-Saxon England are the groups of buildings related to an enclosure or compound, which have been termed farm modules (Arnold 1984b). These are in contrast to the settlements of 300 or 400 years later, and there are signs that this type of layout was less common after *c.* AD 700 (Addyman 1964; 1972). The widespread desertion of known settlements and the hints of an intensification of agriculture may represent the nature and cause of the change in the form and location of settlements. Many of these changes may be linked to an overall growth in population.

Another significant change that takes place at the same time is the development of a greater range of settlement types. In addition to rural settlements, the seventh and eighth centuries witness the appearance of centralised places of exchange and royal sites, acting as stimuli to urban growth. Only one of each has been extensively excavated, the royal administrative centre at Yeavering (Hope-Taylor 1977) and the port of *Hamwic*, Saxon Southampton (Addyman and Hill 1968; 1969; Holdsworth 1976; 1980). Other settlements of these types are known from more limited excavations, inference or documentary evidence.

A four-step road to the state has been suggested in terms of economic development by Hodges (1978; 1982a). The first step consists of the 'early state module' (Renfrew 1975), groups of territories which form early state civilisations when unified. Such territories would have an incipient trading site, a central person, with kin-exchange and tribal exchange. The second stage is described as a polity with large, spasmodically-used trading sites with trade as before, with the addition of long-distance prestige trade; a criticism is that such trade was in existence earlier than the existence of known trading sites. Thirdly, the protostate, which is associated with the first markets and market exchange, and a defined bureaucracy. The final step is the state with its hierarchy of markets and a more developed market exchange.

Long-distance trade is in evidence well before the appearance of even 'incipient trading sites'. It may seem more probable that leaders gained control of imports because of their local eminence, based on powers created locally, which served to reinforce their position. Geographic location, as is the case with Kent, may be an important factor in an argument for powers being created by preferential access to imports. For an individual to achieve this preferential position implies, as do the later ports of trade, that a surplus was being created by the working population, but to what extent leaders were provided with a surplus through the allegiance of the population or by a slave class is not known. The observable commodities of this prestige exchange include amber, gold, glass, garnet, cowrie shells, mercury, wine jars, ivory, rock-crystal, amethyst. That many of these materials were necessary pre-requisites for established manufacturing processes as in the case of jewellery, suggests this was a more regular activity than the haphazard payment of tribute, ransoms, etc. (Grierson 1959), although it would be foolish to deny that such systems may also have existed. There is also a marked patterning in their distribu-tions; those from the Mediterranean and other eastern sources have a concentrated distribution in southern England, whereas those from Scandinavia are dispersed. Detailed studies have yet to be made of many of these commodities (Huggett forthcoming), but it is clear at present that they are most commonly found in graves with a greater overall wealth. Of the observable imported materials in evidence by the eighth century, finished metalwork, ceramics and quernstones are amongst those virtually absent in the sixth century, emphasising the very different nature of exchange at these times, the earlier emphasis being on raw materials, the later on finished articles and goods which had the potential to make production more efficient.

Hodges has suggested that incipient trading settlements might be identified, but the archaeological evidence used to argue for such sites are the sets of weights and scales, dated to the late sixth and seventh centuries, which have been found in cemeteries close to the suggested sites; they are also found elsewhere in England (Arnold 1980, pp. 90–1). Their distribution certainly implies exchange in luxury goods but need not, in the absence of any clear evidence, be taken to indicate that this was carried out at a fixed trading site at this time, as opposed to a point of entry and/or the presence of a local power base; the two may, of course, constitute the same thing. More importantly, the regular unit of weight used in the sets implies a level of agreement between traders and/or administrators in each area.

The earliest occupation of the south coast port of *Hamwic* is dated to the period AD 700–750 on the basis of a silver coinage, the secondary series of *sceattas*. This series of coins has a lower silver content than the primary series found particularly in Kent (Rigold and Metcalf 1977). *Hamwic* is characterised by houses laid out along the spine of the Southampton peninsula, beside gravel streets. The settlement may not have originated as a single large unit, although there is no evidence to the contrary. On the Continent such ports often developed as dispersed clusters of buildings, but *Hamwic*, like other such sites, Ipswich, Canterbury, London, are currently only conceivable as large units (Vince 1984; Biddle 1984). The imported pottery found there is from a variety of regions in northern France, probably connected with a trade in wine, just as the earlier evidence for exchange between Kent and the Continent is in part involved with wheel-turned bottles which may also have served to carry wine (Evison 1979). This phase of *Hamwic*'s occupation 'terminates' towards the middle years of the eighth century, followed by a hiatus in coin production and occupation. The major crafts represented on the site are metalworking, carpentry, textiles and boneworking, and a similar range of activities are represented at Ipswich. It is not yet clear whether such production was to satisfy the towns' needs or for the export market, or whether to some extent these traditionally rural crafts had been relocated in these new environments; this is critical for the understanding of the relationship between such ports and their hinterland. As at *Hamwic* the imported material at Ipswich includes glass, pottery and quernstones from the Continent.

Hodges takes the relationship between the origins of the medieval market and the formation of the state as his central theme, and sees exogenous activities, particularly trade, as the principal stimulus to change (Hodges 1982a; 1982b). Settlements such as *Hamwic* may originate as inlets for international trade directed towards a central person in a territory and its existence would, therefore, be affected if the role of that central person were to change. An increase in *wergeld* payments for the king by the early eighth century is taken to indicate the growth in power of the central person, a development which underlines the new and distant role of kingship in a larger territory. *Hamwic* and other eighth-century ports are viewed as being dependent on a rural surplus but whether the surplus 'came first' and was therefore available to the traders from other territories bringing prestigious items, or vice versa, is unclear (Hodges 1982a, p. 130ff).

Royal centres have been indicated using a variety of evidence, as discussed above, at Eastry (Hawkes 1979; see also Arnold 1982c), Canterbury, Dorchester-on-Thames (Dickinson 1974), York, Goodmanham (Yorkshire), Rendlesham (Suffolk), Hatton Rock (Rahtz 1970), Northampton and Winchester. At least four of them have a close geographic relationship with an early port of trade (Figure 6.1) in which royal interest was very close.

Whatever their precise roles, by the eighth century there were at least three levels of settlement in England: ports, royal centres and rural settlements. The rural settlements, presumably, were principally concerned with food production and supporting, to an increasing extent, the resident population of the ports and royal centres; food production, commerce and administration. The structure of the church was grafted onto this structure at various levels. This development emphasises the self-sufficiency of the rural settlements of fifth and sixth century date, with craft production at a local level and some prestige trade in luxuries. It is important to emphasise that this three-tiered system had evolved through the sixth and seventh centuries from one of farmsteads with no obvious distinguishing features. Products were moved through a system of redistribution between kin and a limited movement between territories. By the eighth century such rural settlements may have lost their 'central persons' who had removed themselves to royal sites, and some of the craft specialists had been relocated, and centralised, at the ports of trade. We have already seen that there is evidence for an horizon of settlement abandonment around AD 700 and it may also be observed that by AD 800 the early building tradition was changing with structures less precisely laid-out in different shapes and employing different techniques. Thus the small rural settlements of the sixth century were largely self-contained, the 'lord' with his 'retainers', with a redistributive form of economy which became dismembered, at least, during the seventh and eighth centuries. Is this also a reflection of a move away from the rarity of private ownership of land to the growth of state control? Sawyer has indicated how, prior to the eighth century 'land held by individuals was thought to belong either to their families or to their lords'. Individuals could not make grants of land having only a life interest (1978, p. 155). A change appears to have taken place from the seventh century onwards, partly because of a need to give churches permanent rights over land through royal charters. At least, certain sections of the population were gradually freed for full-time specialisation, be it craft/industry or administration.

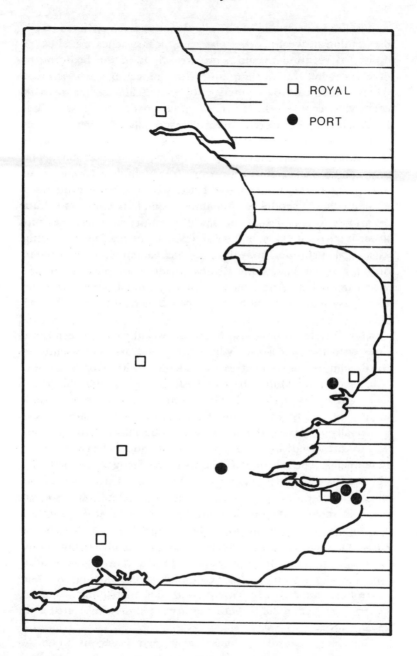

Figure 6.1: The distribution of royal sites and ports of trade in early Anglo-Saxon England known from written sources or by excavation

Such a redistribution of the population may be reflected in the distribution of wealth. One way in which societies are able, or desire, to accumulate and store wealth, is in the hoarding of precious metal. It is one of the surprising aspects of the period that there is no hoarding known until the middle of the seventh century, except in the form of grave-goods which were not intended to be recovered. Hoards, especially of silver coinage, become more frequent from the late seventh century onwards which may be a reflection of the role of the new silver coinage. The removal of the ruling minority from rural settlements to administrative tasks in central places also implies a centralised accumulation of capital and the imposition of taxation and tribute on a more formal basis. The seventh century also sees the start towards the codification of laws and punishment, although kinship as a legal institution may have remained immensely strong in ordinary social life. While forms of the kinship structure are visible in the later Anglo-Saxon period, Loyn has argued that the kinship system never fully developed in Anglo-Saxon England (1974).

The centralisation of wealth and the wealthy can be seen more directly in the rich graves which are found associated with the royal administrative centres; Cuddesdon with Dorchester-on-Thames, Sutton Hoo with Rendlesham, Winchester, the royal Christian graves at Canterbury, and those probably of high rank at such sites as St Paul-in-the Bail, Lincoln. Others are known, principally in Wessex, the majority being burials with conspicuous wealth displayed in their grave-goods under large earthern monuments. The role of Christianity in the changes that are being observed is difficult to gauge. The new religion not only caused the redirection of wealth into an alternative system, but also into the construction of churches, at least the sees at Dorchester, Winchester and Canterbury, minster churches and the earliest rural churches identified, which are the first public monumental buildings known in the post-Roman period. They are therefore yet another reflection of the centralisation of resources and the control of manpower. Inevitably, with their need for patronage, churches erected in the seventh century are closely associated with royal centres.

Certain structural changes have been observed in rural settlements of the seventh and eighth centuries; the increasing rarity of the hall-enclosure module as the norm, and the abandonment of many rural settlements at about the same time; an intensification of agriculture in the use of new soil types and possibly new field systems (Arnold and Wardle 1981). Such changes should be related to the structure found in the pagan cemeteries which we have analysed. In the sixth century the cemeteries of isolated groups reveal the wide disparity in wealth distribution with small membership of the wealthier groups while the majority have few grave-goods. In the seventh century the pattern changes. The overall levels of wealth are much lower, there is far less differentiation on that basis, and the groups are very small. This can hardly be the result of an overall reduction in population as only certain classes are absent. Are we to believe that society was becoming more egalitarian on this road to statehood? The alternative may be to view this as the result of the isolation of the rich and the removal of craftsmen to the central places, leaving subsistence farmers in the countryside to be increasingly dependent on the developing market economy for their support. We have seen that the rich graves of the seventh century are also associated with royal sites, which are in close association with ports of trade where the debris from the activities of craftsmen is to be found in profusion. These ports, however, need be no more than a centralisation, or formalisation, of the processes of exchange that had existed earlier.

The implication of this change would be the formation of a politically organised society based on territorial principles as opposed to the earlier one based on kin ties. The establishment of such territories may in part be seen as the result of recurring aggression documented between the various 'kingdoms'. Such aggression shows signs of giving way to statemanship in the late seventh century. Thus the integration of Early State Modules in early Anglo-Saxon England takes place largely as the result of the desire to control access to resources.

A synthetic approach to the matter of state formation is most successful in establishing effects; causes may continue to elude us. The role of the growing population is hard to assess but may be crucial. The two most apparent elements in the data (admittedly in the terms that it has been examined) are wealth and power, whose importance grows with centralisation and specialisation. It was perhaps inevitable in early Anglo-Saxon England that social change would be brought about by the increasing wealth of a minority, a wealth that could only be achieved with power. A growth in population would have necessitated an intensification in agriculture and in technology, and any moves towards mass-production and commercial activity would have required control and administration, emphasising the role if kingship. The wealthy class's desire for luxuries must have been a major incentive for the regularisation and control of international trade; intensification and specialisation ultimately require a market to maximise efficiency. The maintenance of power implies the production of a surplus and a change that, it is suggested, took place from the self-contained rural settlement in which a surplus was produced for the maintenance of leaders, to that of a system of taxation in which a surplus was provided more formally. In the space of two centuries many of the prerequisites for the formation of a unified English state had rapidly been brought into existence. After the confusion which followed the collapse of Roman Britain, order was restored.

Bibliography

Åberg, N. (1926) *The Anglo-Saxons in England during the early centuries after the invasion*, Uppsala

Addyman, P.V. (1964) 'A Dark-Age Settlement at Maxey, Northants.', *Medieval Archaeol, 8*, pp. 20–73

—— (1972) 'The Anglo-Saxon house: a new review', *Anglo-Saxon England, 1*, pp. 273–307

—— (1977) 'York and Canterbury as ecclesiastical centres' in M.W. Barley (ed.), *European Towns: their archaeology and early history*, London, pp. 499–509

—— and Hill, D.H. (1968) 'Saxon Southampton: a review of the evidence', *Proc Hampshire Fld Club Archaeol Soc, 25*, pp. 61–93

—— (1969) 'Saxon Southampton: a review of the evidence' *Proc Hampshire Fld Club Archaeol Soc, 26*, pp. 61–96

—— Leigh, D. and Hughes, M.J. (1972) 'Anglo-Saxon houses at Chalton, Hampshire', *Medieval Archaeol, 16*, pp. 13–32

Akerman, J.Y. (1855) *Remains of Pagan Saxondum*, London

Alcock, L. (1978) '*Her . . . gefeaht with Walas*: Aspects of the warfare of Saxons and Britons', *Bull Board Celtic Stud, 27*, pp. 413–24

—— (1981) 'Quantity or quality: the Anglian graves of Bernicia' in V.I. Evison (ed.), *Angles, Saxons and Jutes*, Oxford, pp. 168–86

Anstee, J.W. and Biek, L. (1961) 'A study in pattern welding', *Medieval Archaeol, 5*, pp. 71–93

Arnold, C.J. (1978) 'George Hillier: an Isle of Wight Antiquary', *Proc Hampshire Fld Club Archaeol Soc, 34*, pp. 59–64

—— (1980) 'Wealth and Social Structure: a matter of life and death' in P. Rahtz, T. Dickinson and L. Watts (eds), *Anglo-Saxon Cemeteries 1979, Brit Archaeol Rep, 82*, Oxford, pp. 81–142

—— (1981) 'Early Anglo-Saxon pottery: production and distribution' in H. Howard and E.L. Morris (eds), *Production and Distribution: a Ceramic Viewpoint, Brit Archaeol Rep, 120*, Oxford, pp. 243–55

—— (1982a) *The Anglo-Saxon Cemeteries of the Isle of Wight*, London

—— (1982b) 'Stress as a factor in social and economic change' in A.C. Renfrew and S. Shennan (eds), *Ranking, Resource and Exchange*, Cambridge, pp. 124–31

—— (1982c) 'Excavations at Eastry Court Farm, Eastry, Kent', *Archaeol Cantiana, 98*, pp. 121–35

—— (1983) 'The Sancton-Baston Potter', *Scottish Archaeol Rev, 2*, pp. 17–30

—— (1984a) *Roman Britain to Saxon England*, London

—— (1984b) 'Social Evolution in Post-Roman western Europe' in J. Bintliff (ed.), *European Social Evolution*, Bradford, pp. 277–94

—— (1987) 'Territories and Leadership: frameworks for the study of emergent polities in early Anglo-Saxon southern England' in S. Driscoll and M. Nieke (eds), *Early Historical Archaeology*, Edinburgh

—— and Wardle, P. (1981) 'Early Anglo-Saxon settlement patterns in southern England', *Medieval Archaeol, 25*, pp. 145–9

―――― and Wilkinson, J.L. (1984) 'Three Anglo-Saxon cremations from Girton', *Proc Cambridge Antiq Soc, 73*, pp. 23–7

Arnold, D.E. (1985) *Ceramic Theory and Cultural Process*, Cambridge

Arrhenius, B. (1971) *Granatschmuck und Gemmen aus nordischen Funden des Frühen Mittelalters*, Stockholm

―――― (1973) 'East Scandinavian Style I — a review', *Medieval Archaeol, 17*, pp. 26–42

―――― (1975) 'Die technischen Voraussetzungen für die Entwicklung der germanischen Tierornamentik', *Frühmittelalterliche Studien, 9*, pp. 93–109

―――― (1978) review of Bruce-Mitford (1975) *Medieval Archaeol, 22*, pp. 189–95

Arthur, B.V. and Jope, E.M. (1963) 'Early Saxon pottery kilns at Purwell Farm, Cassington, Oxfordshire', *Medieval Archaeol, 6-7*, pp. 1–12

Astill, G. and Lobb, S. (1982) 'Sampling a Saxon settlement site: Wraysbury, Berks.', *Medieval Archaeol, 26*, pp. 138–42

Atkinson, D. (1916) *The Romano-British Site on Lowbury Hill in Berkshire*, Reading

Atkinson, R.J.C. (1953) 'Technical notes on the construction of the Swords, Scabbards and Shields', in E.T. Leeds and H. de S. Shortt, *An Anglo-Saxon cemetery at Petersfinger, near Salisbury, Wilts.*, Salisbury, pp. 55–60

Avent, R. (1975) *Anglo-Saxon Garnet inlaid disc and composite Brooches*, Brit Archaeol Rep, *11*, Oxford

―――― and Leigh, D. (1977) 'A study of cross-hatched gold foils in Anglo-Saxon jewellery', *Medieval Archaeol, 21*, pp. 1–46

―――― and Evison, V.I. (1982) 'Anglo-Saxon Button Brooches', *Archaeologia, 107*, pp. 77–124

Bakka, E. (1958) *On the beginnings of Salin's Style I in England*, Bergen

Bateman, T. (1861) *Ten Years' Diggings in Celtic and Saxon Grave Hills*, London

Beck, C.W. (1970) 'Amber in Archaeology', *Archaeology, 23*, pp. 7–11

Beckwith, J. (1972) *Ivory Carvings in Early Medieval England*, London

Bell, J.A. (1981) 'A Reconstruction of Anglian Female Dress in Yorkshire and Lincolnshire', unpublished BA dissertation, University of Leeds

Bell, M.G. (1977) 'Excavations at Bishopstone in Sussex', *Sussex Archaeol Coll*, p. 115

―――― (1978) 'Saxon settlements and buildings in Sussex', in P. Brandon (ed.), *The South Saxons*, Chichester, pp. 36–53

Biddick, K. (1984) 'Field edge, forest edge: early medieval social change and resource allocation' in K. Biddick (ed.), *Archaeological Approaches to Medieval Europe*, Kalamazoo, Mich., pp. 105–18

Biddle, M. (1976) 'Hampshire and the Origins of Wessex' in G. de G. Sieveking, I.H. Longworth and K.E. Wilson (eds), *Problems in Economic and Social Archaeology*, London, pp. 323–42

―――― (1984) 'London in the Strand', *Popular Archaeol, 6*, (1), pp. 23–7

Bimson, M. (1985) 'Dark-Age Garnet Cutting', *Anglo-Saxon Studies in Archaeology and History, 4*, pp. 125–28

Bimson, M., La Neice, S. and Leese, M. (1982) 'The characterisation of

Mounted Garnet', *Archaeometry*, *24*, pp. 51–8

Blair, P.H. (1948) 'The Northumbrians and their Southern Frontier', *Archaeologia Aeliana* (4th Series), *26*, pp. 98–126

Böhner, K. (1958) *Die fränkischen Altertümer des Trierer Landes*, Berlin

Bonnet, C. and Martin, M. (1982) 'La modèle de plomb d'une fibule anglo-saxonne de Saint-Pierre à Genève', *Arch Suisse*

Bonney, D.J. (1972) 'Early Boundaries in Wessex' in P.J. Fowler (ed.) *Archaeology and the Landscape*, London, pp. 168–86

—— (1976) 'Early Boundaries and Estates in southern England' in P.H. Sawyer (ed.), *Medieval Settlement*, London, pp. 72–82

Bourdillon, J. (1979) 'Town life and animal husbandry in the Southampton area, as suggested by the excavated bones', *Proc Hampshire Fld Club Archaeol Soc*, *36*, pp. 181–92

Bradley, R. and Lewis, E. (1968) 'Excavations at the George Inn, Portsdown', *Proc Hampshire Fld Club Archaeol Soc*, *25*, pp. 27–50

Brenan, J. (1985) 'Assessing Social Status in the Anglo-Saxon Cemetery at Sleaford', *Bull Institute Archaeol*, *21-22* (1984-85), pp. 125–31

Brisbane, M. (1980) 'Anglo-Saxon Burials: Pottery, Production and Social Status' in P.A. Rahtz, T.M. Dickinson and L. Watts (eds), *Anglo-Saxon Cemeteries 1979, Brit Archaeol Rep*, *82*, Oxford, pp. 209–18

—— (1981) 'Incipient Markets for early Anglo-Saxon Ceramics' in H. Howard and E.L. Morris (eds), *Production and Distribution: a Ceramic Viewpoint, Brit Archaeol Rep*, *120*, Oxford, pp. 229–41

—— (1983) 'The period 4 pottery', *Archaeol Journ*, *140*, pp. 254–7

Briscoe, T. (1981) 'Anglo-Saxon Pot Stamps', *Anglo-Saxon Studies in Archaeology and History*, *2*, pp. 1–36

British Museum Guide (1923) *British Museum Guide to Anglo-Saxon Antiquities*, London

Brown, B.J.W. *et al.* (1957) 'Excavations at Grimstone End, Pakenham', *Proc Suffolk Institute Archaeol*, *26*, pp. 188–207

Brown, D. (1974) 'So-called "needle-cases"', *Medieval Arachaeol*, *18*, pp. 151–4

—— (1977) 'Firesteels and Pursemounts again', *Bonner Jahrbücher*, *177*, pp. 451–80

—— (1981a) 'Swastika Patterns' in V.I. Evison (ed.), *Angles, Saxons and Jutes*, Oxford pp. 227–40

—— (1981b) 'The Dating of the Sutton Hoo Coins', *Anglo-Saxon Studies in Archaeology and History*, *2*, pp. 71–86

Brown, G.B. (1903-1937) *The Arts in Early England* I (1903), II (1903), iii-iv (1915), V (1921), VIi (1925), VIii (1937), London

Brown, P.D.C. (1976) 'Some Notes on Grass-tempered Pottery', *Records of Buckinghamshire*, *20*, pp. 191–3

Browne, T. (1658) *Hydriotaphia, or Urne buriall*, London

Bruce-Mitford, R.L.S. (1970) 'The Sutton Hoo Lyre, Beowulf and the Origins of the Frame Harp', *Antiquity*, *44*, pp. 7–13

—— (1974) *Aspects of Anglo-Saxon Archaeology*, London

—— (1975) *The Sutton Hoo Ship Burial I*, London

—— (1978) *The Sutton Hoo Ship Burial II*, London

—— (1983) *The Sutton Hoo Ship Burial III*, London

Bullough, R.A. (1965) 'Anglo-Saxon Insititutions and Early English

Society', *Annali della Fondazione Italiana per la Storia Amministraria*, 2, pp. 647–59

Campbell, J.A., Baxter, M.S. and Alcock, L. (1979) 'Radio-carbon dates for the Cadbury massacre', *Antiquity*, 53, pp. 31–8

Capelle, T. and Vierck, H. (1971) 'Modeln der Merowinger- und Wikingerzeit', *Frühmittelalterliche Studien*, 5, pp. 42–101

—— (1975) 'Weitere Modeln der Merowinger- und Wikingerzeit', *Frühmittelalterliche Studien*, 9, pp. 110–42

Chadwick, H.M. (1905) *Studies in Anglo-Saxon Institutions*, Cambridge

—— (1907) *Origin of the English Nation*, Cambridge

Chadwick, S.E. (1958) 'The Anglo-Saxon cemetery at Finglesham, Kent: a reconsideration', *Medieval Archaeol*, 2, pp. 1–71

Childe, V.G. (1933) 'Is prehistory practical?' *Antiquity*, 7, pp. 410–18

Claessen, H.J.M. (1978) 'The Early State: a structural approach' in H.J.M. Claessen and P. Skalnik (eds), *The Early State*, The Hague, pp. 533–96

—— and Skalnik, P. (eds) (1978) *The Early State*, The Hague

Clark, A. (1960) 'A cross-valley dyke on the Surrey-Kent Border', *Surrey Archaeol Colls*, 57, pp. 72–4

Clark, A.J., Hampton, J.N. and Hughes, M.F. (1983) 'Mount Down, Hampshire: The reappraisal of evidence', *Antiq Journ*, 63, pp. 122–4

Cleere, H. (1972) 'Anglo-Saxon Iron-working Debris' in A.C.C. Brodribb, A.R. Hands and D.R. Walker, *Excavations at Shakenoak Farm, near Wilcote, Oxfordshire III*, Oxford, pp. 117–18

Clough, T. Mc.K., Dornier, A. and Rutland, R.A. (1975) *A guide to the Anglo-Saxon and Viking antiquities of Leicestershire and Rutland*, Leicester

Coffin, S. (1975) 'Linear earthworks in the Froxfield, East Tisted and Hayling Wood district', *Proc Hampshire Fld Club Archaeol Soc*, 32, pp. 77–82

Collingwood, R.G. and Myres, J.N.L. (1937) *Roman Britain and the English Settlements* (2nd Edition), Oxford

Cook, A.M. (1974) 'The Evidence for the Reconstruction of Female Costume in the Early Anglo-Saxon Period in the South of England', unpublished MA thesis, University of Birmingham

—— and Dacre, M.W. (1985) *Excavations at Portway, Andover 1973–1975*, Oxford University Committee for Archaeology Mono 4, Oxford

Copley, G. (1986) *Archaeology and Place-names in the Fifth and Sixth Centuries Brit Archaeol Rep*, 147, Oxford

Corney, A. *et al.* (1967) 'A Prehistoric and Anglo-Saxon Burial Ground, Portsdown, Portsmouth', *Proc Hampshire Fld Club Archaeol Soc*, 24, pp. 20–41

Cramp, R.J. (1957) 'Beowulf and Archaeology', *Medieval Archaeol*, 1 pp. 57–77

Crowfoot, E. and Hawkes, S.C. (1967) 'Early Anglo-Saxon gold braids', *Medieval Archaeol*, 11, pp. 42–86

Crowfoot, G.M. (1952) 'Anglo-Saxon tablet weaving', *Antiq Journ*, 32, pp. 189–91

Cunliffe, B. (1972) 'Saxon and Medieval settlement patterns in the region of Chalton, Hampshire', *Medieval Archaeol*, 16, pp. 1–12

Daniel, G.E. (1981) *A Short History of Archaeology*, London

Darrah, R. (1982) 'Working unseasoned oak' in S. McGrail (ed.), *Woodworking Techniques before AD 1500, Brit Archaeol Rep, 129,* Oxford, pp. 219–30

Davidson, H.R.E. (1962) *The Sword in Anglo-Saxon England: its archaeology and literature,* Oxford

Davies, S.M. (1980) 'Excavations at Old Down Farm, Andover. Part I: Saxon', *Proc Hampshire Fld Club Archaeol Soc, 36,* pp. 161–80

—— (1984) 'The excavation of an Anglo-Saxon cemetery (and some prehistoric pits) at Charlton Plantation, near Downton', *Wiltshire Archaeol Nat Hist Mag, 79,* pp. 109–54

Davies, W. (1977) 'Annals and the origin of Mercia' in A. Dornier (ed.), *Mercian Studies,* Leicester, pp. 17–29

—— (1982) *Wales in the Early Middle Ages,* Leicester

—— and Vierck, H. (1974) 'The contexts of the *Tribal Hidage*: social aggregates and settlement patterns, *Furümittelalterliche Studien, 8,* pp. 223–93

Deanesley, M. (1943) 'Roman traditionalist influence among the Anglo-Saxons', *English Hist Rev, 58,* pp. 129–46

Denton, G.H. and Karlén, W. (1973) 'Holocene climatic variations — their pattern and possible cause', *Quaternary Research, 3*

Dickinson, T.M. (1974) *Cuddesdon and Dorchester-on-Thames, Brit Archaeol Rep, 1,* Oxford

—— (1978) 'British Antiquity: Post-Roman and Pagan Anglo-Saxon', *Archaeol Journ, 135,* pp. 332–44

—— (1982) 'Ornament Variation in Pairs of Cast Saucer Brooches: a case study from the Upper Thames Region' in L. Webster (ed.), *Aspects of Production and Style in Dark Age Metalwork,* London, pp. 21–50

—— (1983) 'Anglo-Saxon Archaeology: twenty-five years on' in D.A. Hinton (ed.), *25 Years of Medieval Archaeology,* Sheffield, pp. 38–43

Dixon, P. (1982) 'How Saxon is the Saxon House?' in P.J. Drury (ed.), *Structural Reconstruction, Brit Archaeol Rep, 110,* Oxford pp. 275–87

Doran, J.E. and Hodson, F.R. (1975) *Mathematics and Computers in Archaeology,* Edinburgh

Dornier, A. (1977) *Mercian Studies,* Leicester

Douglas, J. (1793) *Nenia Britannica,* London

Driscoll, S. and Nieke, M. (eds) (1987) *Early Historical Archaeology,* Edinburgh

Dumville, D.N. (1977) 'Kingship, Genealogies and Regnal Lists' in P.H. Sawyer and I.N. Wood (eds), *Early Medieval Kingship,* Leeds, pp. 72–104

Dunning, G.C. (1932) 'Bronze-Age settlements and a Saxon hut near Bourton-on-the-Water, Gloucestershire', *Antiq Journ, 12,* pp. 279–93

—— (1959) 'The Anglo-Saxon plane from Sarre', *Archaeol Cantiana, 73,* pp. 196–201

Eagles, B.N. (1979) *The Anglo-Saxon Settlement of Humberside, Brit Archaeol Rep, 68,* Oxford

Ekwall, E. (1936) 'Some notes on English place-names containing tribal names', *Namn och Bygd, 24,* pp. 178–83

Evans, A.J. (1890) 'On a Late-Celtic Urn-Field at Aylesford, Kent', *Archaeologia, 52,* pp. 315–88

Evison, V.I. (1955) 'Early Anglo-Saxon inlaid metalwork', *Antiq Journ,*

35, pp. 20–45

────── (1958) 'Further Anglo-Saxon inlay', *Antiq Journ*, *38*, pp. 240–4

────── (1963) 'Sugar-loaf shield bosses', *Antiq Journ*, *43*, pp. 38–96

────── (1967) 'The Dover ring-sword and other sword rings and beads', *Archaeologia*, *101*, pp. 63–118

────── (1968) 'Quoit brooch style buckles', *Antiq Journ*, *48*, pp. 231–49

────── (1972) 'Glass cone beakers of the 'Kempston' type', *Journ Glass Stud*, *14*, pp. 48–66

────── (1975) 'Pagan Saxon Whetstones', *Antiq Journ*, *55*, pp. 70–85

────── (1979a) 'The body in the ship at Sutton Hoo', *Anglo-Saxon Studies in Archaeology and History*, *1*, pp. 121–38

────── (1979b) *A Corpus of Wheel-thrown Pottery in Anglo-Saxon Graves*, London

Farley, M. (1976) 'Saxon and Medieval Walton, Aylesbury: Excavations 1973-4', *Records of Buckinghamshire*, *20*, pp. 153–290

Faull, M.L. (1976) 'The location and relationship of the Sancton Anglo-Saxon cemeteries', *Antiq Journ*, *56*, pp. 227–33

────── (1977) 'British survival in Anglo-Saxon Northumbria' in L. Laing (ed.), *Studies in Celtic Survival*, *Brit Archaeol Rep*, *37*, Oxford, pp. 1–55

Fell, C.E. (1975) 'Old English *BEOR*', *Leeds Stud Eng* (New Series), *8*, pp. 76–95

Foard, G. (1978) 'Systematic fieldwalking and the investigation of Saxon settlement in Northamptonshire', *World Archaeol*, *9*, pp. 357–74

Fortes, M. (1968) 'Of Installation Ceremonies', *Proc Roy Anthrop Inst for 1967* pp. 5–20

Fox, C. (1923) *The Archaeology of the Cambridge Region*, Cambridge

Fox, A. and Fox, C. (1958) 'Wansdyke reconsidered', *Archaeol Journ*, *115*, pp. 1–48

Gelling, M. (1978) *Signposts to the Past*, London

Goodier, A. (1984) 'The formation of boundaries in Anglo-Saxon England: a statistical study', *Medieval Archaeol*, *28*, pp. 1–21

Green, B. and Rogerson, A. (1978) *The Anglo-Saxon cemetery at Bergh Apton, Norfolk, East Anglian Archaeol Rep*, *7*, Gressenhall

Green, C. (1963) *Sutton Hoo: the Excavation of a Royal Ship-burial*, London

Green, F.J. (1983) 'The plant remains', *Archaeol Journ*, *140*, pp. 259–61

Grierson, P. (1959) 'Commerce in the Dark Ages: a critique of the evidence', *Trans Roy Hist Soc* (5th Series), *9*, pp. 123–40

────── (1961) 'La fonction sociale de la monnaie en Angleterre au VIIe-VIIIe siècles', *Settimane di studio del Centro italiano di stude sull'alto medioevo*, *7*, pp. 341–85

Griffith, A.F. and Salzmann, L.F. (1914) 'An Anglo-Saxon cemetery at Alfriston, Sussex', *Sussex Archaeol Coll*, *56*, pp. 16–51

Hall, D.N. (1979) 'New evidence of modifications in open-field systems', *Antiquity*, *53*, pp. 222–4

────── (1981) 'The origins of open-field agriculture — the archaeological fieldwork evidence' in T. Rowley (ed.), *The Origins of Open Field Agriculture*, London, pp. 22–38

Hallam, S. (1961) 'Wash coast-line levels since Roman Times', *Antiquity*, *35*, pp. 152–5

Harden, D.B. (ed.) (1956a) *Dark Age Britain. Studies presented to E.T. Leeds*, London
———— (1956b) 'Glass vessels in Britain and Ireland, A.D. 400–1000' in D.B. Harden (ed.), *Dark Age Britain. Studies presented to E.T. Leeds*, London, pp. 132–70
———— (1978) 'Anglo-Saxon and later medieval glass in Britain: some recent developments', *Medieval Archaeol*, *22*, pp. 1–24
Härke, H. (1981) 'Anglo-Saxon laminated shields at Petersfinger — a myth', *Medieval Archaeol*, *25*, pp. 141–4
———— and Salter, C. (1984) 'A technical and metallurgical study of three Anglo-Saxon sheild bosses', *Anglo-Saxon Studies in Archaeology and History*, *3*, pp. 55–66
Harrison, K. (1976) *The Framework of Anglo-Saxon History to AD 900*, Cambridge
Hawkes, C.F.C. (1956) 'The Jutes of Kent' in D.B. Harden (ed.), *Dark Age Britain. Studies presented to E.T. Leeds*, London, pp. 91–111
———— and Smith, M.A. (1957) 'On some buckets and cauldrons of the Bronze and Early Iron Ages', *Antiq Journ*, *37*, pp. 131–98
Hawkes, S.C. (1961) 'The Jutish Style A. A study of Germanic Animal Art in Southern England in the Fifth Century A.D.', *Archaeologia*, *98*, pp. 29–74
———— (1968) 'Richborough-the physical geography' in B. Cunliffe, *Fifth Report on the Excavations of the Roman Fort at Richborough, Kent*, London, pp. 224–30
———— (1969) 'Early Anglo-Saxon Kent', *Archaeol Journ*, *127*, pp. 186–92
———— (1973) 'The Dating and Social Significance of the burials in the Polhill Cemetery' in B. Philp, *Excavations in West Kent 1960-1970*, Dover, pp. 186–201
———— (1977) 'Orientation at Finglesham: sunrise dating of death and burial in an Anglo-Saxon cemetery in East Kent', *Archaeol Cantiana*, *92*, pp. 33–51
———— (1979) 'Eastry in Anglo-Saxon Kent: its importance and a newly found grave', *Anglo-Saxon Studies in Archaeology and History*, *1*, pp. 81–114
———— and Dunning, G.C. (1961) 'Soldiers and settlers in Britain, fourth to fifth century: with a catalogue of animal ornamented and related belt-fittings', *Medieval Archaeol*, *5*, pp. 1–70
———— Merrick, J.M. and Metcalf, D.M. (1966) 'X-ray flourescent analysis of some Dark Age coins and jewellery', *Archaeometry*, *9*, pp. 98–138
———— and Page, R.I. (1967) 'Swords and runes in South-east England', *Antiq Journ*, *47*, pp. 1–26
———— and Pollard, M. (1981) 'The gold bracteates from sixth-century Anglo-Saxon graves in Kent, in the light of a new find from Finglesham', *Frühmittelalterliche Studien*, *15*, pp. 316–70
———— and Wells, C. (1975) 'Crime and Punishment in an Anglo-Saxon cemetery?', *Antiquity*, *49*, pp. 118–22
Hedges, J.D. and Buckley, D.G. (1985) 'Anglo-Saxon burials and later features excavated at Orsett, Essex, 1975', *Medieval Archaeol*, *29*, pp. 1–24

Hedges, M.E. (1977) 'The excavation of the Knowes of Quoyscottie, Orkney', *Proc Soc Antiqs Scotland, 108*, pp. 130–55

Hewlett, H.G. (ed.) (1886) *The Flowers of History, by Roger Wendover,* London

Hillier, G. (1856) *The History and Antiquities of the Isle of Wight,* London

Hills, C. (1977a) 'A chamber grave from Spong Hill, North Elmham, Norfolk', *Medieval Archaeol, 21*, pp. 167–76

——— (1977b) *The Anglo-Saxon Cemetery at Spong Hill, North Elmham. Part 1, East Anglian Archaeol Rep, 6,* Gressenhall

——— (1979) 'The archaeology of Anglo-Saxon England in the pagan period: a review', *Anglo-Saxon England, 8*, pp. 297–329

——— (1980a) 'Anglo-Saxon chairperson', *Antiquity, 54*, pp. 52–4

——— (1980b) 'Anglo-Saxon Cremation Cemeteries with particular reference to Spong Hill, Norfolk' in P.A. Rahtz, T.M. Dickinson and L. Watts (eds), *Anglo-Saxon Cemeteries 1979, Brit Archaeol Rep, 82,* Oxford pp. 197–208

——— (1980c) 'The Anglo-Saxon Settlement of England' in D.M. Wilson (ed.), *The Northern World,* London, pp. 71–94

——— (1981a) 'Barred zoomorphic combs of the migration period' in V.I. Evison (ed.), *Angles, Saxons and Jutes,* Oxford, pp. 96–125

——— (1981b) *The Anglo-Saxon Cemetery at Spong Hill, North Elmham, Part II, East Anglian Archaeol Rep, 11,* Gressenhall

——— (1984) *The Anglo-Saxon Cemetery at Spong Hill, North Elmham, Part III: Catalogue of Inhumations, East Anglian Archaeol Rep, 21,* Gressenhall

Hines, J. (1984) *The Scandinavian Character of Anglian England in the pre-Viking Period, Brit Archaeol Rep, 124,* Oxford

Hockey, S.F. (1977) 'Stolen manuscripts: the case of George Hillier and the British Museum', *Archives, 13*, pp. 20–8

Hodges, H. (1964) *Artifacts. An Introduction to early Materials and Technology,* London

Hodges, R. (1977) 'Some early Medieval French Wares in the British Isles' in D.P.S. Peacock (ed.), *Pottery and Early Commerce,* London pp. 239–56

——— (1978) 'State formation and the role of trade in Middle Saxon England' in D. Green , C. Haselgrove and M. Spriggs (eds), *Social Organisation and Settlement, Brit Archaeol Rep,* Internat Series 47, Oxford, pp. 439–54

——— (1982a) *Dark Age Economics. The origins of towns and trade AD 600–1000,* London

——— (1982b) 'The evolution of gateway communities: their socio-economic implications' in C. Renfrew and S. Shennan (eds), *Ranking, Resource and Exchange,* Cambridge, pp. 117–23

Hogarth, A.C. (1973) 'Structural features in Anglo-Saxon graves', *Archaeol Journ, 130*, pp. 104–19

Hogg, A.H.A. (1941) 'Earthworks in Joydens Wood, Bexley, Kent', *Archaeol Cantiana, 54*, pp. 10–27

Holdsworth, P. (1976) 'Saxon Southampton: a new review', *Medieval Archaeol, 20*, pp. 26–61

——— (1980) *Excavations at Melbourne Street, Southampton, 1971-76, Council Brit Archaeol Res Rep, 33,* London

Holmqvist, W. (ed.) (1961) *Excavations at Helgö I*, Uppsala
—— (ed.) (1964) *Excavations at Helgö II*, Uppsala
—— (ed.) (1970) *Excavations at Helgo III*, Uppsala
—— (ed.) (1972) *Excavations at Helgö IV, Workshop. Part I*, Uppsala
—— (1975) 'Helgö, an early trading settlement in central Sweden' in R.L.S. Bruce-Mitford (ed.), *Recent Archaeological Excavations in Europe*, London, pp. 111–32
Hope-Taylor, B. (1977) *Yeavering: an Anglo-British centre of early Northumbria*, London
Horsfield, T.W. (1835) *History, Antiquities and Topography of Sussex*, Lewes
Huggett, J. (1982) 'Prestige grave-goods and the pagan Anglo-Saxon Economy', unpublished BA dissertation, University of Leeds
Humphreys, J. *et al*, (1923) 'An Anglo-Saxon cemetery at Bidford-on-Avon, Warwickshire', *Archaeologia, 73*, pp. 89–116
Hunter, J.R. (1985) 'Glass and Glass-making' in P. Phillips (ed.), *The Archaeologist and the Laboratory, Council Brit Archaeol Res Rep, 58*, London, pp. 63–6
Hurst, J.G. (1976) 'The Pottery' in D.M. Wilson (ed.), *The Archaeology of Anglo-Saxon England*, London, pp. 283–348
Hyslop, M. (1963) 'Two Anglo-Saxon cemeteries at Chamberlains Barn, Leighton Buzzard, Bedfordshire', *Archaeol Journ, 120*, pp. 161–200
Jackson, D.A. *et al*. (1969) 'The Iron Age and Anglo-Saxon site at Upton, Northants.', *Antiq Journ, 49*, pp. 202–21
James, E. (1977) *The Merovingian Archaeology of south-west Gaul, Brit Archaeol Rep*, Supp Series 25, Oxford
James, S., Marshall, A. and Millett, M. (1984) 'An Early Medieval Building Tradition', *Archaeol Journ, 141*, pp. 182–215
Janaway, R.C. (1985) 'Textile fibre characteristics preserved by metal corrosion: the potential of SEM studies', *The Conservator, 7*, pp. 48–52
Jarvis, K. *et al*. (1983) 'The Bargates pagan-Saxon cemetery with late Neolithic and bronze age sites' in K. Jarvis (ed.), *Excavations in Christchurch 1969–1980, Dorset Nat Hist Archaeol Soc Monog 5*, Dorchester, pp. 102–44
Jessup, R.F. (1975) *Man of many talents*, London
Jones, M.U. (1979a) 'Saxon Mucking — a post Excavation note', *Anglo-Saxon Studies in Archaeology and History, 1*, pp. 21–38
—— (1979b) 'Saxon Sunken Huts: problems of interpretation', *Archaeol Journ, 136*, pp. 53–9
—— (1980) 'Metallurgical finds from a multi-period settlement at Mucking, Essex' in W.A. Oddy (ed.), *Aspects of early metallurgy*, London, pp. 117–20
—— and Jones, W.T. (1975) 'Crop-mark sites at Mucking, Essex, England' in R.L.S. Bruce-Mitford (ed.), *Reent Archaeological Excavations in Europe*, London, pp. 133–87
Kemble, J.M. (1863) *Horae Ferales*, London
Kendrick, T.D. (1938) *Anglo-Saxon Art to AD 900*, London
Kennett, D.H. (1975) 'The Souldern burials', *Oxoniensa, 40*, pp. 201–10
Kidd, D. (1976) review of Myres and Southern (1973) *Medieval Archaeol, 20*, pp. 202–4
Knocker, G.M. (1957) 'Early burials and an Anglo-Saxon Cemetery at

Snell's Corner near Horndean, Hampshire', *Papers Proc Hampshire Field Club Archaeol Soc, 19*, pp. 117–70

Kuhn, H. (1940) *Die Germanischen Bügelfibeln der Völkerwanderungszeit in der Rheinprovinz*, Bonn

Lamm, K. (1973) 'The manufacture of jewellery during the Migration Period at Helgö in Sweden', *Bull Hist Metallurgy Group, 7*, (2), pp. 1–7

────── (1980) 'Early Medieval metalworking on Helgö in central Sweden' in W.A. Oddy *Aspects of Early Metallurgy*, London, pp. 97–116

────── and Lundström, A. (1976) 'East Scandinavian Style I: an answer to Birgit Arrhenius', *Medieval Archaeol, 20*, pp. 16–25

Lancaster, L. (1958) 'Kinship in Anglo-Saxon society', *Brit Journ Sociol, 9*, pp. 230–50, 359–77

Lawson, G. (1978) 'The Lyre from Grave 22' in B. Green and A Rogerson, *The Anglo-Saxon Cemetery at Bergh Apton, Norfolk, East Anglian Archaeol Rep, 7*, Gressenhall, pp. 87–97

Leeds, E.T. (1912) 'The distribution of the Anglo-Saxon saucer brooch in relation to the Battle of Bedford A.D. 571', *Archaeologia, 63*, pp. 159–202

────── (1913) *The Archaeology of the Anglo-Saxon Settlements*, Oxford

────── (1916) 'An Anglo-Saxon cemetery at Wheatley, Oxfordshire', *Proc Soc Antiq London, 29*, pp. 48–64

────── (1923) 'A Saxon village near Sutton Courtenay, Berkshire', *Archaeologia, 72*, pp. 147–92

────── (1924) 'An Anglo-Saxon Cremation-burial of the seventh century in Asthall Barrow, Oxfordshire', *Antiq Journ, 4*, pp. 113–26

────── (1927) 'A Saxon village near Sutton Courtenay, Berkshire (second report)', *Archaeologia, 76*, pp. 59–79

────── (1933) 'The Early Saxon Penetration of the Upper Thames Area', *Antiq Journ, 13*, pp. 229–51

────── (1936) *Early Anglo-Saxon Art and Archaeology*, Oxford

────── (1945) 'The distribution of the Angles and Saxons archaeologically considered', *Archaeologia, 91*, pp. 1–106

────── (1947) 'A Saxon village near Sutton Courtenay, Berkshire (third report)', *Archaeologia, 92*, pp. 79–93

────── (1949) *A Corpus of Anglo-Saxon Great Square-Headed Brooches*, Oxford

────── (1953) 'Anglo-Saxon Exports: a criticism', *Antiq Journ, 33*, pp. 208–10

────── and Harden, D.B. (1936) *The Anglo-Saxon cemetery at Abingdon, Berkshire*, Oxford

────── and Pocock, M. (1971) 'A survey of the Anglo-Saxon cruciform brooches of florid type', *Medieval Archaeol, 15*, pp. 13–36

────── and Riley, M. (1942) 'Two early Saxon cemeteries at Cassington, Oxon., *Oxoniensia, 7*, pp. 61–70

────── and Shortt, H. de S. (1953) *An Anglo-Saxon Cemetery at Petersfinger, near Salisbury, Wilts*, Salisbury

Leigh, D. (1980) 'The Square-Headed Brooches of Sixth Century Kent' unpublished D. Phil thesis, University College, Cardiff

────── (1984a) 'Ambiguity in Anglo-Saxon Style I Art', *Antiq Journ, 63*, pp. 34–42

────── (1984b) 'The Kentish Keystone-Garnet Disc Brooches: Avent's

Classes 1–3 Reconsidered', *Anglo-Saxon Studies in Archaeology and History*, *3*, pp. 65–74
——— (1985) 'Differential abrasion and brooch usage', *Science and Archaeol*, *27*, pp. 8–12
Lethbridge, T.C. (1931) *Recent excavations in Anglo-Saxon cemeteries in Cambridgeshire and Suffolk*, *Cambridge Antiq Soc*, quarto publications, Cambridge
Losco-Bradley, S. (1977) 'Catholme', *Current Archaeol*, *59*, pp. 358–64
Loyn, H.R. (1962) *Anglo-Saxon England and the Norman Conquest*, London
——— (1974) 'Kinship in Anglo-Saxon England', *Anglo-Saxon England*, *3*, pp. 197–209
MacGregor, A. (1985) *Bone, Antler, Ivory and Horn: the technology of skeletal materials since the Roman Period*, London
Manser, J. (1977) 'A Technological Study of the "Bronze" Brooches excavated at Spong Hill, Norfolk, 1972-76', unpublished dissertation, University of London
Meaney, A. (1964) *A Gazetteer of early Anglo-Saxon Burial Sites*, London
——— (1981) *Anglo-Saxon Amulets and Curing-Stones*, *Brit Archaeol Rep*, *96*, Oxford
——— and Hawkes, S.C. (1970) *Two Anglo-Saxon Cemeteries at Winnall, Winchester, Hampshire*, *Soc Medieval Archaeol Mono 4*, London
Meeks, N.D. and Holmes, R. (1985) 'The Sutton Hoo Garnet Jewellery', *Anglo-Saxon Studies in Archaeology and History*, *4*, pp. 143–58
Millett, M. (1983) 'Excavations at Cowdery's Down, Basingstoke, Hampshire 1978-81', *Archaeol Journ*, *140*, pp. 151–279
Montelius, O. (1908) 'The Chronology of the British Bronze Age', *Archaeologia*, *61*, pp. 97–162
Moore, D.T. and Oddy, W.A. (1985) 'Touchstones: some aspects of their Nomenclature, Petrography and Provenance', *Journ Archaeol Sci*, *12*, pp. 59–80
Moore, W.J. and Corbett, M.E. (1971) 'The distribution of dental caries in ancient British poulations I: Anglo-Saxon period', *Caries Res*, *5*, pp. 151–68
Morris, J. (1974) review of Myres and Green (1973) *Medieval Archaeol*, *18*, pp. 225–32
Morris, R.K. (1983) *The Church in British Archaeology*, *Council Brit Archaeol Res Rep*, *47*, London
Musty, J. and Stratton, J.E.D. (1964) 'A Saxon cemetery at Winterbourne Gunner, Near Salisbury', *Wiltshire Archaeol Mag*, *59*, pp. 86–109
Myres, J.N.L. (1969) *Anglo-Saxon Pottery and the Settlement of England*, Oxford
——— (1970) 'The Angles, the Saxons and the Jutes', *Proc Brit Academy*, *56*, pp. 145–74
——— (1977) *A Corpus of Anglo-Saxon Pottery of the Pagan Period*, Oxford
——— (1978) 'Amulets or small change', *Antiq Journ*, *58*, p. 352
——— and Green, B. (1973) *The Anglo-Saxon Cemetery at Caistor-by-Norwich and Markshall, Norfolk*, London
——— and Southern, W.H. (1973) *The Anglo-Saxon cemetery at Sancton, East Yorkshire*, Hull

Nelson, J.L. (1975) 'Ritual and Reality in the Early Medieval "ordines"', *Stud Church Hist, 11*, pp. 41–51

────── (1977) 'Inauguration Rituals' in P.H. Sawyer and I.N. Wood (eds), *Early Medieval Kingship*, Leeds, pp. 50–71

────── (1980 'The earliest royal *Ordo*: some liturgical and historical aspects' in B. Tiernay and P. Linehan (eds) *Authority and Power: Studies on Medieval Law and Government*, Cambridge, pp. 29–48

Oddy, W.A. (1980) 'Gilding and tinning in Anglo-Saxon England' in W.A. Oddy (ed.), *Aspects of Early Metallurgy*, London, pp. 129–34

O'Niell, B.H. St. J. (1967) 'Monastic mining and Metallurgy in the British Isles', *Metals and Materials, 3*, pp. 182–90

Ordnance Survey (1966) *Britain in the Dark Ages*, Southampton

Owen, G.R. (1981) *The Rites and the Religions of the Anglo-Saxons*, London

Pader, E. (1980) 'Material Symbolism and social relations in Mortuary Studies' in P.A. Rahtz, T.D. Dickinson and L. Watts (eds) *Anglo-Saxon Cemeteries 1979, Brit Archaeol Rep, 82*, Oxford, pp. 143–60

────── (1982) *Symbolism, Social Relations and the Interpretaiton of Mortuary Remains, Brit Archaeol Rep*, Internat Series 130, Oxford

Page, R.I. (1970) *Life in Anglo-Saxon England*, London

────── (1973) *An introduction to English Runes*, London

Peebles, C.S. (1972) 'Monothetic divisive analysis of the Moundville burials: an initial report', *Newsletter of Computers in Archaeology, 8*, pp. 1–13

Pelteret, D. (1981) 'Slave Raiding and Slave Trading in Early England', *Anglo-Saxon England, 9*, pp. 99–114

Penny, L.F. (1974) 'Quaternary' in D.H. Rayner and J.E. Hemingway (eds), *The Geology and Mineral Resources of Yorkshire*, Leeds, pp. 145–64

Philp, B.J. (1973) *Excavations in West Kent 1960–1970*, Dover

Rahtz, P.A. (1961) 'An excavation on Bokerley Dyke, 1958', *Archaeol Journ, 118*, pp. 65–99

────── (1970) 'A possible Saxon palace near Stratford-upon-Avon', *Antiquity, 44*, pp. 137–43

────── (1976) 'Buildings and rural settlement' in D.M. Wilson (ed.), *The Archaeology of Anglo-Saxon England*, London, pp. 49–98

────── (1978) 'Grave Orientation' *Archaeol Journ, 135*, pp. 1–14

Reilly, P. and Zambardino, R. (1986) 'Boundary associations and the manipulation of ancient boundaries: A computerized approach' in A. Voorips and S.H. Loving *To Pattern the Past* PACT 11, Strasbourg, pp. 15–30

Renfrew, C. (1975) 'Trade as action at a distance: questions of integration and communcation' in J.A. Sabloff and C.C. Lamberg-Karlovsky (eds), *Ancient Civilisation and Trade*, Albuquerque, New M., pp. 3–60

Reynolds, N. (1980) 'The King's whetstone: a footnote', *Antiquity, 54*, pp. 232–7

Richards, J.D. (1982) 'Anglo-Saxon pot shapes: cognitive investigations', *Sci and Archaeol, 24*, pp. 33–46

────── (1984) 'Funerary symbolism in Anglo-Saxon England: further social dimensions of mortuary practices', *Scottish Archaeol Rev, 3*, pp. 42–55

——— (1987) *The Significance of Form and Decoration of Anglo-Saxon Cremation Urns*, Brit Archaeol Rep, *166*, Oxford

Richards, P. (1986) 'Byzantine Vessels in England and Europe: the Origins of Anglo-Saxon Trade', unpublished PhD thesis, University of Cambridge

Rigold, S. (1975) 'The Sutton Hoo coins in the light of the contemporary background of coinage in England' in R.L.S. Bruce-Mitford, *The Sutton Hoo Ship Burial I*, London, pp. 653–77

——— (1977) 'A group of three sceattas from excavations at Mucking, Essex', *Brit Numism Journ*, *47*, pp. 127–8

——— and Metcalf, D.M. (1977) 'A check-list of English finds of sceattas', *Brit Numism Journ*, *47*, pp. 31–52

Robinson, M. (1981) 'The Iron Age to Early Saxon Environment of the Upper Thames Terraces' in M. Jones and G. Dimbleby (eds), *The Environment of Man*, Brit Archaeol Rep, *87*, Oxford, pp. 251–86

Rodwell, W. (1984) 'Churches in the Landscape: aspects of topography and planning' in M.L. Faull (ed.), *Studies in Late Anglo-Saxon Settlement*, Oxford, pp. 1–24

Roosens, H. and Thomas-Goorieckx, D. (1970) 'Die Merowingische Goldscheibenfibel von Rosmeer', *Archaeol Belgica*, *123*, pp. 5–18

Russel, A.D. (1984) 'Early Anglo-Saxon Ceramics from East Anglia: A Microprovenance Study', unpublished PhD Thesis, University of Southampton

Russell, J.C. (1976) 'The Early Medieval Plague in the British Isles', *Viator*, *7*, pp. 65–78

Salin, B. (1904) *Die altgermanische Thierornamentik*, Stockholm

Sanderson, D.C.W. and Hunter, J.R. (1980) 'Major element glass type specification for Roman, post-Roman and medieval glasses', *Rev Archéometrie*, *3*, pp. 255–64

——— and Warren, S.E. (1984) 'Energy dispersive X-ray flourescence analysis of 1st millenium AD glass from Britain', *Journ Archaeol Sci*, *11*, pp. 53–69

Sawyer, P.H. (1978) *Fron Roman Britain to Norman England*, London

——— (1983a) 'English Archaeology before the Conquest: a historian's view' in D.A. Hinton (ed.), *25 Years of Medieval Archaeology*, Sheffield, pp. 44–7

——— (1983b) 'The royal *tūn* in pre-Conquest England' in P. Wormald (ed.), *Ideal and Reality in Frankish and Anglo-Saxon Society*, Oxford, pp. 273–99

Scull, C. (1985) 'Further Evidence from East Anglia for Enamelling on Early Anglo-Saxon Metalwork', *Anglo-Saxon Studies in Archaeology and History*, *4*, pp. 117–24

Seebohm, F. (1911) *Tribal Customs in Anglo-Saxon Law*, London

Service, E.R. (1978) 'Classical and Modern Theories of the origins of government' in R. Cohen and E.R. Service (eds), *Origins of the State*, Philadelphia, Penn., pp. 21–34

Shephard, J.F. (1979) 'The social identity of the individual in isolated barrows and barrow cemeteries in Anglo-Saxon England' in B.C. Burnham and J. Kingsbury (eds), *Space, Hierarchy and Society*, Brit Archaeol Rep, International Series *59*, Oxford, pp. 47–80

Bibliography

Smith, C.R. (1848–1880) *Collectanea Antiqua* (7 vols.), London
——— (ed.) (1856) *Inventorium Sepulchrale*, London
Smith, R.A. (1905) 'The evolution of late-Keltic pins of the Hand-type', *Proc Soc Antiq London*, *20*, pp. 344–54
Speake, G. (1980) *Anglo-Saxon Animal Art*, Oxford
Spratling, M.G. (1980) 'The Sutton Hoo Purse: Analysing the Weights of its contents' in P. A. Rahtz, T. Dickinson and L. Watts (eds) *Anglo-Saxon Cemeteries 1979*, Brit Archaeol Rep, *82*, Oxford, pp. 363–72
Stamper, P. (1978) 'Early Anglo-Saxon buckets' unpublished BA dissertation, University of Southampton
Sutherland, C.H.V. (1948) *Anglo-Saxon gold coinage in the light of the Crondall Hoard*, Oxford
Swanton, M.J. (1973) *The spearheads of the Anglo-Saxon settlements*, London
——— (1974) *A Corpus of pagan Anglo-Saxon spear types*, Brit Archaeol Rep, *7*, Oxford
Tainter, J.A. (1975) 'Social inference and mortuary practices: an experiment in numerical classification', *World Archaeol*, *7*, pp. 1–15
Taylor, C.C. (1977) 'Polyfocal settlement and the English village', *Medieval Archaeol*, *21*, pp. 189–93
——— (1978) 'Aspects of village mobility in medieval and later times' in S. Limbrey and J.G. Evans (eds), *The effect of man on the landscape: the Lowland Zone*, Council Brit Archaeol Res Rep, *21*, London, pp. 126–34
——— (1983) *Village and Farmstead*, London
——— and Fowler, P.J. (1978) 'Roman fields into Medieval Furlongs' in H.C. Bowen and P.J. Fowler (eds), *Early Land Allotment in the British Isles: a Survey of Recent Work*, Brit Archaeol Rep, *48*, Oxford, pp. 159–62
Tester, P.J. (1968) 'An Anglo-Saxon cemetery at Orpington', *Archaeol Cantiana*, *83*, pp. 125–50
Thompson, F.H. (ed.) (1980) *Archaeology and Coastal Change*, London
Tooley, M.J. (1978) *Sea-level Changes: North-West England during the Flandrian Stage*, Oxford
Turville-Petre, G. (1964) *Myth and Religion of the North: the religion of ancient Scandinavia*, London
Vierck, H. (1967) 'Ein Relieffibelpaar aus Nordendorf in Bayerisch Schwaben: zur Ikonographie des germanischen Tierstils I', *Bayerische Vorgeschichtsblätter*, *32*, pp. 104–43
——— (1972) 'Redwalds Asche', *Offa*, *29*, pp. 2–49
——— (1976) 'Ein südskandinavische Relieffibel: zum Felinguss im frühen Mittelalter' in K.J. Narr (ed.), *Aus der Sammlung des Seminars für Ur- und Fruhgeschichte der Universität Munster*, Münstersche Beiträge zur Ur- und Fruhgeschichte, *9*, Munster, pp. 137–209
——— (1987a) 'Trachtenkunde und Trachtgeschichte in der Sachsen-Forschung, ihre Quellen, Ziele und Methoden' in C. Ahrens (ed.), *Sachsen und Angelsachsen*, Hamburg, pp. 231–43
——— (1978b) 'Die anglische Frauentracht' in C. Ahrens (ed.), *Sachsen und Angelsachsen*, Hamburg, pp. 245–53
——— (1978c) 'Zur seegermanischen Männertracht' in C. Ahrens (ed.), *Sachsen und Angelsachsen Hamburg*, pp. 263–70
Vince, A. (1984) 'The Aldwych: Mid-Saxon London discovered?', *Curr Archaeol*, *93*, pp. 310–2

Bibliography

Wade-Martins, P. (1980) *Fieldwork and excavation on village sites in Launditch Hundred, East Anglian Archaeol Rep, 10,* Gressenhall

Walker, J. (1978) 'Anglo-Saxon traded pottery' in M. Todd (ed.), *Studies in the Romano-British Villa,* Leicester, pp. 224–8

Wallace-Hadrill, J.M. (1971) *Early Germanic Kingship in England and on the Continent,* Oxford

Webb, M.C. (1975) 'The flag follows trade' in J.A. Sabloff and C.C. Lamberg-Karlovsky (eds), *Ancient Civilisation and Trade,* Alburquerque, New M., pp. 155-210

Welch, M.G. (1983) *Early Anglo-Saxon Sussex, Brit Archaeol Rep, 112,* Oxford
————— (1985) 'Rural settlement patterns in the Early and Middle Anglo-Saxon Periods', *Landscape History, 7,* pp.13–25

Wells, C. (1960) 'A study of cremation', *Antiqvity, 34,* pp. 29–37
————— and Green, C. (1973) 'Sunrise dating of death and burial', *Norfolk Archaeol, 35,* pp. 435–42

Werner, J. (1935) *Münzdatierte Austrasische Grabfunde,* Berlin
————— (1957) 'Zwei gegossene Koptische bronze-flaschen aus Salona' in *Antidoron Michael Abramić I, Vjesnik za arheologija i historiju dalmatinsku, 56-59,* 1954–57, pp. 115–28
————— (1961) 'Fernhandel und Naturalwirtschaft im östlichen Merowinger-reich archäologischen und numismatischen Zeugnissen', *Bericht der Römisch-Germanisch Kommission, 42,* pp. 307–46
————— (1970) 'Zur Verbreitung frühgeschichtlicher Metallarbeiten', *Early Medieval Studies, 1,* pp. 65–81

West, S.E. (1969) 'The Anglo-Saxon village of West Stow', *Medieval Archaeol, 13,* pp. 1–20
————— (1978) 'Die Siedlung West Stow in Suffolk' in C. Ahrens (ed.), *Sachsen und Angelsachsen,* Hamburg, pp. 395–412
————— (1985) *West Stow: The Anglo-Saxon Village, East Anglian Archaeology Rep, 24,* Ipswich

Wheeler, R.E.M. (1934) 'London and the Grim's Ditches', *Antiq Journ, 14,* pp. 254–63

Williams, J.H. (1984) 'A Review of some aspects of Late Saxon Urban Origins and Development' in M.L. Faull (ed.), *Studies in Late Anglo-Saxon Settlement,* Oxford, pp. 25–34
—————, Shaw, M. and Denham, V. (1985) *Middle Saxon Palaces at Northampton,* Northampton

Wilson, D. (1985) 'A Note on OE *hearg* and *wēoh* as Place-Name Elements representing different types of Pagan Saxon Worship Sites', *Anglo-Saxon Studies in Archaeology and History, 4,* pp. 179–84

Wilson, D.M. (1968) 'Anglo-Saxon carpenters' tools' in M. Claus *et al.* (eds), *Studien zur europäischen Vor- und Frühgeschichte,* Neumunster, pp. 143–50
————— (1976a) (ed.) *The Archaeology of Anglo-Saxon England,* London
————— (1976b) 'Craft and Industry' in D.M. Wilson (ed.) *The Archaeology of Anglo-Saxon England,* London, pp. 253–82

Wood, I.N. (1983) 'The Merovingian North Sea', *Occasional Papers on Medieval Topics, 1,* pp. 1–26

Wylie, W.M. (1852) *Fairford Graves. A record of researches in an Anglo-Saxon burial-place in Gloucestershire,* Oxford

Index